Successful Real Estate Negotiation

Successful Real Estate Negotiation

Peter G. Miller
and
Douglas M. Bregman

HarperPerennial
A Division Of HarperCollinsPublishers

A hard-cover edition of this book was published in 1987 by Harper & Row, Publishers, Inc., under the title *The Common-Sense Guide to Successful Real Estate Negotiation*.

SUCCESSFUL REAL ESTATE NEGOTIATION *(Revised Edition)*. Copyright © 1994 by Peter G. Miller and Douglas M. Bregman. All rights reserved. Printed in the United States of America. No part of this book may be used or reproduced in any manner whatsoever without written permission except in the case of brief quotations embodied in critical articles and reviews. For information address HarperCollins Publishers, Inc., 10 East 53rd Street, New York, NY 10022.

HarperCollins books may be purchased for educational, business, or sales promotional use. For information, please write: Special Markets Department, HarperCollins Publishers, Inc., 10 East 53rd Street, New York, NY 10022.

FIRST EDITION

Library of Congress Cataloging-in-Publication Data

Miller, Peter G.
    Successful real estate negotiation/Peter G. Miller and Douglas M. Bregman—Rev. ed.
        p.   cm.
    Rev. ed. of: The common-sense guide to successful real estate negotiation. 1st ed. c1987.
    Includes index.
    ISBN 0-06-273264-1
    1. Real estate business. 2. Real property. 3. Real estate agents. 4. House buying. 5. House selling. I. Bregman, Douglas M. II. Miller, Peter G. Common-sense guide to successful real estate negotiation. III. Title.
HD1379.M597   1994
333.33'83—dc20   93-31859

96 97 98 ❖ / RRD 10 9 8 7 6 5

*With love to the Reverend and
Mrs. Herbert Nash Tucker from Peter*

*With love to Benjamin, Lauren,
and Daniel from Doug*

Contents

Acknowledgments

The authors wish to thank the individuals and organizations who made this edition possible. In particular, we are grateful to Jennifer A. Blum, who proofread our revisions; Karen L. Scullen, who typed substantial portions of the revised materials; and Jeffrey M. Guelcher, Esq., who researched the law in various areas.

The model language used in this text is based upon wording developed by the authors and material compiled and edited by the authors and privately published in 1982 as a compendium of forms entitled *Model Contingencies for Real Estate Sales.*

Part of Chapter 38, "How Brokers Can Protect Their Interests," was originally published by *Real Estate Today,* the nationwide magazine of the National Association of Realtors, in an article by the authors entitled, "Contingencies and the Contracting Process." This material is reprinted from the January 1984 issue of *Real Estate Today* by permission of the National Association of Realtors, copyright 1984, all rights reserved.

Major portions of "Condition and Inspection: The Buyer's Perspective" in Chapter 19 were originally published in the February 1981 issue of *The Washingtonian* in an article entitled, "How to Avoid Doghouses." The section on "Fixing Up: The Seller's Perspective" in Chapter 19 is based on "Prepping for Sale," an article that appeared in *The Washington Post* on July 9, 1977.

The material concerning facilitation first appeared in the November/December 1992 issue of *The Real Estate Professional* (Suite 5, 1492 Highland Avenue, Needham, MA 02192). The material has been edited for this guide.

Portions of the material regarding radon were first published in 1992 in the real estate area of America Online, a nationwide electronic bulletin based in Vienna, Virginia. The material is reprinted with permission of the author, Peter G. Miller. (America Online may be reached at 800-827-6264. At the time of publication, free software and time online were available by mentioning extension #5764.)

Preface

This is a book about real estate negotiation, how it works and how deals are made in the marketplace. It assumes that all players in the negotiating system behave rationally and act in their own self-interest, and that the interests of reasonable people frequently clash. Resolving these clashes in the essence of negotiation.

In writing this guide we have not attempted to develop an all-inclusive manual that addresses every issue in real estate, for the simple reason that such a guide, in theory and in practice, cannot be written. There are too many issues, too many variations of every issue, and too many perspectives to consider.

Instead, we have viewed the concerns and interests raised by clients, students, and readers, and the result is a guide which discusses real estate contracting in general, examines selected negotiating issues, and looks at the special interests of realty brokers in the bargaining process. Our approach has been to provide a foundation from which readers can better understand real estate bargaining and identify issues of concern before they develop into problems. Most importantly, we hope this guide will encourage readers to understand that everything in real estate is negotiable and that everyone—from the first-time home buyer to the realty pro—has a right to protect his or her self-interest.

This book was developed with a variety of users in mind. Because of its modular format, readers can quickly identify and turn to issues of particular interest with great speed. Also, because of its format, this guide can be adopted by real estate educators. Instructors can assign material on a topical basis consistent with course outlines, while students, in turn, can use this guide as a textbook in class and as a practical field reference upon graduation.

It should be clear that real estate negotiation is potentially profitable, but at the same time possibly hazardous to one's economic welfare. Because of the complexities involved in the bargaining process and the specialized areas of expertise which every negotiator faces, we urge readers to consult with brokers, attorneys, tax advisers, structural engineers, and other professionals as required *before* making marketplace commitments.

PETER G. MILLER

DOUGLAS M. BREGMAN

Model Language Subject Directory

Timesharing

Title

Zoning

See: Permits

Successful Real Estate Negotiation

I

How the Negotiation System Really Works

Each year millions of people buy and sell real estate, but for many the marketplace is tinged with a sense of foreboding. While the idea of owning real estate is attractive, the process of negotiation is often complex and intimidating. Fear and anxiety are common; people worry not only about possible cash losses but also about the unknown, the unstated, and the undisclosed.

It's hardly surprising that the bargaining process produces discomfort. Few of us buy or sell property more than three or four times in our lives, enormous sums of money are involved, and where we live is an important index of our social status and economic standing.

Yet with so much at stake, what frequently passes for "negotiation" is nothing more than a kind of ritual dance held together by boilerplate language and great trepidation. In a typical home sale, the "art" of bargaining often consists of nothing more than filling in a few blank spaces on a standardized contract form.

What we have today is a negotiating process that attempts to channel the diverse needs of buyers and sellers into uniform agreements and patterns of behavior. The result is that, in the best circumstances, the average negotiator comes out with an average deal, a deal where benefits and advantages worth thousands of dollars are often lost.

But many buyers and sellers do better than average. They understand that the purchase and sale of real estate is a package arrangement where profits are often buried in obscure clauses and seemingly harmless wording, that it pays to bargain because the "bottom line" is rarely the apparent sales price, and, finally, that all the strategies, gamesmanship, and ploys in the world are worthless if they're not clearly written into a contract. The winners in real estate prosper not because they're seduced by form agreements or standardized deals, but because *they customize each transaction* to get the best possible package of values.

1
Real Estate as a Package Deal

When people talk about housing values, what they usually mean is pricing. Purchase prices are highly visible, but they represent only one portion of a real estate deal.

The actual value of real estate can be measured from two perspectives. To sellers, the minimum value of real estate is the lowest acceptable combination of price and terms. To buyers, the maximum value of real estate is the greatest possible package of price and terms available for what they are willing to pay.

The "zone of negotiation" is the area where deals are made. It is bounded on top by the buyer's perception of value and on the bottom by the seller's perspective. If the package value of the property is too great, buyers won't buy. Conversely, if the package value is too low, owners won't sell. Only when the package value is somewhere within the zone of negotiation is a deal feasible.

What's in the zone of negotiation?

Price, certainly, is a major issue. No one wants to pay too much or receive too little. But pricing is only one of many issues in real estate, and pricing alone can be deceptive. For example, a property sold for $100,000 may come with the clothes washer and dryer, require the seller to pay "points" (fees to the buyer's lender), and include extensive repairs. In another $100,000 sale, the seller may keep the washer and dryer, refuse to pay points, and leave repairs to the buyer. Thus, while the apparent purchase prices are the same, the deals are different.

Price is an observable measure and it might seem as though other issues within the zone of negotiation could also be identified, classified, and numbered, but this is not entirely possible. Every buyer and seller has an individual agenda of issues that is regarded as important (or unimportant). That agenda is always in flux and includes visible items (such as who gets the window air-conditioners), values (such as personal preferences and judgments), and economics (tax benefits, cash flow, inflation, interest rates, concessions by the other party, the availability of credit, etc.).

Thus while the zone of negotiation has bounds, those bounds are endlessly elastic, and the bargaining process can include, or exclude, a limitless variety of potential issues and opportunities. Unfortunately, most realty sales today are structured within the framework of standardized contracts and forms. These forms, if used without modification, constrict the bargaining process by limiting the zone of negotiation to a few preselected issues, and the result is that valuable bargaining opportunities are lost.

THE ALLURING WORLD OF STANDARDIZATION

Every trade, industry, and profession has its particular way of doing things and real estate is no exception. Rather than reinvent the wheel with every transaction, brokers, agents, and lawyers tend to work from a basic set of assumptions that are contained in uniform documents.

In theory and in practice there is much to recommend standardized forms. They save time, they're efficient, and offers prepared with uniform documents are easy to compare and evaluate. But for all their value, standardized forms camouflage a significant number of problems.

First, all real estate transactions are one-of-a-kind events: they involve people with different and opposing interests, unique properties, different jurisdictions, and economic conditions that are always in transition. Trying to fit these diverse interests into a single, standardized contract form makes no more sense than requiring everyone in town to wear size 10 shoes.

Second, standardized forms have evolved into a kind of social and economic bludgeon. Buyers and sellers are told that "everybody" uses one form, that a particular document is "our standard agreement," and that "all the points you've raised are in the contract." Such assertions are uncontested, not because they're right or wrong, but because it's impolite to argue. Our social training encourages us to be courteous and the result is that the need for personal acceptance dampens our drive for a good deal.

Third, the very idea of a "standard" implies certain values. After all, if something is standard, are not alternative approaches "unstandard" or perhaps substandard? The answer in brief is "No." The real issue concerns not what is "standard" but what is appropriate in a given transaction. If a standardized form works, fine. But if it needs to be modified that's okay too.

Fourth, in the current marketing system standardized forms are treated with an awe and reverence usually reserved for sacred objects. They're so "official" that all too often buyers and sellers believe such forms are also untouchable. Yet no matter how imposing a form may look, it's just a piece of paper, something that can be modified or amended at any point before both buyer and seller sign the document and close the deal.

Fifth, by signing standardized forms, buyers and sellers often bind themselves to a lengthy list of understandings and accommodations that have not been negotiated. For example, a form might divide the payment of realty sales taxes equally between buyer and seller even though such payments are totally negotiable. As a result, buyers and sellers may haggle over prices and terms for hours and then give up hundreds or perhaps thousands of dollars without any discussion, bargaining, or concessions, merely because of an obscure clause buried in the middle of a form document.

HOW STANDARDIZED FORMS HURT THE UNWARY

With all the potential faults, hazards, and liabilities inherent in standardized forms, it might seem as though no one would sign a contract document without carefully reading each word. Unfortunately, this is not the case.

Part of the problem is that buying and selling real estate is more than an academic exercise. Emotions are involved, pressures are great, and in this environment the bargaining that does take place is often confined to a few major issues. As for the contract form, that piece of paper is often looked at as an afterthought when it's really the whole ballgame, as Mr. Whitney discovered.

When Whitney was looking for a home, he found several properties he liked but the best deal was a large house offered by Mr. Nelson. The Nelson home had everything Whitney wanted, from a large lot to a basement rec room with an indoor barbecue. The price was right too at $159,000, and when Whitney offered $155,000—just a little bit less than Nelson had sought—the seller agreed.

Real estate sales, of course, must be committed to paper, and so Whitney was not surprised when Nelson pulled out a contract form, a legal-size document entitled "Official Real Estate Contract for Arcola County." It was a lengthy form that seemed to cover just about every issue of interest to Whitney; in fact, it even provided for a structural inspection of the property. After reviewing the document for a few minutes, Whitney signed.

Later, when the excitement of the day began to wear off, Whitney looked again at the contract. Sure, it was "official," but now he saw some features that had gone unnoticed at first.

- There was a 2-percent sales and recordation tax on the sale which, said the contract, the buyer was supposed to pay. That would cost Whitney an additional $3,100.
- The list of items that came with the house included the furnace, refrigerator, and plumbing system, and all items not listed were excluded from the sale. Among the unlisted items were the clothes washer and dryer, an outdoor shed which could be dismantled and moved, and four window air-conditioners. It would cost Whitney about $2,000 to replace these items.
- The contract form provided for "a structural inspection of the property to be made within ten days by an inspector selected by Purchaser." What the form failed to say was that the inspection had to be "satisfactory" or the buyer could back out of the deal without penalty. The inspection showed that the roof would have to be replaced within two years and that the 40-year-old brickwork was missing mortar and needed to be repaired. Altogether, the estimated repairs totaled $4,800.

- The contract required the buyer to pay the first $500 in settlement expenses.
- The contract said Whitney would pay financing interest at "7 percent per annum or the most favorable rate available at the time of settlement." A check with several lenders showed the best rate for 30-year financing was 7.25 percent. With a $124,000 loan, the difference totaled an extra $20.92 a month or as much as $7,532.46 over the life of the loan.

Whitney took the contract to a local attorney and asked if it was a valid document.

"Yes," said the lawyer. "All the information required in a real estate contract is here. You've got yourself a perfectly good agreement."

Whitney balked. "But that's ridiculous. How can an official contract be so one-sided?"

"Easy," said the lawyer. "Nelson went down to a printer and had his own contract published. What you have here is nothing more than an 'official' Nelson. After all, it merely says that the document is an 'official' contract. Who's to say what's official and what isn't."

Nelson got the best of Whitney not by being unfair or immoral, but by correctly counting on Whitney's failure to use his brains. Having knocked $4,000 off the price, Whitney bargained no further. Nobody denied him the right to think about Nelson's offer for a few days or to show the contract form to friends, brokers, lenders, or lawyers. Nobody held a gun to his head demanding that he sign. Nelson, for his part, may not be a candidate for sainthood, but in the real world he defended his interests. And the real world, as Whitney can testify, is a harsh place.

COMMON-SENSE NEGOTIATION DEFINED

Nelson is notable only in the sense that he used an outlandish ploy to enhance his bargaining position. In principle, however, his behavior is no different from that of thousands of other buyers and sellers who are active in the market every day and who use generally accepted, standardized agreements. The marketplace is full of Nelsons and other sharks who thrive on the unwary, and while being a shark may not seem particularly appetizing, being a victim is even less enthralling. Given the choice, most people will opt for their self-interest, and at a minimum that means being able to defend themselves in the marketplace.

But how can you protect and advance your interests in today's marketplace, especially with so many sharks in the waters? How can you get the best possible deals in an environment geared to producing average results?

There is no single answer to these questions, nor should there be. The needs and goals of millions of buyers and sellers are different, in conflict, and forever changing. If there were a "secret" formula that worked well for buyers, it would undoubtedly offend sellers, and vice versa. If there were a specific plan that generated winning results in one city, it might produce disasters in another.

If there is no single, magical path to successful real estate negotiation—and there isn't—then at least there should be a way to analyze deals and respond to each transaction individually. There is such an approach, what might be called "common-sense negotiation."

Common-sense negotiation is not a secret formula known only to real estate insiders or an obscure technique practiced solely by wealthy gnomes and wizards. Instead of providing absolute answers, common-sense negotiation is both a concept and a process designed to help individual negotiators develop their own strategies, offers, and responses within the bounds of each transaction. In general terms, common-sense negotiators follow eleven basic guidelines.

First, there is no single strategy that works every time in every deal because each deal is different, even in cases where buyers and sellers have dealt with one another before or when property is being resold. Rather than a single path to real estate profits, bargaining is viewed as an unfinished canvas which buyers and sellers paint and repaint until both are satisfied with the results. While every canvas may start with the same basic elements, each finished picture is unique.

Second, one cannot be successful in a vacuum. Smart negotiators, whether buying or selling, prepare for the marketplace by reading, taking classes, and visiting open houses. They ask questions about properties and about the other parties with whom they will negotiate. They study local form agreements and speak with as many people as possible, including buyers, sellers, brokers, lenders, tax advisers, and lawyers. The educational process, in turn, is an ongoing effort because new information, ideas, and opportunities are always coming into the marketplace.

Third, deals are made on paper. Except in the rarest circumstances, if it's not on paper, it didn't happen, it hasn't been accepted, it's not part of the deal, and it can't be enforced.

Fourth, the world is full of "standard" agreement forms. If left untouched, such documents establish negotiating positions according to someone else's interests and perspectives. Such boilerplate contracts have value only as a place to start the negotiating process. Smart bargainers are familiar with the standardized forms used in their communities, including those which give an edge to buyers or sellers.

Fifth, it is not illegal, antisocial, immoral, or unfair to modify a standardized form or to pick one form and not another. Negotiators have an absolute right to defend their interests, even if someone else claims to be shocked or offended. There is no law, regulation, or requirement restricting buyers and sellers to the use of a particular contract form, and smart negotiators will select forms and provisions that favor their interests.

Sixth, every real estate deal is a package arrangement that includes both price and terms. The success of each transaction is measured according to which side of the deal you're on—sellers want the most valuable package possible after expenses while buyers want the biggest possible package at the lowest cost. Whitney, in the example above, concentrated on price and not terms. Nelson traded a marginally lower price for better terms, a more valuable package, and ultimately a better deal.

Seventh, within the package of price and terms found in every transaction are issues of unequal importance. Some items are "nickels," some are "dimes," and some are "quarters." Recognizing that concessions are made in virtually every deal if only to salve tender egos, smart negotiators gladly trade nickels for dimes or dimes for quarters.

Eighth, every deal has its "shoulds," "musts," and "extras."

- A "should" is an item that is important to the deal but not sufficiently significant in and of itself to kill the transaction if left out.

If Mintner can't get the microwave oven, he'll still go through with the deal if all other terms are attractive.

- A "must" is a potential deal killer: If it's not in the transaction, there can be no deal. For example, Fenton offers to buy the Waterford house but only if he can also get the vacant lot next door. If the lot isn't available, there's no deal.
- An "extra" is an unexpected goody that somehow gets thrown into the deal. When the Crocketts sold their home, they left the outdoor swing set behind for Carleton's children, even though the contract allowed them to take it.

Ninth, offers and counteroffers are somewhat similar to arrows: not every one hits its mark. Just as hunters carry extra arrows in case their first shot misses, good negotiators have back-up offers in mind so they can react quickly if their first tries are not accepted.

Tenth, buyers and sellers should recognize that they are competitors rather than buddies, pals, or chums. At the same time, negotiators should treat one another with respect so that extraneous personal issues are not introduced into the bargaining process.

Eleventh, top bargainers willingly pay for professional help and use specialists such as brokers, lawyers, structural engineers, surveyors, and tax advisers. Such services are a bargain in the context of real estate deals, where substantial amounts of money are likely to be involved.

HOW TO PROFIT WITH THIS BOOK

This book is designed to serve buyers, sellers, and brokers by explaining how the bargaining system works and what the authors regard as the major issues to consider when negotiating real estate deals.

Part I of this manual contains background information to study before entering the marketplace. Basic words and terms are described in Chapter 2, while contract elements are covered next in Chapter 3. Chapters 4 and 5 explain how contracts can be modified with addenda and contingencies. In Chapter 6, three "silent" issues are discussed, issues which should be known to all negotiators: the doctrine of merger, the idea of satisfaction, and the use of notices. Finally, Chapter 7 describes the place of warranties in the contracting system.

Part II explores the basic issues found in most standardized form agreements, matters such as titles, deeds, and termites. Comparing the information found here with the clauses and terms found in local form agreements (or left out) will allow you to determine if a form is pro-seller or pro-buyer. Part III follows a similar pattern except that the issues presented here are important yet unlikely to be addressed in most form contracts. The chapters in Part II and Part III generally begin with model language related to the chapter's subject and close with a series of separate negotiating strategies for buyers and sellers.

Written for both realty professionals and the general public, Part IV examines areas where brokers and their clients may have conflicting interests and explores steps that brokers can take to limit business risks.

HOW TO LOSE YOUR SHIRT WITH THIS BOOK

In writing this guide, we have not attempted to develop a legal text or an encyclopedic manual that minutely explores every possible issue associated with real estate bargaining. Instead, our goal has been to explain in plain English how the real estate marketing process works and alert readers to frequent areas of concern. *Given its limited intent, readers should realize that this book is not designed as an alternative to the professional services offered by brokers, lawyers, tax advisers, and others.*

Throughout this guide readers will find model language designed to illustrate how various issues can be reduced to writing in the bargaining process. In the same way that standardized forms should not be used without careful review or modification, the model language found in this guide is not intended for use in actual transactions without the prior advice of a competent professional person.

The advantage of model language is that it speeds the negotiating process because wording is easier to modify than to create. In effect, the model language provided here is nothing more than a benchmark from which alternative wording and strategies can be developed.

Model language should be seen as a general response to selected problems. The model language used in each chapter thus represents only one approach to given situations; different negotiators, writing their own agreements, will employ different wording, raise different concerns, and possibly exclude some of the points that we regard as important. Therefore, model language should be viewed as nothing more than a starting point from which specific terms and phrases can be modified for individual transactions with the assistance of brokers, attorneys, and other professionals as required. *Readers who elect to use the model language found in this guide—without prior review by a competent professional person—do so at their own risk.*

2

The Inside Language of Real Estate Negotiation

The process of negotiating successful real estate deals is often difficult to understand because real estate pros frequently speak in a language that seems foreign to most buyers and sellers. Words that have one meaning to the general public sometimes have entirely different definitions in the context of real estate sales.

Part of the problem is that real estate has special words, terms and phrases that most of us never use in everyday conversation, but which negotiators need to know. An even more difficult issue concerns the conversion of spoken terms into written documents. Because real estate agreements are designed to be legally enforceable contracts, they contain numerous phrases which have specific legal meanings that are known and accepted in the legal community. By using standardized legal wording, the so-called "language of art," debates over who meant what can often be quickly resolved or avoided entirely.

The fact that the real estate negotiating process may include obscure terms or unique meanings should not deter buyers or sellers from having a solid understanding of the special words and phrases they are likely to encounter. Here's a selected list of key real estate expressions defined in general terms.

Acceptance: A positive response to an offer or counteroffer. There are conditional acceptances ("I'll accept if you'll pay another $1,500 for the property"), express or written acceptances, implied acceptances

("I'm not going to say anything if you move in early"), and qualified acceptances ("I'll accept your offer subject to my lawyer looking at the deal").

Addenda: Clauses, documents, or statements added to a contract that alter it in some way. To be enforceable, an addendum must be signed or initialed by both buyer and seller and clearly referenced in the body of the contract. For example, a contract might refer to an addendum by saying that "An addendum is attached to and made a part of this contract."

Addendum: Singular of *addenda*.

Agent: Has two meanings in real estate. First, in general terms, someone who acts on behalf of another frequently for a fee, such as a real estate broker or an attorney. Second, a type of real estate licensee who works under the authority of a real estate broker.

Appraisal: An estimate of value produced by an appraiser. Appraisals are typically based on such factors as replacement costs, past sales of like properties, and the ability to produce income.

Appraiser: A person familiar with local real estate values who estimates the worth of particular properties. Compensation for the appraiser cannot be related to a specific estimate of value ("I'll pay you $500 if you say the property is worth $150,000"), nor can the appraiser have an undisclosed interest in the property ("Come up with a good appraisal and you can act as a broker in the deal").

"AS IS" Agreements: Situations where property is sold without warranty and in whatever physical condition it may be in as of the time a contract is signed. Before entering such deals, both buyers and sellers should check state and local regulations and warranty rules to see if and how "AS IS" sales are affected by such laws.

Balloon Notes: Real estate loans where some portion of the debt will remain to be paid off in a lump sum at the end of the loan term. Second trusts, for example, are frequently short-term loans (say three to five years), where a single large payment is due at the end of the loan term.

Brokers: A licensed real estate professional employed by a buyer or seller to assist in a purchase or sale of real property. A broker's duties may include determining market values, advertising properties for sale, showing properties to prospective purchasers, assisting in the preparation of contracts, advising clients with regard to the acceptance or rejection of an offer or counteroffer, and dealing with a wide variety of related matters. While brokers have traditionally represented sellers, they can also be hired by purchasers, a concept known as "buyer brokerage." *For purposes of this guide, the term* broker *is often used in a general sense when either a broker or agent (or both) might be appropriate in certain situations.* For instance, a sentence saying that "brokers frequently spend many weeks working with prospects" could just as easily apply to agents.

Co-owners: Two or more people with an interest in a single parcel of property. Co-ownership is an extremely important issue, since the form of co-ownership shown on a title may affect such matters as estates, inheritances, and personal liability in the event of a lawsuit.

Co-signer: A person who signs and assumes joint liability with another. For instance, Mr. Daly may agree to co-sign a loan with his son so that a lender will provide a mortgage. Note that a co-signer may share liability to repay the loan but that such an individual is not necessarily a co-owner.

Contingent Contract: A contract with a qualification or condition that must be resolved before the contract is final.

Contingency: A provision that makes a contract conditional until a certain event occurs. For example, if buyer Lanham offers to purchase the Hartford property "subject to a structural inspection satisfactory to Purchaser," there is no enforceable contract unless Lanham says the structural inspection is satisfactory to him.

Contract: In real estate, a binding, written agreement between two or more people to attain a common goal, typically the purchase or sale of property.

Credit Report: A report from an independent source which outlines a person's creditworthiness by listing debts, liabilities, and related information. Used by lenders to assess the creditworthiness of potential borrowers. (Note: It's a good idea to check your own credit report on a regular basis to be sure that it's accurate. Contact local credit reporting agencies for more information.)

Damages: An entitlement to compensation for a loss or injury. Damages may be recovered by any person who has suffered loss, detriment, or injury through an unlawful act, omission, or negligent act of another.

Deposit: Usually money delivered by a buyer to a seller in advance of full performance to assure that the buyer's contract obligations will be fulfilled.

Deed: A document that transfers title to real estate from one party to another and is recorded among the governmental land records in the jurisdiction where the property is located.

Easement: A right to use someone else's property. Beware! Sometimes easements are created without an owner's permission or knowledge.

Encroachment: An intrusion, obstruction, or invasion of someone else's property. For example, if a neighbor just built a fence and the fence is six inches over your property line, it's an encroachment.

Facilitator: An individual who works with buyers and sellers in an effort to help both parties complete a real estate transaction. Unlike a traditional real estate broker, a facilitator does not represent either a buyer or a seller.

Fixtures: Items that usually convey to the buyer in a realty transaction unless specifically excluded from the sale. Fixtures are generally attached to the property and intended to be a part of the property. Examples of common fixtures include built-in dishwashers, furnaces, and plumbing.

Gift: The voluntary transfer of money, property, or something of value from one person to another without any duty or expectation of repayment. Since gifts in the context of a real estate transaction may be large, donors should check with a CPA or tax attorney before making a gift commitment to assure that all tax consequences are understood.

Inspection: An examination to determine the condition or quality of any aspect of a real estate transaction.

Loan Origination Fee: A fee charged by lenders to cover loan processing costs, often equal to 1 percent of the loan's value.

Language of Art (Legal Wording): Standardized language with specific legal meanings. A trap for the unwary, legal language may contain definitions, meanings, shadings, and implications not found when the same words are used in everyday conversation.

Merge: To absorb or fuse one document or right into another. In real estate, this usually means the sales contract is merged into or becomes a part of the deed. Once this merger takes place, the terms of the real estate contract are no longer in effect. However, if a real estate contract says that a portion of the document—or the complete document—is to "survive," then that material will not be merged into the deed.

Offer: A proposal which, when accepted, will become a contract. In real estate the buyer commonly makes a written offer to purchase property, which may then be accepted, rejected, or countered by the seller. Offers may be withdrawn without penalty at any time prior to acceptance, unless the offer provides otherwise. If a proposal is rejected, it may not be resurrected without permission of the person who made the offer.

Option: A right to act under certain terms and conditions. For example, if Mr. Clermont can purchase the Mullin property for $150,000 if he acts by June 1st, he has an option. If he does not act by June 1st, the option is expired.

Points (Loan Discount Fees): An interest fee charged by lenders at settlement equal to 1 percent of a mortgage. The purpose of points is to raise the lender's yield above the apparent interest rate.

Quitclaim Deed: A deed that says, in effect, "whatever title I have, I hereby give to you." Unfortunately, the seller who offers a quitclaim deed may have no rights or interests to sell. *Always consult an attorney before agreeing to any deal that involves a quitclaim deed.*

Remedies: Forms of compensation, such as money or actions, that are granted by a court in response to a wrongful situation or condition.

Satisfaction: Acceptance by one or both parties on the completion of an obligation. As an example, Mr. Brody offers to buy the Kent residence if he decides the roof inspection is satisfactory. If he accepts the inspection report, the contract will be finalized.

Settlement (Closing): The act or process of adjusting and finalizing all dealings, money, and arrangements for real estate buyers and sellers. At settlement, all adjustments are made as of the date of the settlement, all money is properly disbursed, the deed is prepared with the new owner's name, and the property is conveyed in accordance with the terms of the contract and the intentions of the parties.

Subject To: An offer or contract that depends on a separate condition or action. In real estate, this phrase is usually found in a provision such as, "This property is being sold subject to a right-of-way granted to the electric company allowing its electrical lines to cross the front yard."

Survey: An examination of the boundaries of real property and the improvements on it. A survey can reveal the quantity of land, boundary distances, the location of improvements on the property such as the house, and other vital information about the property.

Tenancies: Interests in real estate defined in the deed. A vitally important matter which shows how title to the property is held.

Tenant: An individual or entity, such as a business, that occupies someone else's property. Note that while "tenancies" usually describe forms of property ownership, a "tenant" does not own property.

Termites: Wood-boring insects that can infest and damage homes. Most realty sales require a termite inspection, showing the property is free and clear of termites and other wood-boring insects. Such inspections should also list insect damage, if any.

Title: The right of property ownership. Such ownership can be held solely, jointly, or in common. In many states title can be held in corporate or in partnership form.

Title Insurance: Policies purchased at settlement, which insure that one's ownership or interest in the property is protected against loss if a title defect is found or if title claims are made after ownership is transferred. Policies differ and may contain exclusions and exceptions. Also, policy coverage may be expanded to include additional protection. Speak to the person conducting settlement for complete information.

Warranties: Guarantees, promises, and protections provided by one party to another. In real estate contracts, there are usually warranties regarding the condition of the appliances and certain fixtures. New homes often have extensive warranties covering not only fixtures and appliances, but the overall structure of the house as well. There can be "express" (written) warranties, "implied" warranties (guarantees that the parties intended even though they may not have stated them specifically in the contract), and "imposed" warranties (guarantees created, for example, by state law).

3

What Is a Contract?

Each year millions of homes are bought and sold, and in virtually all cases there is a written agreement that binds both buyer and seller together, an agreement called a "contract."

Contracts can be long, complex documents or short statements of not more than a few sentences. But regardless of length, all contracts have certain elements that are either written into an agreement or assumed.

In its most basic form, a contract can be seen as a voluntary arrangement between at least two parties who consent to a set of clearly understood terms and conditions—either set out in writing or assumed because of the parties' actions—to achieve a specific purpose and a mutual benefit.

We use contracts every day. Buying a rake from a hardware store, for instance, is an example of a basic contract. There is an offer ("Rakes for sale") and an acceptance ("Hey, I'll take one"). Buyer and seller act voluntarily for a mutual benefit—the seller receives money and the buyer acquires a rake.

But contracts and the contracting process can get far more complex, particularly when dealing with commercial transactions such as the purchase and sale of real property. Indeed, visit any law school library and you can probably find hundreds, if not thousands, of lengthy books that discuss contracting in general and real estate sales in particular.

Even though real estate agreements can be complex, buyers and sellers should still have an idea of how the contracting process works.

Here, in basic terms, is an overview of the major elements that can be found in every real estate agreement.

Offer and Acceptance: An essential part of every contract is an "offer" made by one person and an "acceptance" made by another. The offer must be in terms that both buyer and seller understand, and any acceptance must be equally understandable.

By definition, all offers have limits. If Harkness makes an offer to buy the Baker property for $125,000, he has set a price, and that price is a limit. Another limit might be seen in terms of time. Harkness might say that his offer will automatically expire by noon Friday. If not accepted by that time, the offer is withdrawn.

To create a contract, there must be both "offer" and "acceptance." In most real estate transactions it is the seller who sets the negotiating process in motion by making an offer ("My home is for sale. Give me $150,000, and you can have it"), and the buyer who responds with an acceptance ("You've offered your home for $150,000, and I'm willing to pay that price") or a counteroffer ("Gee, you want $150,000 for that place! I'll offer $135,000"). In response to the buyer, a seller can agree to the buyer's proposal, reject it, or suggest a counteroffer. *A counteroffer, in turn, automatically replaces the original offer.*

Price or Other Duty: The formation of a contract is complete when one party understands the other's offer and accepts it. When both parties perform their obligations under the contract it's fulfilled. In terms of real estate, the general obligation of the buyer is to pay for the property, while the seller must deliver a deed.

Modification: Once made, contract terms may be modified but *only with the agreement of both buyer and seller.*

Competency of Parties: In order for a contract to be valid, both buyer and seller must be legally and mentally competent. "Legally competent" means being of legal age, 18 or older in most jurisdictions. "Mentally competent" means being able to make a reasonable decision unclouded by mental illness, drug dependency, or similar afflictions.

Mutual Benefit: A contract must create a mutual benefit between the parties. In a real estate sale, the seller gets the money and the buyer gets the property.

Bargaining Position: Both buyer and seller must be able to negotiate as equals to have a valid contract. In situations where one party feels compelled to act because he believes he has no choice, or he does not have a valid opportunity to understand the agreement, or he finds the complex and technical language used in the contract is over his head, then such contracts may, in certain instances, be declared invalid by the courts because these deals lack a true "bargaining over terms." A contract in which the language cannot be understood equally by both parties is a so-called "contract of adhesion."

Voluntary Action: A contract will not be enforceable if it was signed under pressure or duress. "An offer you can't refuse" might make for a good story, but it would not be legally enforceable.

Reciprocal Benefit or "Consideration": A contract must require that each party does something for the other. Doing something to fulfill a contract is called "consideration." "Consideration" can be the payment of money, an exchange of goods and services, or even an exchange of a promise for a promise. A valid contract can even include "good consideration," the exchange of love and affection between two people.

Quality of Goods/Acceptability of Subject Matter: A reasonable expectation in every contract is that the goods (or "subject matter") being purchased are not defective. Selling a house that does not have an occupancy permit, for example, would mean that the property could not be used as a home, and so the seller's "goods" (the house) would not be acceptable, the contract would have failed, and the purchaser would have cause to seek damages.

There are limitations, though, on both "use" and "damages." The limitation of "use" is that the purchaser must employ the product for its generally intended purpose. A home seller has no obligation to assure that his property can be used as a distillery, nuclear dump, or for any purpose other than as a residence. Damages, in turn, are limited to necessary repairs or reasonable compensation.

Not only must goods be usable, they must also have an "acceptable level of quality." The definition of what is, or is not, an acceptable level of quality can vary greatly, depending on whether one is providing goods or receiving them.

Discovering a Defect: Problems also arise as to who should be "on notice" concerning defects and who is responsible for their repair.

In connection with real estate contracts, "defects" could involve both title problems as well as the physical condition of the property.

Generally, it is up to the seller to be sure that no title defects exist. Thus, if there are any problems preventing the buyer from obtaining complete and clear title, the seller is obligated to resolve them. Defects in title can include liens, unreleased judgments, or questionable prior deeds. *A major exception here concerns sales that involve so-called "quitclaim" deeds—deeds where the seller makes no warranties whatsoever and may not even own the property.*

At times, it is not the title but the condition of the property that is an issue. If a defect is so plain as to be obvious by visual inspection or other reasonable examination, then the purchaser might well be "on notice." Being on notice, in turn, means the buyer cannot later claim that he was unaware of the defect. However, if a defect is known to the seller and cannot be seen by the purchaser, then the seller generally must inform the purchaser of the problem.

Language for Breach: Just as contracts are made every day, so are they broken every day. Difficulties may arise when one side does not "perform," some event takes place that makes performing impossible, or the buyer and seller disagree about the exact meaning of a clause or phrase.

Sometimes the failure to perform is serious. When this happens, the contract is said to have been "broken," and a "breach of contract" has taken place. Generally, real estate contracts have provisions that define breaches and provide remedies if one party or the other fails to perform.

Signatures: All signers must have the capacity and authority to sign and their signatures must be valid.

"Capacity" refers to the requirement that all signers must be of legal age and of sound mind. The "authority" of the parties refers to the requirement that someone signing a contract must have the right to bind himself or others he may represent. This can be a tricky issue in the case of corporations (does the corporation have the right to purchase or sell real estate?), partnerships (what is the authority of the signing partner or partners?), and multiple owners (whose signature is required on a contract and whose signature, if anyone's, can be left off?).

A related issue concerns responsibility. It sometimes happens that one person signs for others, as in the case of an assignment. Suppose, for example, that a property is sold by London to Mays, and buyer Mays turns around and assigns his interest to a third party, Kepler. Three problems can arise. First, London may not wish to deal with Kepler. Second, if the contract wording does not prohibit assignments or require London's approval of an assignment, there may be nothing he can do to prevent Kepler from coming into the deal. Third, Mays—who signed the contract—remains responsible for its fulfillment.

Signatures, to be valid, must correctly state the name of the person who is contracting and match the name that is typed or written into the body of the contract and represent the free and informed choice of each signer.

To say that each signature must match the name in the contract may seem like an obvious point, but it often happens that "G. Willard Simpson" signs his name "Sonny Simpson." In such cases, it is remotely possible that there may not be a contract at all if the person named in the contract can convince a court that he never signed.

Damages: Once a contract is broken, the matter of "damages" must be considered. Rather than leave the matter to endless debate, many real estate contracts establish how breaches and damages are to be handled in case of a problem.

Damages can range from symbolic sums ($1) to huge monetary awards. In assessing breaches and damages, courts will take into account such matters as the language in the contract, the conduct of the parties, and whether all the elements for a valid contractual agreement were present in the first place.

4

Customizing Forms: The Use of Addenda and Contingencies

We live in a world of forms and blank spaces, a society where the expression "Just fill in the blanks" is virtually a national battle cry. Yet in the case of real estate, relying on preprinted forms and the completion of a few blank spaces to cement a deal can be costly. Standardized forms simply cannot reflect the individual interests of every buyer or seller. If you're going to negotiate real estate deals, you either have to accept somebody else's idea of how a sale should be structured or customize standardized forms to your advantage.

How are forms customized?

In many instances current contract wording can be changed by adding or deleting words. This is usually done with standardized form agreements by making additions between paragraphs or in margins or by striking out words in the body of the agreement. *All such changes must be initialed or signed by all buyers and sellers to be valid.*

But it often happens that standardized form agreements cannot be altered so easily. It may not be possible to express certain ideas adequately or properly in just a few words. Some topics may require more space than can be found in the margins of a form agreement.

In many cases, it is necessary to add an extra page or pages to the basic contract form, additions called addenda (the singular term is "addendum").

An addendum is nothing more than an addition or amendment to a contract—extra material not found in the body of the document, which may be used to replace, negate, augment, or explain incomplete or unacceptable standardized contract wording. For example, a statement saying that "The dining room light fixture shall not be included in the sale of the property" is an addendum. It clarifies the status of the light fixture in writing so there will be little opportunity for dispute at settlement or any other time.

An addendum may also describe a change made in the contract after it has been signed. If settlement is set for October 1st but money a buyer expected from an estate is delayed, both buyer and seller might agree to have settlement a month later. Rather than write a new agreement, they could simply modify the old one with an amendment saying, "Buyer and seller agree that settlement shall be held on or about November 1st of this year. This addendum shall take precedence over any conflicting or contrary language found in the contract between the parties dated August 10th."

Another type of addendum is the "contingency," a requirement within a contract concerning an event or action (or the lack of an event or action) that can affect an entire agreement. For example, if a purchase is made "subject to a physical inspection of the property satisfactory to buyer" and the buyer is not satisfied with the examination, then the deal is finished and the contract is terminated.

The most common contingency in real estate concerns financing ("If Buyer Ludak cannot get a 30-year mortgage at 7.5 percent interest and two points the deal is off"), but contingencies for structural inspections and legal reviews are widely used as well. *There is no limit to the number or variety of contingencies that a single offer may contain; however, as a practical matter, sellers will prefer offers with few, if any, contingencies.*

Unlike certain parts of the real estate contract which may be mere notices, contingencies are clauses that must be accomplished if a deal is to succeed. If the contingency fails—if an event does not take place as expected or something is unsatisfactory—there may be no contract. Everything can stop.

To have validity, a contract addition, deletion, or addendum must be signed or initialed by all parties to the agreement as an indication of their acceptance. In addition, the fact that there is an addendum (sometimes titled an "Exhibit") should be mentioned in the main body of the contract as being "incorporated by reference." The phrase "incorporated by reference" is a bit of legal jargon that tells the buyer and seller that there is an addendum and that it is part of the contract. Using such language and having the addendum signed or initialed will prevent later claims by either the buyer or the seller that he was unaware extra language had been added to the agreement or that he disagreed with the additional wording.

There is no standardized form or language for addenda, and thus they are sometimes innocently seen as minor contract modifications without any importance or substance. *This attitude is a mistake.* Once an addendum is signed or initialed, it becomes "as one" with the original contract. Addenda have the same weight and value as any contract language found in the body of the agreement, and they need to be written, reviewed, and negotiated with the same attention that one would otherwise use throughout a real estate transaction. Failure to abide by an addendum is no less serious than the failure to act in accordance with any requirement in the main body of the contract.

In fact it can be argued that addenda are even more important than basic contract language. Why? Because if there is a conflict between the addendum language and language in the body of the contract, the addendum wording will usually prevail if the matter goes to court. The reason is that courts generally view the addendum as an item given special attention by buyers and sellers and thus one that should take precedence over the form language found in the body of a contract.

5

How to Add Addenda and Contingencies to a Contract

Although it is true that addenda and contingencies can be written in any form acceptable to both buyers and sellers, it would seem that as a matter of convenience there should be some basic format. The advantage of a standardized format is that it can automatically incorporate many important features to make addenda and contingencies more understandable.

At a minimum, a basic addendum should have six standard elements:

First, clear notice in the main body of the contract that there are one or more addenda.

Second, page notations showing the total number of pages that have been added to the contract.

Third, an identification of the property.

Fourth, a basic statement of attachment. For purposes of clarity and to ward off future claims and disputes, a paragraph of attachment should identify the buyer and seller, show the date of the original offer or agreement to which the addenda is attached, state that the addenda has the "same binding force and effect" as the original contract language, and state that the wording in the addenda shall "take precedence over any and all conflicting or contrary language."

Fifth, the addendum itself. Each addendum on a page should be numbered or identified with a capital letter.

Sixth, a signature block at the bottom of each page.

How an Addendum Might Look

Page _____ of _____ Pages

Subject Property _____

This Addendum made and entered into this _____ day of _____, 19 _____, is attached to and made a part of the Agreement/Contract/Offer dated _____, 19 _____, between _____, Purchaser, and _____, Seller, and shall have the same binding force and effect on all parties hereto as does the Agreement/Contract/Offer, and shall take precedence over any and all conflicting or contrary language contained in the Agreement/Contract/Offer to which this Addendum is attached and made a part, or any prior addendum or addenda attached thereto and made a part thereof, and states as follows:

[A], This Agreement/Contract/Offer is contingent upon a property inspection which, in the sole judgment of Purchaser, is deemed "satisfactory." Such inspection shall be arranged and paid for by Purchaser and if Purchaser does not remove or act on this Contingency or notify Seller or Seller's agent in writing by _____ M. (TIME) on _____ (DATE) of any dissatisfaction associated with subject property inspection, then this Agreement/Contract/Offer dated _____ shall be in full force and effect. If Purchaser or Purchaser's agent notifies Seller or Seller's agent by the time and date specified in this paragraph that subject property inspection is unsatisfactory then this Agreement/Contract/Offer shall be null and void and any deposit made by Purchaser shall be returned in full.

_____ Purchaser/Date

_____ Purchaser/Date

_____ Seller/Date

6

Three Important Ideas for Real Estate Negotiators

All contracts, at least in theory, should contain the same elements and features. Although the basics are the same, different areas of commerce require different approaches to the contracting process. In real estate, there are three special areas buyers and sellers should watch when negotiating a deal: the ideas of merger, satisfaction, and notice.

THE IDEA OF MERGER

It's not unusual for buyers and sellers in a real estate transaction to pass several offers back and forth before a final agreement is reached. And while each side may have made promises, demands, and concessions during the bargaining process, only the understandings written into the final contract will be binding.

The problem with realty contracts, however, is that while they may be binding, they're only binding until closing. At settlement the sales contract is "merged" into the deed, the document that actually transfers title and truly establishes the rights and responsibilities of each party.

Once the sales contract is merged, it no longer exists in the eyes of the courts. And since it no longer exists, buyers and sellers can't go back and rehash the deal unless they both elect to do so. In real terms, the merger doctrine raises several important points.

First, if something can't be done by settlement, say the landscaping, then the buyer and seller must provide a mechanism to assure that the work is completed. For example, the agreement might say that if the landscaping isn't completed by closing, the settlement provider will set aside $3,000 in an escrow account to assure completion of the work. If the builder doesn't do the work by a certain date, then money in the escrow fund can be used for landscaping. If the builder does the work, the money in the fund will be turned over to him upon completion.

Second, oral promises at settlement are worthless. If the landscaping isn't done but the builder says, "Don't worry about it. I'll take care of the problem next week when my foreman gets back from vacation," a buyer has no enforceable way to get the work finished. Two weeks after settlement the builder might say to the buyer, "Look, if you want extra work I'll have to charge $1,000 to putter around in your backyard. If you don't want to pay, don't bother me."

Third, unless otherwise stated, it is assumed that all contract provisions will be merged with the deed at settlement.

Fourth, the doctrine of merger can be avoided in instances of fraud, duress, mistake, or undue influence, but such conditions are difficult to prove.

Fifth, there are times when buyers or sellers *do not* want the sales agreement, or portions of the sales agreement, merged into the deed. Instead, they may want something to "survive" settlement.

A seller, for instance, might want a statement in the contract to survive if it told the buyer that a portion of the property used by the seller actually belonged to the local government. If this statement "survived" the merger, it would discourage the buyer from coming back years later and claiming that the seller had misled him about the size of the property.

The merger doctrine represents one very good reason why a careful contract review is required prior to the final acceptance of a written agreement. If there are oral commitments that have not been incorporated into the written agreement, then it makes sense to delay signing until every important promise has been outlined in writing. And if something written into a contract isn't completed by settlement, beware of losing your rights and benefits once the agreement is merged into the deed and lost forever.

THE IDEA OF SATISFACTION

To most people the word "satisfaction" means simply that one is pleasantly content. But in contract negotiations generally—and in real estate bargaining in particular—the term "satisfaction" represents a perfectly valid negotiating tactic that can give a buyer or seller an effective veto over the entire contracting process.

To understand how "satisfaction" works, one must first understand that this is an example of an ordinary word used in a specialized manner. In contract jargon it conveys not only its general meaning but also a sense and context that goes beyond everyday usage.

One specialized definition of the term "satisfaction" means "performing," doing the things that are supposed to make a deal succeed. For example, if a buyer is supposed to get a loan and promptly makes an application for financing, supplies needed information, and works with a lender to get the needed loan, that person is said to be "performing." If the buyer does not apply for financing, however, it could be said that a provision of the contract has not been satisfied and therefore the agreement has been breached.

A second special usage of "satisfaction" in contract lingo refers to personal acceptance. For example, an offer may be made subject to "a structural inspection satisfactory to buyer." This means the contract will be final only when the buyer says the inspection is satisfactory.

But what standards are imposed on the purchaser? What standards can be imposed? When the issue of satisfaction is raised, who other than the buyer in this case can say what "satisfaction" means? As long as the evaluation seems within the realm of logic and good sense—what a "reasonable" person might conclude—courts generally will not interfere.

How a "reasonable" person might think is a matter that courts and attorneys would debate eternally if allowed. For example, suppose the inspection report for the above buyer came back with a notation from the inspector that "this property is the best home I have ever seen. There is no work required, nothing needs to be replaced." Surely with such a glowing recommendation, a "reasonable" person would have to say the report was "satisfactory." Maybe not, particularly if the purchaser was looking for a home to fix up, a property in something less than top condition that could be bought for less money and then improved with "sweat equity."

Buyers and sellers should use great care when entering into agreements which require "satisfaction."

- Be aware that many savvy negotiators use satisfaction clauses to effectively create an option. A buyer, for instance, may purchase a property subject to his attorney's satisfaction with the contract papers. The buyer has perhaps ten days to complete the review and in that time he goes out and seeks a second purchaser for the property. If he can't find a buyer who will pay a higher price, he instructs his attorney to declare the papers "unsatisfactory." Now the deal is off and the real loser is the seller who has given up valuable marketing time.
- If you're a seller, beware of contracts where dissatisfaction can lead to penalties or excess costs.
- If you're a buyer, make sure your deposit will be returned if you are dissatisfied.
- If a report or examination must be satisfactory to the other party, be certain all reporting and examining is done within a certain time frame—say, three to ten days. Otherwise, the opportunity to claim dissatisfaction should end.
- The opportunity to claim dissatisfaction should also end if one party fails to act. For example, if a sale depends on a structural inspection satisfactory to the buyer but the purchaser never orders an inspection within the allotted time frame, then the buyer's right to an inspection should end without penalty or liability to the seller.
- Avoid "satisfaction" clauses when they can lead to unnecessary disputes and conflicts. A contract that requires a seller to replace an old clothes washer with a model that is satisfactory to the buyer may lead to continuing strife. The buyer may expect a brand-new mechanical marvel with gold handles while the seller may be thinking in terms of a washboard. In this case it would be much easier simply to name a specific brand and model in the contract so everyone knows what is expected.

THE IDEA OF NOTICE

Part of the process of negotiating real estate deals (and, indeed, contracts of every type) concerns the issue of "notice." In very broad terms, "notice" means there are some things you should be told, some things you should know, and some things which should not be withheld.

Suppose, for example, Mr. McGrue, a seller, markets his home to a buyer, Mr. Talbott. McGrue has a $20,000 mortgage on the property, money he borrowed from his father, and a debt he has not disclosed to Talbott or recorded in local land records. But even though $18,000 is still owed to McGrue's father at the time of settlement and the property has been used to secure the loan, Talbott is not responsible for repaying the debt. Why? Because he had no way of knowing that there was a debt; he had no "notice" from McGrue.

If, however, McGrue's loan was a matter of public record or McGrue or his father told Talbott of the debt, then it is possible that Talbott might be responsible for the loan if the property was sold to him subject to all liens and debts.

Publication of the debt in local land records is called "actual notice." But what happens if Talbott never looked at the public records? In such instances there is an "implied" or "constructive" notice. Constructive notice is notice that the law will impose on a seller or buyer because the legislature or courts have decided that individuals should have some level of responsibility. Looking at public land records is a responsibility for buyers, even if nobody says so.

Another form of constructive notice concerns items that are plainly visible or clear. If the basement of the McGrue house is full of mildew and there are damp spots on the floor, Talbott should immediately assume there is a leakage problem or, at least, should ask if such a problem exists. If he doesn't ask, McGrue might claim constructive notice—all the signs of leakage were there, but Talbott ignored them.

Sellers, in turn, may not conceal conditions, defects, or situations that may materially affect the use, value, or habitability of the property. Sellers must respond completely and adequately to buyer questions. If, for example, McGrue covers the basement wet spots with old cartons, he could be liable for fraud. In such situations, it is possible that the contract could be rescinded, and McGrue would have to return Talbott's deposit. In addition, Talbott might be entitled to recover expenses from McGrue.

A major problem here concerns the term "material." Not everyone will agree that one problem or another is important, so it makes sense to disclose potential issues and thus prevent or limit future claims.

Another form of "notice" concerns the issue of communication between buyers and sellers.

To the extent possible, communication between buyer and seller should be in writing to avoid misunderstandings and discrepancies. Where it is inappropriate or unreasonable to provide written information, notes detailing conversations should be kept for future reference. Show when and where conversations took place, who participated, and the topics discussed.

It is also important to read the contract to see how, if at all, notices are to be handled. Suppose, for example, an offer is made subject to a structural inspection satisfactory to the purchaser. The buyer has ten days to notify the seller if he is unhappy. But how must he notify the seller? Can he just call the seller or the seller's agent? Can he write? If he mails a letter but the letter is delayed in the mail, what happens then? (A suggestion: If a notice is hand-delivered, get a receipt showing the hour, date, and place the letter was received and who received it.)

To resolve these issues, some contracts use standardized language to show how notices will be handled, language such as the following:

> Notices required to be given to Seller or Buyer under this contract shall be in writing and effective as of the date on which such notice is delivered to the party or the party's agent. If the notice is mailed to the party at the address provided herein, it shall be mailed, certified mail, postage prepaid, and it shall be deemed received three (3) days after mailing.

If this standardized notice provision, or a similar one, is not in your contract, consider adding it. It is very important that notices be in writing whenever possible, and it should be clear how the notice shall be sent and when the notice shall be regarded as received. Notice provisions may become very important if contract terms change, promises are unfulfilled, or disputes arise.

II
Basic Contract Issues

Even the simplest real estate transactions involve a variety of issues and concerns. What is being sold and what is the price? What warranties are given? How will the property be financed?

Unfortunately, real estate transactions—particularly when something goes wrong—are rarely simple. Real estate is a complex field, where both actual and potential problems are forever lurking. And while no contract can defend against all possible issues and disasters, buyers and sellers can at least create agreements that spell out, define, address, and resolve common concerns before they evolve into major disputes.

What follows in this portion of the book is a discussion of basic issues and concerns that are probably addressed in standardized form agreements used throughout the country. But "addressing" an issue does not guarantee that a given form contains language that benefits the user. Worse yet, because some forms are silent on basic issues, they may cause more harm than good when disputes arise.

Because there are many "standard" contract forms, readers should look for those forms used locally that best meet their needs, forms that require as little change as possible and thus do not alert opposing buyers or sellers to your negotiating interests. After all, why negotiate over recordation taxes or some other matter if the form says the buyer (or seller) will pay such costs?

7
The Wide World of Warranties

In every real estate deal both buyers and sellers exchange promises and understandings. Among the most important are warranties concerning the condition of the home and its mechanical components. For buyers, warranties represent a basic protection against unanticipated expenses and repairs, while for sellers, warranties may mean additional costs even after title to a property has changed hands.

THREE TYPES OF WARRANTIES

The word "warranty" refers to a promise or a guarantee concerning the quality, acceptability, performance, or worthiness of a particular item, product, service, or act. As an example, an appliance's warranty might state that the product will be free of defects and function properly with careful use and maintenance for a given period of time. If the appliance does not function properly and the buyer notifies the seller within the warranty period, he may be able to get the item repaired or replaced at little or no cost.

What a warranty guarantees, in addition to performance, quality, or fitness, is that the buyer will be able to obtain some response from the seller if the item under warranty is not up to the guaranteed standard. Thus a warranty has two features: First, it states that a product—in this case a house—will meet certain standards or guarantees; and second, it grants a right to the buyer to obtain some action from the seller—such as correction, replacement, or repair—if the guarantees are not met.

In connection with real estate there are three basic warranties: implied, express, and imposed.

Implied warranties are those for which the law will hold a builder or seller accountable even though no promises are written in the contract. Implied warranties must be honored, since they can seldom be limited or eliminated in a contract.

What is an implied warranty? There are at least three that relate to real estate. Buyers can assume that properties they purchase will be constructed in a "good and workmanlike" manner, that homes will be "reasonably fit" for their intended purpose, and that houses will be "habitable."

Of course, not everyone will give the same definition to these terms. If the upstairs windows don't close correctly, has the property been built in a "good and workmanlike" manner? If the heating system fails after three weeks, is the property "reasonably fit" for its intended purpose? And what if the builder hasn't gotten occupancy permits by the date of settlement? Can the property be considered habitable?

Express warranties are guarantees specifically written into a contract. If a seller, for example, promises to deliver all mechanical equipment on the property in "good working order" and the central air-conditioner is not working on the day of settlement, then either the equipment must be fixed by the seller, or the contract has been broken.

As the term suggests, express warranties are stated in plain language, hopefully, and in the contract itself. These warranties can either be inserted by the seller to encourage the sale of the house or required by the purchaser to protect against defects or problems that may not be covered by implied or imposed warranties. Express warranties can extend the time of implied warranties—perhaps for two years rather than one—or provide protection in areas not normally covered by implied warranties, items such as the quality of window seals or the life of certain fixtures. In addition, express warranties can include remedies for loss not normally found in implied warranties.

Express warranties are critical contract clauses that are likely to be included by new home sellers (to limit liability) and by existing home buyers (for protection in the event of a problem). Regardless of the type of property involved, however, express warranties should be carefully read, for although they may appear to be plainly written, their meaning is often in dispute. In the event that wording, coverage, obligations, or limitations seem unclear, both buyers and sellers would be well advised to spell out what they are trying to say before an agreement is finalized.

Imposed warranties are not warranties so much as rules, regulations, or restrictions that apply by law to the house itself. As legislated interests, they generally cannot be limited or eliminated by contract clauses. Because they are established by governmental action, imposed warranties differ in applicability and duration from jurisdiction to jurisdiction.

One type of imposed warranty might arise from local building codes. The builder's obligation to meet the code is a form of imposed warranty. If the home he constructs does not meet the standards established by the code, the builder could be sued by a purchaser for damages that are at least equal to the cost of making repairs in the construction.

Implied and imposed warranties generally apply only to the first purchaser of a new house, since any subsequent owners of the house could be dealing with defects aggravated or caused by a previous owner. It is thus important to be sure that something marketed as a "new" house has not been owned previously. There have been instances where unscrupulous builders have sold property for a short period of time to a captive buyer and then resold the property in an effort to avoid warranty obligations.

WARRANTIES AND PRODUCT LIABILITY

Another form of warranty relates to the major appliances found in a typical house—heating and cooling systems are good examples. With these systems the builder of the house, as well as the manufacturer of the product, may be liable for any damage caused to the occupants or guests of the house due to the poor quality of the product.

If a pipe bursts because of poor welding in its manufacture or construction, and leaking water causes the ceiling to collapse, thereby injuring people living in the house, the builder as well as the pipe manufacturer could be liable. This is an extension of the rule of product liability that applies to many other appliances and items on the market—including appliances that may be in the home but not related to its construction.

Product liability at times can go beyond the first purchaser of the home, so that second or later occupants or owners of the house might also be protected by this policy. The liability for these conditions cannot be eliminated by clauses placed in the contract by the builder and cannot be limited or waived by agreement between the manufacturer and builder. Buyers should be aware that even if there are product liability waivers in the sales contract, such waivers almost always have no effect.

Implied, express, and imposed warranties are separate and distinct from the guarantees and rules that deal with the sale of land itself. For further information about these specialized warranties, see Chapter 15 concerning deeds.

8
Where's the Property: Surveys and Encroachments

Model Language:
Sale Subject to Satisfactory Survey

This Agreement/Contract/Offer is contingent on a survey which shows that there is no encroachment onto subject property, that there is no encroachment from subject property onto the property of others and that all property lines are satisfactory to Purchaser. Such survey shall be arranged and paid for by Purchaser. If this contingency is not removed and/or acted upon by Purchaser for any reason whatsoever, or if Seller or Seller's agent is not notified in writing by _____ M. (TIME) on _____ (DATE), then this contingency shall be removed automatically and this offer shall otherwise be in full force and effect. If Purchaser or Purchaser's agent notifies Seller or Seller's agent by the time and date specified in this paragraph that subject survey has disclosed an encroachment or that the property lines are unsatisfactory to Purchaser based on subject survey, then this Agreement/Contract/Offer may be declared null and void at the time of notification at the option of Purchaser; provided, however, that Seller shall have _____ days from notification to correct subject defects. If this Agreement/Contract/Offer is declared null and void by Purchaser, then any deposit made by Purchaser shall be returned in full. In exchange for the right to survey the property, Purchaser shall provide Seller with copies of all survey documents upon receipt and without charge and shall be responsible for any damage done to the property by the surveyor.

Real estate has a physical presence, something that can be seen, felt, measured, and walked upon. Given the physical nature of property, it might seem that location—establishing where the property begins and ends—is a minor issue, something that should seem obvious. Unfortunately, there is often a difference between where property is actually located and where people think it is.

Location is typically stated in two ways. First there is the common description of property. The house you like might be found at an address generally known as 2414 Tulip Lane. In addition, there is a legal description of the property, perhaps "Lot 5, Block 92, Square 12 in the subdivision known as Goodluck Estates, located among the Land Records at Liber 919, Folio 247." The legal description shows the property's precise location in community land records.

Offers to purchase real estate typically describe property by both common and legal designations. Using both descriptions helps assure that the correct property is being transferred.

But even though the street address and legal description are properly stated in an offer form, a potential problem remains: The paper description of the property and the actual boundaries of the property may not match.

When Mr. Smathers bought the house on Toledo Drive, he liked the idea that it had a separate garage. Eventually, he figured, it could house the art studio he had always wanted. But the garage was on the back of the property, and after the sale was closed and Smathers moved in, his neighbor, Mr. Timmons, mentioned that the garage was partially on his property.

"Don't mean to be a pest," said Timmons, "but that garage is an eyesore, and it's over the property line by at least a foot. I don't like it at all, but I'll make you a deal: Either move it, tear it down, or pay me for the right to use my land. I figure that ground must be worth at least $3,000."

Can Smathers be forced to pay $3,000? In this example, $3,000 may be cheap. Unless the garage was there for a long time (creating a right to use the property by what is called "adverse possession") or there is a written agreement allowing the garage to encroach on Timmons's property, Smathers faces several unpleasant choices—tear down the garage, move it, fight Timmons in court, or pay out the $3,000.

Another possibility is for Smathers to file a claim with the company that issued his title insurance policy at settlement. While some policies may help Smathers, errors due to poor surveying are often *excluded* from standard policies. Smathers may also be able to make a claim against the surveyor (if the survey was incorrect), the contractor who built the garage (depending on when it was built), or the settlement provider (if the person conducting settlement knew or should have known about the boundary problem but failed to point it out at closing).

What Timmons found is an "encroachment," a situation where property is occupied by a neighbor without an owner's permission.

In the situation above it was a neighbor who was encroached upon, but it could just as easily have been Smathers. Smathers may find on the other side of his property that a fence has been placed six inches over the boundary. Smathers might be able to demand its removal or compensation for the use of his land. Or, possibly, the fence has been in place for so many years that again it's a case of "adverse possession," and Smathers is stuck. Most likely, if a minor encroachment is involved, Smathers will do nothing, preferring instead to have good relations with his neighbor.

Encroachments are not normally shown in property descriptions or community records; the only way to find encroachments is through the use of a survey, a study showing the precise boundaries of the property and therefore whether any encroachments exist. The cost of a survey varies, depending on the size and shape of the property, whether a plat (a map made by a surveyor) is created, if there has been a recent survey from which to work, and the type of markers (wooden or steel), if any, used to show boundaries.

The Buyer's Strategy

1) A survey may be unnecessary. However, buyers will not know with certainty if location problems exist unless a survey is ordered. Surveys should be especially considered (a) when the property has a large lot, (b) when the lot is unfenced or unmarked, (c) when the house or other improvements are near boundary lines, or (d) when neighbors have improvements that abut property lines.

2) Lenders almost always require a survey as part of the loan application process. Both lender and borrower have a mutual interest to assure that the property does not have encroachments.

3) If an encroachment is found, the property may still represent an attractive purchase. If the encroachment is serious, however, then buyers should consider either abandoning the purchase or seeking a better price and terms.

The Seller's Strategy

1) If the buyer wants a survey, fine.

2) As a condition of permitting a survey, sellers should insist on receiving copies of all survey documents, at the purchaser's expense.

3) If any damage is done to the property by the surveyor, the buyer should be responsible.

4) If the survey shows a problem, the sellers should have the right to remedy the defect at their cost before the buyer can back out of the deal.

9
Easements, Covenants, and Restrictions

> **Model Language:**
> **Offer Subject to Buyer Satisfaction Regarding Easements, Covenants, and Restrictions**
>
> This Agreement/Contract/Offer is contingent on a review, satisfactory to Purchaser, of all easements, covenants, restrictions, and zoning. If this contingency is not removed and/or acted upon by Purchaser for any reason whatsoever, or if Seller or Seller's agent is not notified of Purchaser's dissatisfaction in writing by _____ M. (TIME) on _____ (DATE), then this contingency shall be removed automatically and this Agreement/Contract/Offer shall otherwise be in full force and effect. If Purchaser or Purchaser's agent notifies Seller or Seller's agent by the time and date specified in this paragraph that subject review is unsatisfactory to Purchaser, then this Agreement/Contract/Offer may be declared null and void at the time of notification and at the option of Purchaser. If this Agreement/Contract/Offer is declared null and void by Purchaser, then any deposit made by Purchaser shall be returned in full.

Hidden away in many realty transactions is a series of easements, covenants, and restrictions that may seriously affect the use and enjoyment of given properties. Although some limitations and qualifications are obvious, such as basic zoning regulations, others are not, and it is the responsibility of prospective purchasers to know about any limitations before a contract is signed. The reason: Once a property with

---

Model Language:
Warranty Concerning Easements, Covenants, and Restrictions

Seller warrants that as of the date of settlement there are no easements, covenants or other restrictions, except zoning, which limit or qualify the use of subject property except as stated herein:

_____

_____. Subject property is currently zoned _____. The provisions of this paragraph shall not be extinguished by the merger of the deed and contract for sale but shall expressly survive the transfer of subject property.

---

easements, covenants, or restrictions is sold, it is enormously difficult to void an agreement because of such limitations.

An easement is simply a grant, reservation, or right that allows a non-owner to use someone's property. For example, suppose Mr. Hansen wants to sell several acres at the back of his farm to Mr. Chaney. However, since the back land does not abut any roads, Hansen must create an easement which will give Chaney the right to cross his farm to reach a roadway.

Although easements are entirely common (the right of a utility to string electrical wires across a front yard is an example of a typical easement), they do raise several significant issues.

First, while easements can be created in deeds and clearly shown in local land records, they can also be established in sales contracts and private agreements to which the public may not have access. Easements can also develop when buyers and sellers intend to create an easement, even if such an intention is never put in writing. For instance, suppose farmer Jenkins owns two adjacent lots and sells one to Hansen. Jenkins can grant by implication all the easements necessary for the reasonable use of the property—even if the easements are not shown in the sales contract or the deed.

Second, easements may restrict land usage. Farmer Hansen, for example, could not erect a fence that would deny Chaney access to the road.

Third, an easement that "runs with the land" cannot be revoked by the property owner alone if the easement benefits someone else. In contrast, in our example with Hansen, if Hansen's farm and Chaney's land are ever owned by the same person, the easement will end or, as lawyers say, it will be "extinguished."

Fourth, an easement can be created without the owner's permission, a so-called "easement by prescription." This is a right to use another's property, consistent with the owner's rights, which is acquired by a use that is open, notorious, adverse, and continuous for a certain length of time. If the owner does not object or prevent the easement, or sue for the invasion of his property rights, an easement could be created by prescription after a period of continued use, say 10, 15, or 20 years, depending on local laws.

Fifth, in some situations easements can be created by "estoppel." An owner, for instance, may object to the unauthorized use of his land, but courts may reject his claim because it would be unfair to end the easement. If Jenkins crossed the Hansen farm for 10 years and Hansen finally objected, a court might allow the easement because Hansen had not objected sooner, and it would now be unfair to stop Jenkins's daily crossing.

Sixth, an easement may be created by condemnation, such as when a city takes land for a sidewalk or road.

Easements can be terminated, but the process is often difficult. Depending on the type of easement involved, it can end if properties are combined under one owner, if the easement is abandoned, or if the user of the easement releases the property owner from any further obligation.

"Covenants" are regulations and guidelines commonly found in subdivisions, condominiums, cooperatives, planned unit developments (PUDs), and even in deeds for raw land. Covenants have been used to ban television antennas on houses, drinking alcoholic beverages on a property, home-selling practices (such as the size of signs), specific activities (such as using a property for commercial purposes), certain types of fences, outdoor clotheslines, and even particular paint colors. Most of these covenants have been upheld as constitutional, but some have been found to be illegal restrictions. Other covenants, such as those that bar property sales to members of racial or religious groups, violate public policy and cannot be enforced.

Unlike many easements, covenants are quite specific and are readily found in land records. The problem, however, is that once in place, covenants tend to be permanent, something buyers should consider when looking at property. While there have been instances where covenants have been negotiated or "waived," such instances are rare.

"Restrictions" on land may involve not only easements and covenants, but zoning laws as well. Zoning is usually seen as an issue that primarily concerns commercial real estate deals, but zoning can affect residential sales as well. For instance, zoning controls land usage, and someone who purchases a home with the intent of expanding it may find that zoning prohibits new construction because any addition to the house will be too close to the property lines. Another example of zoning concerns rentals. If an area is zoned for single-family homes, it may not be possible to create an "in-law suite" with a second kitchen because additional kitchens are usually not permitted with such zoning.

Zoning should be checked to see how sale properties are classified and how adjoining land can be used. By examining local master plans, you can make certain that the nearby woods, which are now so bucolic, have not been set aside for an all-night gas station or a nuclear dump.

The Buyer's Strategy

1) Always ask about easements, covenants, and restrictions.

2) Check master plans to see how development is anticipated in your community.

The Seller's Strategy

1) Tell buyers about easements, covenants, and restrictions.

2) Be familiar with prospective development in your community, and know what is planned for the area where your property is located.

10
Pricing and Down Payments

Model Language:
Price Established

Purchaser agrees to a purchase price of $_____ for subject property. A $_____ deposit shall be submitted with this Agreement/Contract/Offer, held in an escrow account and applied in whole at settlement as a credit toward the purchase price.

Every real estate deal revolves around the issue of cost, and it's difficult to imagine a standardized agreement form that doesn't show a selling price. Given the seemingly basic nature of a sales price and the attention it receives, how could any contract form subvert or misrepresent the interests of either buyer or seller?

The answer can be seen in terms of misdirection. While a price is shown, the full cost of the property is not.

For example, virtually every standardized realty agreement shows a sales price that excludes closing costs. Lowell can buy the Crown home for $125,000, plus settlement costs. Settlement costs, in turn, may include thousands of dollars in taxes, fees, and other charges to the buyer. The seller, too, suffers from some element of misdirection. Crown is unlikely to see $125,000 in cash, particularly after he pays off his mortgage, closing fees, and marketing costs.

Why aren't settlement costs shown? One reason is that realty agreements are largely designed to record the passage of funds from buyer to seller rather than to third parties. A second reason is that settlement costs—payments to lenders, tax collectors, lawyers, and others—are not specifically known at the time an offer is accepted.

Another area of misdirection concerns down payments. Many purchasers would like to buy property without any cash investment whatsoever, deals in which there is no deposit and no down payment at closing.

Deals with no money may represent a considerable risk to sellers. If there is no deposit from a buyer, the purchaser may simply walk away from a contract. Sure, you could sue, but this could be a very costly, time-consuming, and potentially fruitless venture.

In many situations, no-money-down deals depend on sellers who are willing to take back financing from buyers. Another ploy is for buyers to offer something other than cash, such as a promissory note, car, or other property.

The problem with accepting goods is that sellers may not be able to convert such items into cash for the full retail value claimed by buyers. Moreover, why should sellers use their time retailing goods to raise money they should have collected in the first place from purchasers?

Although no-money-down deals can work for both buyer and seller, a no-money-down offer should be seen as a large red flag waving in the breeze. Not only is there more risk for sellers, there is also more risk for buyers. With no money down, borrowing must be maximized to the highest possible levels, levels that not every buyer can afford.

There is one form of no-money-down arrangement that works every time—at least for sellers. Qualified buyers can purchase property through the Veterans Administration (VA) insurance program with no money down. There is no risk to sellers because they get 100 percent of their money, minus settlement costs, at settlement. If the buyer later has a problem making payments, it's a matter between the purchaser, the lender, and the VA.

The Buyer's Strategy

1) Use contract forms that state, in writing, that the deposit will be applied in whole as a credit against the purchase price. If the form does not credit the deposit, beware of other tricks and traps.

2) Have your offer clearly state what portion of the purchase price will be made in cash and how much will be financed.

3) Get an estimate of settlement costs so you will know how much cash will be required at closing.

The Seller's Strategy

1) Do not use a contract form that automatically requires you to pay a portion of the buyer's settlement costs, say the first $2,000 or $3,000. This is a matter of negotiation.

2) Beware of offers where the purchaser is putting no money down, except for deals financed with a VA mortgage.

11

Appraisals and Value

Model Language:
Offer Contingent on Adequate Appraisal

This Agreement/Contract/Offer is contingent upon an appraisal which shows the value of subject property is not less than $_____. Such appraisal shall be arranged and paid for by Purchaser and if Purchaser does not remove or act on this contingency or notify Seller or Seller's agent in writing by _____ M. (TIME) on _____ (DATE) that the appraised value is less than $_____, then subject Agreement/Contract/Offer shall be in full force and effect without regard to appraised value. If Purchaser or Purchaser's agent notifies Seller or Seller's agent by the time and date specified in this paragraph that subject property appraisal is less than $_____, then Purchaser may declare this Agreement/Contract/Offer null and void and any deposit made by Purchaser shall be returned in full.

Before Mr. Williams first offered his house for sale, he checked home prices in the neighborhood to see how much he should ask for his property. After visiting many properties over the course of several weeks, he put his house on the market for $150,000.

Not long after Williams began to market his property, a buyer, Mr. Truman, saw the house and made an offer.

"I like it," said Truman, "but I'm worried. See, I only moved into this area a few months ago, and while the house is perfect for me, I don't really know how much it's worth. If I'm not careful I might overpay by thousands of dollars. And if I overpay, I not only lose money up front but I also face additional interest costs over the life of the mortgage that could amount to tens of thousands of dollars."

Truman's situation is hardly unique. It's often enormously difficult to determine property values, particularly in older neighborhoods with a wide variety of housing styles and sizes or in communities which are new to buyers and where pricing patterns are unfamiliar. For Truman and for others, the solution to this problem is an appraisal—a judgment of market value made by a knowledgable, independent authority.

The above definition of an "appraisal" is purposely loaded. An appraisal is not, by its nature, a value created by buyers, sellers, or brokers since each has an interest in the final figure. To have validity, an appraisal must be made by someone who is familiar with local realty patterns and who has no personal or financial involvement in the transaction. The appraiser's fee, in turn, must be wholly unrelated to the property's value. In other words, the appraiser is paid to appraise, not compensated to select a specific price.

Appraisers can be hired by either buyers or sellers, but in the majority of residential transactions they are hired by a third party: the lender. The lender selects an appraiser, but the appraiser's fee is paid by the purchaser. *Thus, although an appraisal may not be mentioned in a contract, an appraisal will be required in most instances by the lender financing the deal.*

Lenders use appraisals to protect themselves from over-lending, and to a certain extent, there is some protection for buyers as well. Suppose Truman is willing to pay $145,000 for the Williams's house with 10 percent down. If the property has an appraised value of only $130,000, lenders will not make the loan. Why? Because the loan-to-value ratio is nearly 100 percent. Lenders prefer mortgages where the amount loaned is equal to only 80 percent of a property's market value, which in this case would mean just $104,000.

Whether an appraisal is ordered by a lender or borrower, the real issue faced by purchasers is this: Even if the lender is willing to finance a transaction, is it a good deal?

Let's go back to Truman. Suppose he is willing to buy the Williams's house for $145,000, but this time he offers to put down 20 percent of the purchase price in cash. Even if the property is appraised at $130,000, a lender might just be willing to loan the necessary $116,000

(80 percent of $145,000) and gamble that in the event of foreclosure all the money loaned can be recaptured. So here we have a situation where there was an appraisal, a lender was willing to make a loan, and yet—if the house was only appraised at $130,000—Truman still overpaid.

Although appraisals are typically made after buyers and sellers have agreed to a contract, there are cases where appraisals are made before a home is marketed. For instance, if FHA or VA financing is attractive, a seller may get an appraisal so the property can be advertised as "VA (or FHA) appraised for $95,000." This would tell prospective purchasers that the property can be bought with federally insured financing and little money down.

VA appraisals, known as "certificates of reasonable value," can be ordered directly from the Veterans Administration (listed in the phone book under "U.S. Government"). FHA appraisals can be ordered through FHA-approved lenders—those lenders in local communities who originate FHA financing. Appraisals for non-governmental loans can also be ordered by contacting appraisers listed in the phone directory.

Sellers who order appraisals before finding a buyer, however, should be aware of a potential problem. What happens if the appraiser thinks your house is worth $15,000 less than your estimate? Certainly the value of that appraisal as a marketing tool is just about zero; it's not something you would want to show to a purchaser. Should sellers ever find themselves with a low-ball appraisal, it may be best to leave the report under a mattress and see how much buyers are willing to offer. You may get a higher offer than the first appraiser estimated, and if that offer is consistent with values in your neighborhood, there is a good chance it will be backed up by the lender's appraiser.

The Buyer's Strategy

1) Use an appraisal contingency in those cases where pricing patterns are unclear—for example, in older neighborhoods with a variety of homes or when moving to a new community where you are not familiar with property values.

2) Look for a realistic appraisal price, something that makes sense in the context of the neighborhood and with homes of similar size and quality.

3) If a contingent appraisal turns out to be low, renegotiate with the seller—it's easier with a written appraisal in your pocket. In some cases it may

be best to renegotiate terms rather than price; that is, ask for the washer and dryer rather than $500 off the sales price.

4) Be reasonable. If an appraisal is $500 low in the context of a $100,000 sale and the property is otherwise attractive, go ahead with the deal.

5) Be aware that factors other than the value of the property can influence a deal. For example, paying a premium price may be okay if you can also get below-rate financing from the seller.

6) Never buy in a vacuum. Look at other properties in the same area and in the same price range. Compare homes and shop around.

The Seller's Strategy

1) If a purchaser wants a property appraisal, be certain you receive a copy for your records. If the buyer backs out of the deal, at least you have an appraisal that may prove valuable with other potential purchasers.

2) Avoid appraisal contingencies requiring the purchaser's "satisfaction." Property values are definable numbers; have the buyer pick one.

12
Clarifying Loan Terms

Model Language:
Sale Subject to Acceptable Financing Terms

It is agreed and understood that Purchaser shall not be required to accept any loan arrangement which fails to provide any of the following: 1. subject financing may be repaid, in whole or in part, at any time and without penalty; 2. Purchaser shall not pay more than _____ points (loan discount fees); 3. Purchaser shall not pay more than _____ percent of the face value of subject financing as a loan placement and/or loan origination fee; 4. the annual interest rate shall not exceed _____ percent; 5. there shall be no prepayment penalties; and 6. the terms and conditions in this paragraph, or terms and conditions otherwise acceptable to Purchaser, shall be included in writing in any loan agreement. If the terms and conditions of this paragraph cannot be met, or if terms and conditions otherwise acceptable to Purchaser cannot be obtained, then subject Agreement/Contract/Offer shall be terminated and Purchaser's deposit, if any, shall be returned in full.

Model Language:
Seller Financing Fee Limited

Seller shall not be required to pay loan placement, loan origination and/or loan discount fees (points) equal to more than _____ percent of the first trust.

Model Language:
Seller to Take Back Financing

It is agreed and understood that Seller shall provide a _____ (first, second or third) _____ (mortgage or deed of trust) in the amount of $_____ for a term of _____ years, bearing simple interest at the rate of _____ percent per annum and payable at the rate of $_____ per month. Financing provided by Seller under subject Agreement/Contract/Offer may not be assumed without Seller's written permission; the loan shall be recorded as a lien against the property with all appropriate governmental entities; all Seller financing documents shall be in a form satisfactory to Seller; Seller shall have the right to assess a reasonable penalty for late payments as specified in the financing documents; Seller shall have the right to substitute trustees, if any, without cause or notice; each installment when paid shall be applied first to the payment of interest; title may not be taken subject to said Seller financing and/or note without Seller's written permission; and subject Seller financing may be prepaid, in whole or in part, without penalty. Seller shall have ten days following receipt to review Purchaser's credit information, including but not limited to a Consumer Report (credit report), past tax returns and such other information and documents as Seller may require. If subject credit review is not satisfactory to Seller then, in that event, subject Agreement/Contract/Offer shall be terminated and all deposits made by Purchaser shall be returned in full. PURCHASER HAS BEEN TOLD AND IS AWARE THAT A BALLOON PAYMENT SHALL/SHALL NOT (CROSS OUT ONE) BE REQUIRED AT THE END OF THE TERM OF SUBJECT FINANCING. This paragraph shall not be extinguished by the merger of the deed and the contract of sale but shall expressly survive the transfer of subject property.

People are often shocked when told the cost of financing is greater than the acquisition price of real estate. Buy a home for $100,000, put down $20,000 at settlement, and $80,000 remains to be financed. If you borrow $80,000 at 8 percent interest for 30 years, there will be a monthly mortgage payment of $587.01, and interest over the loan term will total $131,324.20 ($587.01 x 360 = $211,342.20 less $80,000).

Not surprisingly, people pay a lot of attention to financing and carefully spell out acceptable loan terms when making an offer. For instance, if Mr. Hartley can get $125,000 at 8 percent interest with two points for fixed-rate financing over 30 years, he'll buy the Randall house. If he can't get those precise terms, the sale is off, and his deposit will be returned in full. Or is the deal off?

Although many standardized contract forms contain blank spaces that allow buyers to describe acceptable financing terms in detail, such descriptions are often worthless. The reason, buried in many forms, is language saying that if the buyer can't get the terms he wants, he must accept whatever terms are available.

For example, a standardized contract form may allow a buyer to pay a given interest rate or "the lowest rate obtainable." Suppose that our Mr. Hartley submits an offer that stipulates interest at the rate of "eight percent per annum or the lowest rate obtainable." To what rate is he committed?

It might seem as though Hartley will not have to pay more than 8 percent, but this is not true. The "lowest rate obtainable" may be 10 percent, 12 percent, or any number at all. If Hartley can only get financing at 12 percent and he then refuses to go through with the deal, he could lose his deposit and face other claims by the seller.

It is entirely possible that Hartley will pay more than 8 percent, especially in a market where interest rates are rising. While some lenders "lock in" (guarantee) rates at the time borrowers apply for financing, many do not. Instead, lenders might only agree to a rate commitment when a loan application is approved (perhaps 45 to 60 days after application), or at the time of settlement (perhaps 60 to 90 days after application). By establishing a rate ceiling in their purchase offer, buyers have some leverage—if interest rates go too high, they can walk away from the deal.

In a situation where Hartley has signed an offer sheet with open rates and terms, his only protection against high rates is likely to be a financial contingency designed largely to protect the lender's interest. If rates rise high enough, Hartley will not qualify for a loan and the deal will be dead.

But then two other problems may crop up. First, not all contracts have a financing contingency. If the buyer can't get financing in such arrangements, he loses his deposit and possibly incurs other penalties as well. Second, what happens if Hartley qualifies for a 12 percent loan? Now if he backs out of the deal, he'll lose his deposit because the financing contingency has been met.

Getting money at the higher rate may also lead to other problems. Sure, Hartley can afford 12 percent financing—at least on paper. But in real life a high interest rate may end Hartley's efforts to put money aside for retirement or to take an annual vacation. At 12 percent, his financial cushion is gone.

Another financing contingency that is often less certain than it seems concerns "points" (loan discount fees). A point is equal to 1 percent of the loan, so if Hartley borrows $125,000, then a single point will be worth $1,250. This money is paid to the lender.

Hartley, in his offer, specified his willingness to pay two points while the seller agreed to pay one point. The contract agreement, however, also said that "Purchaser and Seller agree to any reasonable change in subject loan discount fees which are caused by changes in the mortgage market."

In this case both Hartley and the seller have agreed to pay whatever the lender requires. After all, who is to say a change in loan discount fees is "unreasonable," particularly since the cost and availability of money changes daily?

Both buyers and sellers must read form contracts carefully to find what financing contingencies, if any, have been included and to see if any provisions permit higher interest rates and closing costs than are superficially allowed in the offer form.

Not only do form contracts frequently contain financing clauses that need revision, elimination, or clarification, but many are totally silent on matters that should concern buyers and sometimes sellers alike.

There is more to a mortgage than interest rates and points, and a variety of substantial bargaining issues regarding mortgages are often obscured in standardized contract forms. Mortgages are typically made in the "lender's usual form," an expression that says, in effect, the lender has the right to set the rules governing the loan. By agreeing to use the "lender's usual form," borrowers again leave themselves open for such terms and conditions as the lender may elect to impose.

If an offer can specify interest rates and points, why can't it specify other matters as well? The answer is that an offer can incorporate any terms desired by the purchaser and acceptable to the seller. Whether such terms are agreeable to lenders is another matter.

One extremely important loan issue normally untouched in standardized contract forms concerns the matter of loan prepayments. Some lenders charge a fee if borrowers prepay their loans, a fee that in some cases can total thousands of dollars.

As a matter of good economic sense, a buyer should make every effort to find loans without prepayment penalties. If Mr. Hartley borrows $125,000 at 8 percent over 30 years he will pay $917.21 per month. If his salary increases or he makes a killing on the stock market, he might be able to pay $1,200 a month. With extra monthly payments of $277.36 Hartley's loan could be repaid in just 15 years, and his total interest cost would drop from $205,194.06 to $90,021.72—a difference of $115,172.34.

Whether prepaying a loan is a good strategy depends on alternative investments (can you get more putting your money elsewhere?), tax brackets (the higher your bracket, the lower your effective interest rate), and inflation (the higher the rate of inflation, the lower the real cost of fixed-rate mortgages).

There is another reason why buyers should avoid prepayment penalties: due-on-sale clauses. Virtually all loans made today, except VA, FHA, and some adjustable rate mortgages (ARMs), have due-on-sale clauses. If the property is sold, the loan cannot be assumed by a new purchaser, because it must be repaid to the lender at settlement.

A due-on-sale clause is a reasonable protection for lenders, particularly those who make fixed-rate loans. But what is not reasonable is a loan that contains both a due-on-sale clause and a penalty for prepayment.

With both a due-on-sale clause and a prepayment penalty clause, we have a situation where if the house is sold, the loan must be paid off at settlement *and* the borrower/seller may be forced to pay a penalty for "prepayment," an expression which means that in this case, the owner—like almost all home buyers—didn't wait 30 years to sell his home.

Can a buyer require a lender to waive prepayment penalties? No, but a buyer can state as part of a purchase offer that he will only accept financing without prepayment penalties or where prepayment penalties are waived in the event of a sale. If such financing is not available, the deal is off, and the buyer's deposit should be returned.

Many lenders, it should be said, are moving away from prepayment penalties. They would rather have the additional money represented by voluntary prepayments, cash that can be loaned again to other customers, thereby generating additional fees, charges, and interest. Some lenders do not charge prepayment penalties for another reason: in many instances they are prohibited by local laws.

The Buyer's Strategy

1) Read the contract form carefully! Where, in writing, is the interest level limited? Where, in writing, is a maximum requirement for points established? Is there language that lets a lender charge something more than the figures shown in the purchase offer?

2) If a lender will not agree to waive all prepayment charges, can you at least get financing where prepayment penalties are waived in the event of a sale?

3) If your financing terms cannot be met, where does the offer say your deposit will be returned in full?

4) Try to find a lender who will lock in your rate and terms in writing at the time of application. Caution: Many lock-in agreements are conditional rather than absolute. A lender who promises to make a loan with a specific interest rate but a variable number of points can effectively engineer a higher rate. A "lock-in" that depends on a satisfactory property appraisal and credit check is both commonplace and a way for lenders to wiggle out of deals. A "lock-in" that is revocable if market conditions "change" is worthless because rates and terms move daily.

5) Be aware that loan officers may not have the authority to make rate commitments! Always ask if the rate provided by a loan officer must be approved by another officer or a loan committee.

6) Loan rates and terms do change in the marketplace. If you can't get a specific rate, what rate might otherwise be acceptable? Would you be willing to lose a house because interest rates rise one-quarter percent? One-half percent?

The Seller's Strategy

1) As a seller you may be required to pay points at settlement. Is the number of points capped or have you agreed in the purchase offer to pay whatever the market will bear?

2) Look at the buyer's financing contingency. Is it reasonable in the current marketplace? If the rate set in the offer is too low, the house may be under contract, but the contract may be worthless. If the financing provision seems weak, require the buyer to get a mortgage commitment quickly or don't accept the offer.

ASSUMPTIONS AND FINANCING "SUBJECT TO"

Model Language:
Offer Contingent on Special Financing

This Agreement/Contract/Offer is contingent upon the ability of the Purchaser to _____ ("assume" or "take title subject to") Seller's current first deed of trust or first mortgage under rates, terms and conditions enjoyed by Seller as of the date this Agreement/Contract/Offer is made or under such rates, terms and conditions as may otherwise be satisfactory to Purchaser. _____ (Purchaser or Seller) shall be responsible for the payment of any assumption fee or similar cost. If Purchaser cannot assume or take title subject to the financing described herein, then this Agreement/Contract/Offer shall be null and void and any deposits made by Purchaser shall be returned in full.

In many sale situations the best financing in town is not a new loan but an old one. Existing mortgages may feature lower interest rates as well as fewer up-front closing costs, such as points and fees. Another advantage of existing mortgages concerns the relationship between principal and interest.

Suppose Mr. Hastings wants to buy the Loman residence. The property is priced at $150,000, and there is an outstanding 30-year, fixed-rate VA loan with 8 percent interest. The loan is freely assumable, and the interest level is identical to rates for new mortgages.

Hastings prefers to assume the old loan for two reasons. First, with new financing he would have to pay two points (loan discount fees). With an assumption, there would be no points to pay, so Hastings would cut his closing costs by $2,500. (Seller Loman also likes the idea of an assumption, because with a new loan he might have to pay one or more points.)

Hastings is also attracted to this option because of the monthly payments. Loman's original loan was $125,000 and now, after five years, his balance is down to $118,712. While the monthly payments are and always have been $912.67 for principal and interest, the composition of those payments has changed. In month number 1, only $83.88 went to reduce principal. In month number 60, the payment is the same but now $124.96 is being set aside for principal. In effect, by assuming a loan Hastings is able to accumulate equity more quickly.

When we talk about buyers taking over existing loans, we typically speak in terms of "assuming" the old mortgage. In fact, however, there may not be an assumption at all.

Many loans, such as most FHA and VA mortgages, are *assumable,* a term which means lenders will hold both buyers and sellers responsible for repaying the note. If the property is purchased "subject to" the mortgage, however, it means the lender can pursue the original borrower (the seller) and not the purchaser for repayment.

As a practical matter, in those cases where property values are strong and buyers have made meaningful down payments, say 15 to 20 percent, sellers have solid (but not perfect) protection against lender claims. If a buyer defaults, the property will be sold at foreclosure, and it is likely that enough money will be raised so that the seller will have no obligation to the lender. If, however, property values are poor or falling, and deals involve little or no money down, sellers may face substantial risks if buyers default.

The Buyer's Strategy

1) Always compare assumable financing deals with currently available mortgages in terms of interest rates, settlement costs, prepayment penalties, and other terms.

2) Be aware that not all "assumable" financing is freely assumable. In many cases, lenders have a right to grant assumptions "at the lender's option" to purchasers they alone deem "qualified," a definition that may hinge on upfront charges or higher interest rates.

The Seller's Strategy

1) Before placing your home on the market, check with your lender to see if your current financing is assumable at its original rate and terms and if the lender has the right to approve or disapprove a new borrower, change the rate of interest, or require new terms. In addition, ask the lender what, if any, continuing obligation you will have after the loan is assumed. Get the lender's answers in writing.

2) Avoid deals with little or no money down, particularly if they involve taking over old financing. Your buyer will have little risk, but you may face substantial liabilities as a result of such financing techniques.

WHAT TO DO WHEN A SELLER "TAKES BACK" A LOAN

When we think about real estate financing, we typically think in terms of savings and loan associations, mortgage bankers, credit unions and other lending institutions. Yet many sales involve the use of owner take-backs—deals where sellers provide some or all of the financing needed to close the deal.

Sellers take back financing for various reasons. For some owners, taking back a loan is simply a good deal because the rate of return is higher than alternative investments. Moreover, the loan is secured by the owner's former home, a familiar asset with a known value.

In weak markets, when sales are poor or interest rates are high (or both), sellers often take back loans at below-market rates because self-financing is the only effective way to market homes. By giving below-market rates, sellers are marketing their homes at a discount, possibly the best choice in an otherwise difficult sales period.

Buyers, in turn, often like seller take-backs because there are no application costs and points are rare, so that even when sellers and lenders charge the same interest rates, seller financing is cheaper. In addition, seller financing is often available at discounted rates.

Standardized offer documents approach the issue of seller take-backs in various ways. Some forms avoid the matter altogether, while others build in the option of owner financing. For buyers and sellers, however, it is best to spell out carefully the terms and conditions of all owner take-backs.

An offer should certainly include the size of the loan, the interest rate, the monthly payment, and the term of the loan. This information, plus whether the take-back is a first or second "trust" or "mortgage"—a somewhat different financial instrument—can be found in most standardized offer forms.

In addition to basic information, however, it is also wise to include a variety of clarifications when a seller take-back is part of the sale:

- The loan documents must be in a form satisfactory to the seller. In other words, the seller—like any lender—gets to make the rules.

- The offer should state whether the seller's financing is assumable and if the property can be sold "subject to" the seller's loan without the seller's written permission.
- It should be clearly stated if a balloon payment will be due at the end of the loan term.
- Contract financing language should survive settlement.
- A seller who takes back financing should have an absolute right to review a buyer's credit information. If such information is not satisfactory to a seller, then the deal can be terminated and the buyer's deposit refunded in full.
- Sellers should welcome prepayments, since the risk associated with the loan declines as it is repaid. Conversely, interest income will decline as a result of prepayments because less principal is outstanding.

The Buyer's Strategy

1) Look for seller financing when interest rates and closing costs are high.

2) Be aware if any balloon payment is due at the end of the loan term.

3) Prepare credit information for a seller with the same care as you would for a commercial lender.

4) Shop around! See how the seller's financing compares with other loan options.

5) Ask to see the seller's proposed loan documents prior to making a commitment to buy. This can be done as part of a legal review of all papers associated with the sale.

The Seller's Strategy

1) Insist on your right to approve all loan documents.

2) Insist on your right to review the buyer's finances.

3) Make certain your lien is recorded in local property records.

4) Have the buyer acknowledge the existence of a balloon payment, if there is one. This may prevent future claims by a purchaser who says he didn't know about the balloon payment.

5) Be aware that the laws regarding real estate finance are not only complex, but they also vary from jurisdiction to jurisdiction. For instance, certain second trust borrowers in Maryland have the right, as this is written, to defer balloon payments for as long as two years. Review all seller financing terms

with an attorney to assure that your rights as a lender are protected, that you understand all options in the event of the buyer's failure to pay, and that you have not violated usury laws or other regulations.

6) Consider having local, federally insured lenders collect money on your behalf. The money can then be electronically transferred to an account in another city or state if desired. The attraction of a bank or savings and loan association making collections is that you need not worry about checks being "lost in the mail." The down side of this approach is that the lender will charge for this service.

7) Speak to a tax attorney, CPA, or other qualified authority regarding the tax implications of owner financing before offering a loan to a buyer.

8) Make certain you have the right to charge a late penalty in the event payments are delayed.

9) Reserve the right to change trustees without notice or cause if a deed of trust is used to document the debt.

10) If you sell the note to raise cash, be certain to show that it is being sold "Without Recourse to Original Holder." If the note is sold without recourse, it means that the new holder can only pursue the borrower if the terms of the loan are not met. If the new holder has recourse, it means that you—the original holder of the note—may ultimately be liable for its payment.

THIRD-PARTY FINANCING

When people talk about real estate financing sources what they generally mean is money from a commercial lender, a seller, a private lender, or a gift from parents and relatives. There are other places to find mortgage money, however, including loans from individuals and organizations not generally involved with real estate financing.

For instance, there are more than 700,000 private pension plans with more than one participant, according to the Pension and Welfare Benefits Administration. Many of these pensions are office plans for 5 to 20 people that were organized by doctors, lawyers, and small businesses. Because of compound interest, time, and tax sheltering, these pension plans now have multimillion dollar balances. Such money can be used for mortgage financing in certain situations, often with rates and terms as good or better than commercial lenders.

Alternative loan sources are also likely to balloon as a result of programming from Fannie Mae. Under the Community Home Buyer's Program, low- and moderate-income purchasers can buy homes with

> ### Model Language:
> ### Third-Party Financing
>
> Purchaser is to obtain a loan in the amount of $\underline{\hspace{1cm}}$, due in $\underline{\hspace{2cm}}$ years and bearing an interest rate of $\underline{\hspace{1.5cm}}$ percent per annum, compounded quarterly, payable at approximately $\underline{\hspace{1.5cm}}$ per month to $\underline{\hspace{1.5cm}}$.
>
> Subject financing is to be in the form of (check one):
>
> $\underline{\hspace{0.7cm}}$ A loan to be repaid in full.
>
> $\underline{\hspace{0.7cm}}$ A loan from $\underline{\hspace{1.5cm}}$, with the unpaid balance remaining as of $\underline{\hspace{1.5cm}}$ (Date) to be forgiven provided the borrower is still employed as of $\underline{\hspace{1.5cm}}$ (Date) by $\underline{\hspace{1.5cm}}$ and/or its successors and/or assigns.
>
> $\underline{\hspace{0.7cm}}$ A loan from $\underline{\hspace{1.5cm}}$, with all interest and principal to be forgiven provided the borrower is still employed by $\underline{\hspace{1.5cm}}$ and/or its successors and/or assigns as of $\underline{\hspace{1.5cm}}$ (Date).
>
> $\underline{\hspace{0.7cm}}$ A loan for the purpose of buying subject real estate that IS/IS NOT to be secured by the property.
>
> If subject financing is not available with the terms and conditions shown in this clause, or if the lender named in this clause cannot deliver the required funds at closing, then this agreement shall terminate and Purchaser's deposit shall be returned in full.
>
> Within $\underline{\hspace{1.5cm}}$ days following ratification of this Agreement/Contract/Offer, Purchaser is to present to Seller with a letter from the lender named in this clause expressly stating that: one, Purchaser is qualified to obtain subject financing; and two, that the Lender has available all funds required for closing.
>
> (To be signed by the buyer, seller, and lender.)

as little as 3 percent down providing another 2 percent comes from an employer, community group, or government agency. With a total of 5 percent down—3 percent from the buyer and 2 percent from an outside source—it then becomes possible to acquire 95 percent financing.

Under the Fannie Mae program, the 2 percent down payment from outside sources can be in the form of a loan, a grant, or monthly payment assistance. Another alternative is a loan that is forgiven over time. For instance, an employer can loan Walker $2,000 with the understanding that if Walker still works for the company in two years, the entire debt will be forgiven.

A third outside source may well be a broker or group of brokers who pool their money to make loans. The usual arrangement is that a buyer puts down at least 10 percent, assumes an existing mortgage, and the brokers put up the balance. Such financing is attractive because it typically involves no points and little paperwork.

In considering outside loan sources there are a number of special issues which must be addressed.

- The loan papers must be in a form "satisfactory" to the lender.
- The loan must meet all appropriate legal tests. For instance, there may be restrictions on the use of pension monies.
- The borrower must be told if there is to be a balloon payment.
- Prepayments—in whole or in part without penalty—should be allowed.
- The loan source should have an absolute right to check the borrower's credit.
- There should be a title search associated with the loan to assure that the property has a good and marketable title.
- Special terms, such as a forgiveness clause, should be spelled out.

Third-party loans also raise a complex matter that borrowers and lenders need to review with care.

In the usual situation, if Rogers makes a loan to Lipton for the purchase of real estate, the loan is secured by the property. If Lipton fails to pay, Rogers can foreclose on the property and get the money back (or as much money as is available through the foreclosure process).

But with third-party lending there is often a problem. A third-party lender such as Rogers may not be the only lender in the picture.

For example, suppose Lipton is buying a property for $150,000. A commercial lender, Ace Mortgage, will put up 80 percent of the acquisition cost as a first trust, $120,000 in this example. Lipton can put up $10,000 from his funds and Rogers is willing to make a $20,000 second trust.

On paper it would seem that Lipton has the financing to make his deal, but Ace Mortgage may think otherwise. They may not want to make a loan with a second trust on the property.

If the Rogers loan cannot be a second trust, then several issues arise.

First, Rogers may not want to make an unsecured personal loan.

Second, because the loan is unsecured and therefore more risky, Rogers may want a higher rate of interest.

Third, Lipton must repay Rogers. If Lipton is making monthly payments for an unsecured debt—a personal loan—those payments must be reported to the lender. The lender will include those monthly payments with other consumer debt such as credit card and auto loan payments when calculating whether or not Lipton can qualify for a mortgage. The more Lipton must pay each month for consumer debt, the less likely he is to qualify for the financing he needs.

Fourth, if Lipton borrows money from Rogers and the debt is not secured by real estate, then interest on the debt is unlikely to be tax deductible. Speak with a tax attorney, CPA, or enrolled agent for specific information.

For both buyers and sellers the growing availability of mortgage money from outside sources should be seen as good news. More lenders mean more competition to place loans, and more competition pushes rates toward the lowest possible levels. That said, there are barriers to the use of third-party loans that should be considered **before** entering into a real estate transaction.

The Buyer's Strategy

1) Whether a loan comes from a traditional lender or a third party, it's a loan. To be worthwhile, it must be as good as or better than other available mortgage options.

2) Always have private loan agreements reviewed by your attorney prior to acceptance to assure that all terms are fair and appropriate.

3) When using financing from a third party, make certain that the offer shows an interest rate and other terms acceptable to you. The offer should be written so that if the terms cannot be met, or if the third party cannot produce the required funding, then the deal ends and your deposit is returned in full.

4) Speak with lenders before buying to assure that funds from a third-party can be used to purchase real estate. Ask if the lender will allow the third-party loan to be recorded as a lien against the property. Also, ask how third-party funding will alter your ability to qualify for a mortgage.

5) Speak with a tax professional if the third-party loan is not secured by the property to determine if there is any way for the interest to be deductible.

The Seller's Strategy

1) As a seller you don't care how the deal is financed, just as long as money is available for closing.

2) If a buyer wants to use a third-party loan source, insist on a letter from the third-party lender stating that the purchaser qualifies for the loan and that all funds are available for closing. If the loan from the outside party is to be a second trust or second mortgage, also insist on a letter from the primary lender within several days after the contract is signed stating that such financing is acceptable.

GETTING LOAN COMMITMENTS IN ADVANCE

Model Language:
Buyer to Get Prompt Loan Commitment

Receipt by Seller or Seller's agent of a written statement from a bona fide lender shall be required by _____M. (TIME) on _____ (DATE) showing that Purchaser, in lender's view, has sufficient income, credit and assets to qualify for the financing necessary under subject Agreement/Contract/Offer; that lender has such funds available at the rate and terms specified in subject Agreement/Contract/Offer; and that settlement on or before the closing date shown in subject Agreement/Contract/Offer is feasible and reasonable. Purchaser agrees to make prompt application, in good faith, for all financing required to purchase subject property. If written approval satisfactory to Seller cannot be obtained within the time period stated herein then, in that event, this Agreement/Contract/Offer shall automatically be null and void unless the time limit shown herein is extended by written agreement of Seller and Purchaser. Purchaser shall promptly inform Seller of all communication to or from lenders concerning subject property. If subject Agreement/Contract/Offer is terminated as a result of this paragraph, then any deposits made by Purchaser shall be refunded in full.

When interest rates are rising or when purchasers are buying at the limits of their income, sellers may wonder if an offer should be accepted. If Mr. Washington, a seller, is offering his house for $145,000 and Mr. Terhune comes in with a $142,000 bid, Washington must consider this offer. But if Terhune is marginally qualified, Washington may reject the offer because completion is implausible—Terhune seems unlikely to get financing. Or, rather than accept the offer outright, Washington might make a counteroffer taking the $142,000 but requiring Terhune to show within a short period of time that he is financially qualified and has found a lender willing to finance the property.

What Washington is trying to avoid is a situation where a buyer makes an offer but can't get a loan. The problem here, besides the failure of the sale to go through, is that Washington may have his home off the market for many weeks while Terhune searches fruitlessly for a mortgage. By requiring his buyer to locate and qualify for financing within a short period, say 14 to 21 days, Washington can, if necessary, get his property back on the market and available to potential buyers within a brief period. The buyer, Terhune, also benefits since he will quickly know if the property is within his financial reach.

The catch for both seller Washington and buyer Terhune is that assurances from lenders tend to be "porous," a polite expression that means full of holes.

In response to demands for an up-front assurance that a purchaser can obtain financing, lenders are likely to provide what is known throughout the real estate industry as a "hand-holding" letter. This is a finely written document beautifully printed on tasteful stationery which says—in so many words—that the buyer and lender met, that no fatal financial flaws have been found, but that the lender isn't making any commitments until everything associated with the borrower is reviewed, the property appraised, and the title checked.

Viewed another way, the letter might look like this:

Dear Mr. Washington:

Mr. Fred Terhune (purchaser) has provided information to this institution required of those applying for a home loan. Based upon a preliminary review of the information provided by Mr. Terhune, he appears to be qualified to receive a loan in the amount of $140,500, at an 8 percent interest rate over a 30-year term.

This institution has funds available to make such a loan. After proper processing of the loan application, a full review and verification of Mr. Terhune's credit history and income, an appraisal of the property satisfactory to this institution, a title examination satisfactory to us, and the resolution of such minor issues which may arise, a settlement date of May 26th appears feasible.

We are prepared to state that Mr. Terhune made application for financing with regard to your property on May 4th and that our initial evaluation is positive. However, please be aware that because various verifications, examinations, commitments, and other matters remain outstanding, this letter should not be construed as a pledge by this institution to provide financing.

> Sincerely,
> Lolita Crawford
> Vice President

The Buyer's Strategy

1) If a seller asks you to demonstrate financial capacity, do not regard this request as a personal affront.

2) Having a written financial commitment from a lender will quickly show whether a deal is feasible.

3) Be prepared to act promptly. Apply for financing quickly, have your papers arranged and ready to go, and work closely with the lender to process the loan.

4) If a seller wants a hand-holding letter, be certain to provide one. A hand-holding letter should be seen as evidence that you applied for a mortgage on a specific date in an effort to satisfy your contractual obligations. If the mortgage does not come through, at least there is evidence that you made a good-faith effort to obtain a loan.

The Seller's Strategy

1) If you're uncertain of the buyer's financial capacity or the availability of money, require the purchaser to qualify for financing and get a loan commitment within a short period after an agreement has been reached. Whatever period of time you want should be clearly specified in the contract. If the money is not available at rates and terms required in the contract or otherwise acceptable to the buyer, the deal will be off, and the property can again be placed on the market.

2) Require the buyer to inform you of all communication with any lenders who are contacted about financing the property. "All communication" should include letters, telephone calls, and informal notes.

3) Be aware that hand-holding letters are not loan commitments. They merely acknowledge that lender and buyer have met and that, in general terms and without verification, the buyer has the financial capacity to purchase your property. While this information is significant, it does not mean financing is assured.

13
Co-signers

Model Language:
Sale Contingent on Co-signer

This Agreement/Contract/Offer is contingent on the willingness of _____ to act as Co-signer under terms and conditions satisfactory to Purchaser. If this contingency is not removed and/or acted upon by Purchaser for any reason whatsoever, or if Seller or Seller's agent is not notified in writing by _____M. (TIME) on _____ (DATE) that a Co-signer has agreed to terms and conditions satisfactory to Purchaser, then this Agreement/Contract/Offer shall be null and void and the deposit of the Purchaser, if any, shall be returned in full.

The undersigned Co-signer agrees to take all steps and actions required to complete and/or effectuate this transaction, including but not limited to signing documents, submitting credit information, and making tax returns and other financial documents available as required, and failure to do so shall give Seller the right to declare Purchaser's deposit to be forfeited and to retain said deposit and/or to seek such legal and equitable remedies as may be permitted under the terms of subject Agreement/Contract/Offer.

The undersigned Co-signer agrees that title to subject property shall be in the name of the undersigned Purchaser alone. The undersigned Co-signer and Purchaser agree that this Addendum shall be binding upon him/her/them and each of his/her/their respective heirs, executors, administrators, successors, and assigns. (To be signed by purchaser, seller, *and* co-signer.)

In an increasing number of instances, the high cost of housing has changed traditional buying patterns. Where homes were once easily available to individuals and families, today buying a home is beyond the means of many Americans. Indeed, if one looks at the cost of the average house and the size of the average income, it becomes clear that in many instances the income of a *single* wage earner is not sufficient to buy the typical home. Two solutions to the affordability problem are (1) buy a house with someone else or (2) have someone co-sign the mortgage.

Buying jointly is a simple issue in most contract forms. There is typically a space that asks how title will be held, and it is here that buyers can write in "Bill Jones and Laura Jones, as tenants by the entirety" (meaning they're married) or whatever form of title is appropriate.

More complex is the matter of co-signers, people who are liable for the full repayment of the mortgage but who are not always co-owners. While contracts commonly address the issue of title, they rarely provide for the use of co-signers.

Perhaps a purchaser has yet to establish a credit record or is newly employed or just out of school. A co-signer helps by being responsible for the repayment of the loan and allowing the use of his or her credit to help the purchaser qualify for financing. Lenders like co-signers, particularly those with extensive assets, because it gives them additional protection in the event of default.

Co-signers should be aware, however, that their participation in a realty transaction creates a clear liability even if they are not also co-owners. If Bill Hunter co-signs a loan with his son, Bill, Jr., Hunter senior will be fully responsible for its repayment. The extent of such liability may include not only the obligation to repay the mortgage, but also foreclosure costs.

Although the issue of co-signer liability must be taken seriously, it should also be said that not all co-signers face equal risk. For example, in a deal with 20 percent down and rising home prices, a co-signer's risk would be largely limited to his or her original investment, any money that was used for a down payment and settlement. Conversely, if property values are declining, the sale of the property might not produce enough revenue to pay off the loan, in which case the co-signer might be responsible for the shortage.

From the seller's perspective, care should be taken when an offer is contingent upon the involvement of individuals who have not yet agreed to act as co-signers. There is always the risk that prospective co-signers won't want to assist a buyer or provide credit information to a lender, steps which unless completed will end the deal.

Contracts involving co-signers should not be viewed by sellers in a negative context. It is possible that the only person in the entire world who wants to buy your property is someone without enough capital or credit to make a sale, someone who can only be converted from renter to owner with the help of a co-signer.

The Buyer's Strategy

1) If a co-signer is needed, make your offer contingent on that person's, or those persons', agreeing to sign with you. No co-signer, no deal—in which case provide that your deposit will be returned in full.

2) If possible, have a co-signer committed in writing at the time you make your offer. This will make for a much stronger bargaining position.

3) Have the co-signer committed to taking all steps necessary to complete the deal, such as supplying tax records, completing credit forms, and signing documents. As an example, the model language used in this section must be signed by a co-signer to have any value.

4) Clearly show that title (ownership) is to be in buyer's name alone, if that is to be the case.

The Seller's Strategy

1) Accept a deal that depends on a co-signer only if the co-signer signs the purchase offer, so his or her participation will be assured.

2) Make the purchaser responsible if a co-signer fails to go through with the sale once a contract has been ratified.

3) Get basic credit statements from both the buyer and the prospective co-signer.

4) Beware of purchasers who anticipate that it will take a long time (say longer than two weeks) to find a co-signer. Without a co-signer there may be no deal and valuable marketing time can be lost.

5) If the co-signer is married, get the signature of both husband and wife on the purchase offer to create a stronger deal.

14
Holding Title: Ownership and Co-ownership

Model Language:
How Title Shall Be Recorded
Title to subject property shall be recorded as follows:

It is probable that the majority of all private home sales involve two or more owners, the most common sales being to married couples. Most standardized real estate contracts address the issue of ownership by asking how title is to be recorded, a matter of great importance to buyers.

At first it may seem as though the matter of title is fairly simple. If Tom Noble buys a home, he is the outright owner of the property. He can finance the property, rent it, sell it, paint it green, have a pet, or leave it to a nephew in his will. As a sole owner, Noble is in complete control of the property.

But the majority of real estate transactions do not involve individual ownership. Most property is purchased by two or more people and sometimes by such entities as partnerships and corporations as well. With two or more owners, matters of title become far more complex.

When we talk about co-ownership, we talk about "tenancies." The use of the term "tenancies" arose because when the English legal system was first developing—the model for most of our own laws and legal concepts—most land was owned by just a few nobles, and everybody else was a tenant. Today, we still call the co-ownership of property a "tenancy" even though the term does not refer to a landlord/renter relationship.

THE WORLD OF TENANCIES

Perhaps the most common form of co-tenancy is a "tenancy by the entireties," a form of title reserved for married couples. "Tenancy by the entireties" is another aged legal expression that arose from the idea that a married couple was a "full and entire" unit. In early times all property rights, as well as the deed, were, in effect, in the name of the husband alone because it was assumed that the rights of the wife were "merged" into those of the husband when they were married. Today's view of marital relationships is a bit more enlightened, but the consequences of a tenancy by the entireties, as a unified ownership, are still essentially the same.

A property owned as a tenancy by the entireties is held fully and completely by each spouse, but the property cannot be divided by one spouse without the consent of the other. With a tenancy by the entireties:

- Any income or proceeds from the sale of the property is shared equally by husband and wife except if there is an agreement to the contrary.
- The death of one spouse results in the automatic, total ownership of the property by the surviving spouse. Because there is no change in ownership, there is no inheritance or estate tax. (Each spouse already has a 100 percent interest in the property.)
- One spouse cannot sell the property without the consent of the other spouse.

Most important, property held as a tenancy by the entireties cannot be taken, liened, or attached by a creditor of just one of the spouses— only creditors of the husband and wife together can reach the property. So, if one spouse injures someone with an automobile, for instance, the injured person cannot go after property held under a tenancy by the entireties deed to satisfy a claim or judgment. If, however, both husband and wife agree to a debt by signing a promissory note together, then the property can be taken to satisfy a joint obligation.

A different real estate concept in connection with property owned by spouses is called "community property." Several states have enacted community property laws, under the theory that all property acquired by husband and wife during the marriage should be shared equally, but this type of ownership differs somewhat from a tenancy by the entireties.

For example, community property permits husband and wife to share in the property acquired during the marriage if it was acquired by both parties through joint efforts. Property acquired by one of the parties through separate funds, inherited by only one of the parties or owned prior to the marriage itself, may be property in which title is retained by just one spouse. Community property can result in complications if a marriage ends, since the ownership trail of each property must be carefully traced to compute the ownership interest of each spouse (in a divorce) or heir (with the death of a spouse).

Since a tenancy by the entireties is a unique form of ownership reserved only for married couples, it follows that if the marriage is dissolved by divorce, the title must also change. With a final divorce decree, the former husband and wife become "tenants in common," another form of ownership.

A "tenancy in common" is a form of ownership which may involve two or more people and does not require a marital relationship. With a tenancy in common:

- There can be two or more co-owners, but their ownership interests need not be equal. If three people own a lot, one person might have a 50 percent interest, another 35 percent, and a third 15 percent.
- There is no automatic "right of survivorship." Unlike a tenancy by the entireties, a share in the property held by one owner does not automatically pass to any other owner at death. When a tenant in common dies, his interest is transferred to his heirs and not the other tenants in common, unless there is an agreement or will giving title to a co-owner.

- Interests held by tenants in common may be sold separately by individual owners. In many cases, however, tenants in common agree when they first acquire property to give other co-owners a "right of first refusal" to buy out one another if any owner wishes to sell.

Situations also may arise where unmarried people wish to buy property together but with a right of survivorship. There is such a form of ownership and it's called a "joint tenancy."

The conditions of joint tenancy may seem very similar to those of tenants in common, which is why it is important—and required by law—that the parties specify in very clear and precise language in the deed that they are forming a joint tenancy.

The creation of a joint tenancy requires four main conditions, or "unities." Those conditions are as follows:

Unity of Interest. This means that all owners involved in a joint tenancy must have the same form of ownership.

Unity of Time. This means that the time of ownership of the property must be the same for all owners.

Unity of Title. Unity of title requires that all of the people involved in a joint tenancy receive the property out of the same transaction and that their interests are the same.

Unity of Possession. All joint tenants must have undivided and equal rights of possession—even if the actual shares (i.e., percentage of ownership) may be different. In other words, each owner must have equal access to the property and equal use of the property even if one owner has a 40 percent interest and another has a 60 percent share.

With both joint and common ownership, a creditor can claim any individual owner's share to satisfy a debt.

The manner in which title is held can have a significant impact on a variety of important matters such as marital rights, divorces, wills, estates, and general liability. Questions concerning title issues should be discussed in detail with an attorney.

The Buyer's Strategy

If you are buying with others, be certain everyone agrees on the form of title that will be used to hold the property. This decision should be made before entering the marketplace, and in many instances the assistance of a lawyer should be sought.

The Seller's Strategy

Ask how title is to be held when two or more people are buying property together.

EQUITY-SHARING

Model Language:
Sale Contingent on the Creation of an Equity-Sharing Agreement

This Agreement/Contract/Offer is contingent on the creation of a written equity-sharing agreement satisfactory to all Purchasers. If this contingency is not removed and/or acted upon by Purchaser for any reason whatsoever, or if Seller or Seller's agent is not notified of Purchaser's dissatisfaction in writing by _____M. (TIME) on _____ (DATE), then this contingency shall be removed automatically and this Agreement/Contract/Offer shall otherwise be in full force and effect. If Purchaser or Purchaser's agent notifies Seller or Seller's agent by the time and date specified in this paragraph that subject review is unsatisfactory then this Agreement/Contract/Offer shall be null and void and any deposits made by Purchaser shall be returned in full.

It is not at all uncommon for people to buy real estate jointly. Prior to 1981, if one owner lived on the property no owner could claim "excess" investor deductions. What this meant was that if two people bought property and rented it to a third party, the investors could claim tax deductions for such items as mortgage interest, property taxes, and depreciation. These deductions, in turn, typically created paper losses. If the property produced a $5,000 income but real and paper expenses (such as depreciation) totaled $8,000, the owners would not pay taxes on income from the property and $3,000 earned elsewhere could also be sheltered from taxation. If one investor lived on the property, however, the rules were different, and excess losses generally were not allowed.

In 1981, a federal law created a new approach to joint ownership, an arrangement called "equity sharing." Now two or more people can own property together and for tax purposes an owner living on the property will be treated in the same manner as any other property owner, while a non-resident owner will be treated as an investor.

Since equity-sharing residents and non-residents each enjoy a separate tax status, you can imagine that such relationships raise interesting questions. For instance:

- What is the ownership interest of each party? (It's negotiable.)
- What is the market rental for the property? (Check comparable properties in the immediate area and ask local brokers.)
- How much of the fair market rental should be paid to the non-resident owner? (An amount equal to his or her proportionate interest. For example, if the fair market rental for a property is $500 per month and investor Reilly owns 60 percent of the property, Reilly should receive $300 per month from the resident owner.)
- What happens if one party wants to sell but not the other? (A written agreement can provide for each party to have a "first right of refusal" if the other wants to sell or, alternatively, an option to buy the property at a certain price by a certain deadline.)
- Who is responsible for maintenance? (Regular maintenance is generally the responsibility of the resident owner. Capital improvement costs are typically shared according to each party's percentage of ownership.)
- What happens if the original resident wants to move out? (The equity-sharing agreement usually makes the resident owner responsible for finding a new tenant and that tenant will be subject to the approval of the investor owner.)
- How can ownership interests be divided if investment contributions differ; for example, when one buyer puts up cash while the other agrees to make repairs and improvements? (This is a tricky area which must be resolved in the initial ownership agreement.)

These and other questions mean that prospective equity sharers *must have a written agreement in hand prior to acquiring property,* preferably something prepared by a knowledgable attorney. Tax advice, a will, and estate planning are also important, especially if the co-buyers are members of the same family.

The Buyer's Strategy

1) Co-buyers should have a complete understanding of the equity-sharing concept before entering the marketplace. For advice, speak to lawyers and brokers, and check with local colleges to see if seminars concerning the subject are available.

2) Be sure you and your co-purchaser have worked out all details of an equity-sharing arrangement with the help of an attorney and tax authority.

3) If you do not have a written equity-sharing agreement, make your offer subject to the development of an agreement satisfactory to you and your co-buyers.

The Seller's Strategy

1) Whether your property is bought by one person or by a horde of buyers is irrelevant as long as the price and terms you receive are acceptable.

2) Purchases by two or more people may be advantageous in the sense that it may be easier for your purchasers to obtain financing with two or more incomes than with one.

15
Deeds

Although the process of real estate negotiation is necessarily centered on the sales contract and how it is written, deeds are a critically important aspect of each transaction and should not be overlooked.

A deed is a legal document that shows who owns a given property and what type of ownership they have, describes the property, and references what restrictions and covenants, if any, have been recorded concerning the property.

Historically, however, deeds were anything but bland legal documents. Deeds in the Middle Ages were precious pieces of parchment, expertly styled and often bearing unique seals and marks to show their authenticity. Some deeds, in fact, were single sheets of parchment that recorded title information twice, after which the parchment was torn in half, very deliberately, so that two complete copies of the deed were created. If there was a question about the authenticity of a deed—or when title was transferred—the two halves could be brought together to see if they matched, thus guarding against falsified deeds.

A deed today is nothing more (or less) than a device to convey property ownership, something that shows who does the conveying—the *grantor*, or seller—and who gets the property, the *grantee*, or buyer. There are five basic requirements to have a valid deed.

First, as with contracts generally, all parties must be legally "competent," an expression which means of legal age and of sound mind. Legal age is the "age of majority" in the state where the transaction is taking place, traditionally 21 but now 18 in most jurisdictions.

Being of "sound mind" means the individual signing the deed has an awareness of what he or she is doing. Problems such as alcohol and drug abuse or a history of mental instability can raise competency questions.

Second, there must be a statement of consideration. A deed in most cases will specify the dollar value paid for the property.

Third, there must be a description of the property showing, for example, the lot, block, and subdivision of a house located in an urban area. A description of the land is an essential feature of a deed, information that must be carefully verified and recorded. Numerous lawsuits have arisen because land descriptions were faulty, insufficient, or simply unclear. A description of the property may be very dry and uninteresting, but the accuracy and reliability of this description is essential to the validity of a deed.

Fourth, the deed must be signed by the seller.

Fifth, there must be delivery and acceptance.

"Delivery," in this sense, refers to a statement or indication of intention on the part of the seller to pass the property over to the buyer and thereby relinquish his rights. This may require more than a mere signing of the deed. For example, a seller could sign the deed and keep it in a safe place while considering whether to go through with the transaction. If the intended purchaser then made off with the deed, despite the existence of a signed document, there would be no sale because there was no delivery—the seller did not state his intention to transfer the property and, therefore, did not "deliver" the deed.

The seller, then, must take some definite action or use some particular words in order for the deed to be delivered. One way of doing this would be to sit at the settlement table, sign the deed, and hand it over to the buyer saying, "Well, the property is all yours now. I hope you enjoy it as much as I have." This statement would show a clear intention to transfer the property and would be a valid indication of delivery.

On the other hand, the seller may say nothing and yet delivery would be complete. The seller's presence at settlement and his signing the deed in the presence of the buyer, coupled with his failure to object to the buyer taking title, would indicate his intention to transfer the property.

A delivery can also be contingent on some event, and if that event occurs, delivery is then complete. For example, a seller might say that the deed will be valid if he doesn't accept another offer by Friday. If no other offer is accepted, then delivery will be complete as of the close of business on Friday.

In addition to a delivery, there must also be "acceptance"—some indication or statement by the buyer that the transaction is satisfactory. Acceptance here need not mean that the buyer is waiving any rights that he may have if there are problems with the deed or with the warranties in the deed, or if there are any other complications with the transaction. It simply means that there has been consent to a transaction by the buyer and that the property is now his.

All deeds must meet the five basic requirements above, but not all deeds are identical. Some deeds include many "warranties," or promises of good title by the seller, while others offer virtually no guarantees to the purchaser.

In general terms there are three types of warranty deeds. The strongest level of assurance comes with a general warranty; less meaningful is a special warranty deed; and finally there is a quitclaim deed, which offers no assurance of ownership at all.

A "general" warranty is the most extensive guarantee that can accompany a deed. A general warranty says that title to the property is good and valid, that the property is free and clear of all encumbrances and liens except as noted in the deed, and that the seller guarantees title back to the first time an ownership interest in the property was created—back to pre-revolutionary times in some cases.

In contrast to a general warranty, a "special" warranty deed says the seller's title is good and valid but subject to any liens or encumbrances that might be outstanding at the time of settlement. No warranties are made, however, about title prior to the time the seller bought the property, so the seller's responsibility for providing good title is limited. This type of warranty requires a careful check of the land records to determine if there are any difficulties with the title or any encumbrances that were unknown or undisclosed by the seller at settlement.

The final form of warranty is, in fact, little or no warranty at all. A "quitclaim" deed says that the seller is giving a deed to the property without any guarantees, not even a guarantee that he has good title. A quitclaim deed says only that a seller is willing to transfer any interest that he or she has in the land—whatever that interest may be. It is entirely possible that the seller has no valid or legal title to the property. *Even so, this is not an illegal transaction, so long as the buyer understands the limitations of a quitclaim deed and the considerable risk that he or she is taking.*

Are there any situations where a quitclaim deed can make sense? There are such cases, though they are not particularly common. For example, suppose Mr. Wilson dies and his estate includes a home on Conway Lane that is to be given to a cousin, Mr. Hoover. The executor of Wilson's estate may not have full knowledge about the scope—or limitations—of Wilson's title to the property on Conway Lane, but he is obligated to pass title to Hoover. To satisfy the obligations of the estate, the executor may give a quitclaim deed to Hoover that transfers whatever interests Wilson had in the property without the executor saying the title is sound.

Both buyers and sellers will want to make every effort through their attorneys or the party conducting settlement to assure that the deed is correctly drafted. Accuracy at the time a deed is written will do much to prevent complex and costly title challenges in the future.

16

Termites

The issue of termites is as good an example as can be found to show how a seemingly simple matter can evolve into a convoluted and complex set of considerations.

Simply stated, buyers want to purchase real estate free and clear of termites and other wood-boring insects. If there's damage, it should be the seller's job to fix it. Sellers have a different goal: to minimize their liability and pay as little as possible if insects are found or if there has been damage.

Given the basic issues here, a buyer—Fitzroy—could simply state, "Property is to be free and clear of termites as of settlement, and all termite damage shall be repaired by Seller."

The language above seems okay, but it fails to address a variety of problems. What happens if the property has been damaged by carpenter bees rather than termites? Fitzroy's simple sentence doesn't say anything about wood-boring insects other than termites. There may be seven million carpenter bees on the property but the seller—Johnson—has no obligation using the above language to get rid of the bees or repair any damage they have caused. Fitzroy, seeing his omission, fixes his brief sentence by adding "wood-boring insects" here and there.

So now we've got seller Johnson looking for termites and wood-boring insects. But Johnson, for his part, has no incentive to find the little creatures and that means someone else has to do the searching.

The obvious person to conduct a termite search is a licensed exterminator, someone who knows his bugs. Johnson suggests his brother-in-law, a local exterminator, as the perfect candidate for the job. Fitzroy—not being totally naive—demands the right to select an exterminator.

Johnson is not particularly bothered by having an independent inspection, especially since the inspector is only charged with examining "visible and accessible" areas of the property, the customary, usual, and traditional standard for termite inspectors. Given these conditions, Johnson hopes for an inspector with failing vision.

He is, however, bothered by something else. Fitzroy wants the "property" to be free and clear of termites. Does the term "property," wonders Johnson, include the woodpile or a 60-year-old detached garage? Suppose Johnson sprays a woodpile for termites, and the wood is subsequently used for a fire. Who's responsible if the buyer is poisoned by the fumes? Johnson suggests instead that the inspection be limited to his house.

Fitzroy has no interest in spraying a woodpile or making sure a fallen limb is termite-free. But if the inspection is limited to Johnson's house, then a detached garage on the property won't be included in the inspection. He compromises and agrees that the inspection should be limited to "improvements" on the property.

At this point, our buyer and seller have agreed on who will pick the inspector, what the inspector's responsibilities will be, and what is to be inspected. There are now just two more problems left to resolve: what if there are termites, and what if there has been damage to the house?

The seller readily agrees that if termites are found, the house should be treated at his expense. On the matter of repairs, however, there is much disagreement.

Seller Johnson worries that there may be nuisance damage, a minor piece of lumber somewhere that doesn't support the house but will be costly to repair. Fitzroy also has a worry—his being that the property may fall down.

To resolve these problems they create both a limit and a benchmark. It is agreed that the seller's financial obligation for the inspection, extermination, and repairs shall not exceed $750. If the cost for repairs and extermination tops $750, the buyer can end the deal, and his deposit will be refunded.

In this situation both parties gain something. The seller's liability is limited to $750 for insect-related costs, and the buyer can withdraw from the transaction if insect damage is extensive. However, if the buyer goes through with the sale, the seller is committed to pay as much as, but no more than, $750 to offset the buyer's potential repair costs.

The Buyer's Strategy

1) Recognize that insect damage can be significant and that an inspection of the property by a qualified examiner is important.

2) You should choose the inspector and not let the seller or the seller's agent make the choice. Have the seller pay for the cost of all repairs.

3) If damage is extensive, provide that you can terminate the offer and have your deposit returned in full.

The Seller's Strategy

1) Limit termite inspections to houses, garages, and other structures on the property.

2) Limit possible inspection, extermination, and repair costs to a specific dollar amount, preferably as little as possible.

3) Have the purchaser pay for the termite inspection, particularly if the buyer gets to name the inspector.

17
Credit Reports and Bargaining

Model Language:
Permission Given to Obtain Credit Report

Seller and/or Seller's agent is hereby authorized by Purchaser to order and obtain a Consumer Report (Credit Report) from a Consumer Credit Reporting Agency and to disburse information in said report to Seller and/or any other party with direct involvement in subject transaction, including but not limited to lenders, real estate brokers and agents and settlements providers. Purchaser agrees to sign and execute all documents necessary to insure subject Consumer Report is expeditiously provided and to pay all costs required to obtain said Consumer Report. Purchaser agrees that neither Seller nor Seller's agent shall be liable for any statements, reports, or documents included in, or resulting from, subject Consumer Credit Report.

Credit information submitted with subject Agreement/Contract/Offer shall be attached to and made a part of subject Agreement/Contract/Offer but shall not be regarded as a substitute for a Consumer Report (Credit Report) from a Consumer Reporting Agency.

Since the number of real estate purchases made entirely for cash is relatively small, it's clear that most transactions depend on the buyer's ability to borrow. Credit, then, is a central issue in virtually all transactions, something that must concern buyers, lenders, sellers, and brokers.

Model Language:
Seller Satisfaction with Consumer Report Required

If Seller is required to provide financing to Purchaser as a condition of this Agreement/Contract/Offer, then Seller shall have the right to determine if Purchaser's Consumer Report (Credit Report) and all related documents, including but not limited to past tax returns, are satisfactory to Seller. Purchaser shall provide required documents, information, and reports by _____M. (TIME) on _____ (DATE). Purchaser or Purchaser's agent must be notified of any dissatisfaction in writing by Seller or Seller's agent by _____M. (TIME) on _____ (DATE), otherwise this Agreement/Contract/Offer shall be in full force and effect. If Seller is not satisfied, then this Agreement/Contract/Offer shall be terminated and any deposit made by Purchaser shall be returned

---

A lender's interest in credit matters is obvious, but the need for sellers and their agents to have such information is often perceived as less significant, if not an outright invasion of privacy—at least in the eyes of many buyers.

Sellers, however, are surely entitled to credit information, particularly if they're asked to take back financing from a buyer. In such cases sellers are acting as lenders and have as much right as any other lender to credit information.

But even when a deal does not depend on owner financing, sellers still have a reasonable need for credit information, as the following examples illustrate:

- On the first day the Connors' house was held open, three identical offers were received. Connors will want to choose the offer made by the best qualified purchaser because that individual will have the strongest chance of getting a mortgage.
- Grassly received an offer from Emerson but is uncertain whether to accept, since Emerson has not provided any credit information. Without that information, Grassly cannot judge if Emerson has any hope of qualifying for a loan. If Grassly accepts the offer and Emerson is turned down for a loan, Emerson will get back his deposit in full, according to the terms of his offer, but Grassly will

have lost valuable marketing time and perhaps the opportunity to attract a good offer from a more qualified purchaser.

Credit information is normally gathered at two points in the home-buying process. First, basic credit forms are typically submitted by purchasers at the time an offer is made. Second, once a deal has been ratified, an independent financial history will be ordered by a lender from a credit bureau.

Buyers often argue that credit histories should not be shared with sellers, because such information can be used to undermine their bargaining position. If, for example, buyer Conklin says his offer of $125,000 is the most he can afford and his credit report shows assets of $380,000, a seller is likely to feel he can get a better price.

This is a no-win situation for purchasers. *It is true that revealing credit information can damage one's bargaining position.* Conversely, it is also true that sellers have a legitimate need for such figures, and in the battle for bargaining position, this is one fight that sellers almost always win. Why? Because an offer without an adequate credit statement is unlikely to be accepted.

Recognizing that full credit information may put them at a disadvantage, some buyers complete informal credit statements with information that is literally correct, though perhaps understated. For example, if $20,000 is needed at settlement and a purchaser has $30,000 in a money-market account, a buyer might list money-market holdings as "$20,000 plus."

What buyers cannot do is overstate income, inflate assets, or lie about factual matters. If Byron, a buyer, claims a $50,000 income and $200,000 in assets, a seller might accept his offer to buy a $150,000 property because of his financial qualifications. But if Byron lied and only makes $30,000 annually, his income might not support the mortgage necessary to purchase a $150,000 home. In another example, if Byron has been sued for $50,000 but says "no" when asked if he faces any pending judgments or lawsuits, he has made a statement that is materially false.

Serious consequences can result when purchasers inflate or falsify credit information forms. Such forms are commonly submitted to sellers at the time an offer is made and are "attached to and made a part of" the buyer's offer. Since the buyer's offer is secured by a deposit plus the possibility of other damages, materially incorrect information in a credit application may be used by sellers to justify damage claims.

In those sales where a deal depends on the willingness of the seller to take back financing, the transaction will normally be contingent on a review of the buyer's credit report that must be satisfactory to the seller. If the report is not satisfactory, the deal is finished, and the buyer's deposit is returned.

The Buyer's Strategy

1) Recognize that it is virtually impossible to get new financing without a credit report.

2) Do not wait until you are making an offer to gather credit information. Instead, have credit figures in hand before entering the marketplace so you can promptly make a loan application. Here are several steps to take:

3) Ask local real estate brokers and lenders for credit applications. The questions on such forms will suggest what information is generally requested.

4) List assets such as real estate less marketing costs, cash on hand, stocks, bonds, IRAs, Keogh plans, money market accounts, and the cash surrender value of life insurance policies.

5) List liabilities such as home and car loans, alimony, and credit card debt.

6) List all credit cards, savings accounts, IRAs and Keogh plans, stock accounts, etc., showing balances and account numbers.

7) Calculate your gross (before-tax) income. This can include dividends, bonuses, interest payments, rents, royalties, overtime, etc., if such payments are regular.

8) Prepare a cover letter explaining your financial position, particularly if any judgments or lawsuits are anticipated or outstanding or if you expect any change in your economic situation.

9) If you are self-employed, be prepared to submit tax returns for the past two to three years as part of the credit application process.

10) Do not inflate or falsify credit forms.

11) Before entering the marketplace, review your credit file with a local credit agency. Correct errors, if any, as required. Credit bureaus can be found in the Yellow Pages under "Credit Reporting Agencies."

12) *Always require, in writing, the prompt and full return of your deposit in the event that you do not qualify for financing.*

13) *Always require, in writing, the prompt and full return of your deposit if a seller must approve your credit information and such approval is not given.*

14) Establish a deadline by which the seller must either approve or disapprove your credit standing.

15) Ask where, in writing, the offer form states that your deposit is to be returned in full if your credit report is unsatisfactory.

The Seller's Strategy

1) Always ask for financial information from a buyer to determine if an offer is credible.

2) Have the buyer's credit statement "attached to and made a part of" the buyer's offer.

3) Have a deadline by which all credit information must be in your hands.

4) Require the purchaser to release you and your agent from any liability in case a credit report or any statements created from the report are negative, incorrect, or libelous.

5) Require the buyer to pay for the cost of any credit report from a credit reporting agency.

6) If you are taking back financing, make the deal dependent on your satisfaction with the purchaser's credit report. If you are not satisfied with the information and figures submitted, ask for further information or reject the offer.

7) If you receive two or more offers that are equal or essentially equal, favor the buyer with the stronger credit standing.

8) Expressly state that credit information provided by the purchaser is not a substitute for a Consumer Report (Credit Report) from an independent credit reporting agency.

18
Deposits

Model Language:
Deposit to Be Placed in Escrow Account, Damages Limited

Received from _____ (PURCHASER) a deposit in the amount of $_____ and in the form of _____ (a check, cash, a note) to be deposited by Seller or Seller's agent in an escrow account maintained in a local, federally insured bank or savings and loan institution and to be applied toward the purchase of Seller's property located at _____. Interest on Purchaser's deposit, if any, shall be credited to Purchaser, except in the case of default. Under no condition shall deposit monies be commingled with funds of the Seller or Seller's agent. In the event of default, Purchaser's total liability to Seller and Seller's agent shall not exceed the value of the deposit plus accrued interest, if any. In the event of default, broker shall be entitled to one-half of the deposit for services rendered but not more than the value of a full brokerage fee.

When purchasers make an offer to buy real estate, that offer is typically accompanied by some form of "consideration." The idea of consideration is to demonstrate the purchaser's seriousness and to compensate the seller if the purchaser causes the deal to fall through by withdrawing without a legally suitable reason. For instance, if buyer Pendleton places a $3,000 deposit on a home and then decides to back out of the deal because he later feels the price is too high, he may lose his deposit money.

Note that a "deposit" (sometimes called "earnest money") is not the same thing as a "down payment." A deposit is consideration given to the seller when an offer is made. A down payment is additional money paid by a purchaser at settlement to reduce mortgage borrowing requirements. As an example, if a home is bought for $100,000, there might be a $3,000 deposit. That deposit accompanies the offer and is credited to the buyer at settlement. However, the lender in this case will only loan $80,000 on the property. At settlement then, the buyer must come up with settlement costs plus a $17,000 down payment in cash.

How large is an appropriate deposit? There is no numerical guide or "standard" percentage; instead the answer depends on your status. If you're a seller, you want as much as possible—the full purchase price of the property if you can get it at the time you receive an offer. From the buyer's perspective, an adequate deposit might be $5.

Complicating the issue of deposits is the matter of disposition. In the event a buyer defaults, who gets the money? Surely the purpose of a deposit is to protect the seller, but there is usually another interested party as well: the broker. In case of default, brokers are often entitled to receive one-half of the deposit up to the value of their commission.

Brokers have a logical claim to a portion of the deposit. Their work is typically to find a buyer who is "ready, willing, and able" to purchase the property, and so, when a seller accepts a purchase offer, the work required of the broker in a listing agreement is largely completed. If the deal later falls through because the buyer defaults, the fact remains that the broker did his or her job and is entitled to some compensation.

Brokers hold deposits in an "escrow" or trust account, which means the buyer's money is separate and apart from the broker's funds. The funds are released at closing to the party conducting settlement. However, if the money is in dispute, it will not be released without the authority of both buyer and seller. Instead, the money in the broker's escrow account will be turned over to a court until buyer and seller reach a settlement.

Buyers, particularly, should be aware that forfeiting a deposit may not terminate all claims if a deal falls through. Many standardized form agreements provide that not only can buyers lose their deposits, they can also be sued for damages as well. From the buyer's viewpoint, it's best to limit potential claims from both the seller and the seller's agent to the deposit alone.

The Buyer's Strategy

1) Make every effort to require escrow accounts for deposits.

2) When escrow accounts are used, ask that they be maintained with local, federally insured lenders such as commercial banks or savings and loan associations. Otherwise you may have to deal with an institution that is 1,000 miles away.

3) Always tie the *full* return of your deposit to any contingencies associated with the purchase.

4) Have your deposit placed in an interest-bearing account if possible.

5) *Be sure your deposit is a credit toward the purchase price of the property, not an addition.*

6) Complete your deposit check with care. You may want to have a brief statement on the back of the check showing why it has been written. In some cases it may be appropriate to use such language as: "Received from _____ (PURCHASER) a deposit of $_____ to be used toward the purchase of real property located at _____, said deposit to be placed only in an interest-bearing escrow account maintained by broker."

7) Make the smallest possible deposit with your offer.

8) Limit your financial exposure in the event of default to your deposit and nothing else.

The Seller's Strategy

1) Require larger deposits for deals where settlement is set far in the future (more than three months).

2) Be wary of offers where the buyer suggests a note due in the future for a deposit. Such notes may be appropriate for short periods—say a few days to allow the buyer to sell stock—but they offer less security than cash, a check, or other assets. The longer the term of the note, the greater your risk.

3) Try to get the largest possible deposit.

4) Maximize your protection in case of default by having the option to seize the buyer's deposit, sue for damages, or both.

19

Bricks and Mortar: The Issue of Condition

When the Robbins family went house hunting, they found two properties that were equivalent in terms of pricing, location, and size. But while the two homes were essentially the same, one—the Santos house—was freshly painted and well maintained, while the other—the Gaber property—was in "mint" condition—untouched, unrepaired, unpainted, and unmaintained since it was first bought 16 years ago. Not surprisingly, the Santos family had a buyer.

Property maintenance in the form of painting, repairing, and upgrading is a key factor in the sales process. Homes that are well maintained are likely to sell faster and command higher prices than equivalent properties without such characteristics.

With the exception of homes sold "AS IS," purchasers assume that necessary and expected repairs have been made and that a property has been generally well maintained. Given a clue that their assumptions are wrong, buyers will often back away from a property or offer less.

The real buyer issues raised by poor maintenance are cost ("How much will it cost to fix or replace?") and anxiety ("If they didn't even bother to paint the front door, who knows what faults may be hidden from view?").

Physical condition also raises a major concern for sellers. Sure, owners want to fix up their homes to get the best possible prices. But isn't it possible to spend too much on repairs and improvements? You bet.

Buyers—it is said—commonly purchase the "least expensive home in the most expensive neighborhood they can afford." This rule suggests that sellers who make extravagant efforts to fix up properties are unlikely to recoup their expenses. Worse yet, a seller with property that does not blend in with the local market, perhaps a five-bedroom home in a neighborhood of three-bedroom houses, will not get the price that five-bedroom homes command in areas where such properties are common. Why? Because if a buyer can afford a better home (read "more expensive"), he or she will move into a different (again, read "more expensive") neighborhood.

Owners, then, should prepare for selling with both care and a conservative outlook. The idea is to make the house more salable with the needs of a buyer in mind.

For example, suppose seller Thompson is moving after five years. The carpet he bought when he first moved in is now somewhat worn. Should it be replaced?

If it will cost Thompson $3,000 to recarpet, the odds are he will not recapture his investment. Not only is he unlikely to increase the value of the property by the cost of the new carpeting but, even worse, he may even reduce its salability. If the new carpet is green, a potential buyer might look at the home and say, "Well, we like the house but none of our furniture goes with a green carpet. We'd have to buy new stuff if we move in here."

Instead, it makes sense to keep the carpet. It may be better than anything the buyers have ever seen, or it simply may not arise as a negotiating issue. If the carpet does emerge as a bargaining point, Thompson can always give a credit to the buyers for a replacement of their choice, saying "Look, I'll give you a $1,500 credit at settlement if you'll pay my asking price for the property." If $1,500 isn't acceptable, Thompson can always raise his offer until he reaches $3,000, his projected replacement cost.

If carpeting is an issue, buyers may greatly prefer a credit to having Thompson replace the old floor coverings. With a credit, the buyers can choose their own colors, patterns, and styles. Also, with a credit they need not spend the money immediately. Maybe they can live with the old carpet for a while, in which case they are at least $1,500 ahead in the bargaining game.

FIXING UP: THE SELLER'S PERSPECTIVE

Correctly preparing a home means doing many little chores. The best way to begin the preparation process is to list all needed repairs both inside and outside the home. From this list, sellers can then determine how long the fixing-up stage will take, which projects are do-it-yourself jobs, and which repairs should be left to professionals.

Most residential preparation can be done by home owners, but consider professional help as well. For example, *licensed* professionals should be used to fix electrical, plumbing, and gas systems while other specialists should be considered on the basis of workmanship, pricing, and potential time savings.

Here is a list of typical fix-up projects:

- Painting: A fresh coat of paint is probably the easiest way to enhance home values. Bright colors make rooms appear larger and hide years of wear. But to get the most from your paint job, be sure to do it right—patch and sand before dipping the first brush.
- Kitchens: All kitchen surfaces must be thoroughly cleaned. Remove dishes from cabinets to put in new shelf paper. Get rid of aging foods in cabinets and the refrigerator. Use a toothbrush and cleaner to brighten rubber refrigerator-door gaskets and hinges. Replace metal reflectors under stove burners with bright new ones—a $10 or $12 cost that will completely change the stove's appearance.
- Bathrooms: All bathroom tile should be cleaned and grouted. Bathtubs, sinks, and toilets should be cleaned and recaulked. Clear all drain pipes and make sure toilet tanks don't "run."
- Basements: Air them out if they're musty, and clean away cobwebs and other eyesores.
- Junk: To paraphrase a famous observation, the amount of junk one accumulates expands to fill the space available. To create the illusion of greater spaciousness and to cut moving costs, throw out or sell old, excess, and valueless goods before showing your home to potential buyers.
- Outside: Remove dead trees and limbs; they're not only unattrac-

tive, they're also potentially dangerous. Paint front doors—they're where first impressions are made. Trim bushes, mow the lawn, and remove dead and dying plants.

- Major Repairs: Major repairs should be made before placing a home on the market. Save those receipts! They will establish what work was done and possibly justify a tax deduction as well.

Even when homes are in the finest possible condition, some buyers will still want professional inspectors to poke and prod throughout the property. Sellers often take such demands personally as an assault on both their ego and their homes. Other sellers recognize that purchasing a house is a complex process and that professional inspections frequently relieve buyer tensions and hesitation as well as seller responsibility.

The view here is that home sellers should not object to a home inspection. If an owner does object, a purchaser may feel that the home has a hidden defect and shy away from the deal.

Just as important, an independent home inspection may greatly benefit the seller. By having an independent inspection, a buyer cannot later claim he relied exclusively on the representations of the seller or the seller's agent regarding the condition of the property.

The Seller's Strategy

1) If a buyer wants a home inspection, fine.

2) Discuss the purpose of a home inspection with the buyer. Explain that no home, including yours, is perfect and that you understand that the purchaser merely wants to determine the physical condition of the property. If the buyer indicates that he or she expects perfection, it may be wise to find a more rational purchaser.

3) Real estate offer forms commonly provide an opportunity for a buyer to "walk through" a property prior to settlement. With existing homes, however, an overall or structural inspection is typically an additional examination of the property made within a few days after the acceptance of the offer. Sellers should require something of value in exchange for the right of a purchaser to have both a structural inspection and a "walk-through." It is reasonable to couch one's acceptance of a home inspection with a requirement that you receive a copy of any written inspection report at the purchaser's expense.

4) Considering the large number of court cases that involve hidden defect claims, savvy sellers should *want* purchasers to obtain home inspections.

If the buyer declines, the seller would be well advised to have an addendum to the contract stating that the purchaser was offered the opportunity to use a home inspector and declined. If such an addendum is not feasible, then a savvy seller will carefully write down when the offer was made and the buyer's response. Such a memo may come in handy if a purchaser later claims that the seller withheld information regarding the condition of the property.

5) Structural inspections are often based on the "satisfaction" of the purchaser. In such situations, there is no one other than the purchaser who can determine the meaning of "satisfaction." Some buyers will use the concept of "satisfaction" to back out of a deal merely because their interests change. This is an unavoidable risk; therefore, sellers should minimize and limit the time available for a structural inspection. Another approach is to have an inspection contingency that gives the seller an opportunity to repair or replace items mentioned in the inspection report, work which would then satisfy the contingency.

6) Save receipts from repair work and capital improvements made prior to selling. These may have value at tax time when calculating marketing cost and figuring profits.

CONDITION AND INSPECTION:
THE BUYER'S PERSPECTIVE

In happier, more ingenuous times, buying a house was an act of faith. Purchasers rambled through a property, asked a few questions, flicked on the stove, and then bought the place "as is." But times have changed, and today more and more people have come to understand that a house is a complex package of pipes, wires, boards, shingles, bricks, and appliances—each ready to rust, rot, or break the moment a buyer moves in.

Physical condition is a worry for every buyer. If the basement leaks and the prospective buyer knows about it, then the house can be judged accordingly; perhaps it's worth $5,000 less than a similar property with a dry basement. But what happens if the buyer doesn't know about the leaky basement? It is the lack of information rather than the leak itself that is a major cause of buyer anxiety.

The burden of assuring property condition has traditionally fallen to the purchaser, except when the seller knows of a "substantial" defect and deliberately hides the problem. Yet one has to wonder, what is "substantial"? Is a leaking roof a substantial problem? Suppose the leak amounts to three ounces of water per year. Is that substantial? What about one ounce? What if the seller is a roofer? Will his definition of "substantial" vary from that of a buyer who is an accountant or salesperson?

And what happens if there is a defect of which the seller is unaware? If the attic is never used, and the seller has never seen any evidence of a leak, should the seller be responsible?

Going further, imagine a house is purchased, and soon after the buyers discover a leaking roof that will cost less than $75 to repair. Does it make sense for a buyer to sue when the sum involved is so small? Would it be reasonable to sue even if the repair value was higher, say $1,000 or $1,500?

More complex still are disputes that involve not structural conditions but appearance. A nail pop—a nail pulled out of a wall—is not a significant structural problem but, then again, it's not attractive either. What to do?

Buyers will have a costly, difficult, and time-consuming battle forcing sellers to fix defects once a property has been sold, so it makes sense to discover defects before a deal is finalized. This can be done through a careful examination of the property by the purchaser, a professional inspector, or both.

The idea of an inspection is not to uncover every minor flaw and problem with a house! *No house—including the most expensive property in town—is perfect.* Every home has some flaw, some damage, some defect somewhere. What a buyer really wants to know is: What needs to be repaired or replaced? How much will it cost? What steps can be taken to make the house run more efficiently? What repair bills can be expected in the next few years? Considering the defects and problems with a given property, should I make an offer requiring the seller to make certain repairs, or should I make a smaller offer or no offer?

Purchasers should informally inspect a property prior to making an offer. To do this right, you should bring a list showing the dimensions of your major furnishings (to see if your sofa, rugs, or whatever will fit in the new house) plus a pencil and pad, a 25-foot tape measure, a small electric radio (to check wall outlets), and a camera.

Using a camera to take photos of the house may be helpful. For example, if you have a picture showing the front screen door in good condition when you made your offer, but later the door is damaged at the time of settlement, the seller is responsible. But if the damage occurred before you offered to purchase the property, then it is merely a part of the package you bought.

In a similar fashion, notes from an initial inspection can also be important. If you recorded that the dishwasher worked when you inspected the property, but was out-of-order on settlement day, you at least have some evidence to support your claim that the seller has an obligation to deliver a working dishwasher.

What should buyers look for in a home inspection? Here are the major items to check before making a purchase offer.

- Air Conditioning, Freezers, and Refrigerators: Each of these cooling systems uses a compressor, a device with an anticipated life of 15 years or so. Thus, if you're buying a 12-year-old home, it's possible that some of the current systems may have to be replaced in a few years or that they may run less efficiently. As these are large, expensive items, their age and condition should be considered when making a purchase offer. Also, if a property has been enlarged, ask if cooling capacity has been increased as well.
- Attics: Is there an attic and, if so, is it usable? In older homes, large attics are often converted into one or more rooms, while attic areas in newer homes are frequently usable only for storage. With homes of similar value, the property with the usable attic will have a lower cost per usable square foot and thus represent a better bargain.
- Basements: While homes in many areas of the country do not have full basements, they are a terrific bonus when available. Full basements represent additional square footage that can frequently be used for storage, game rooms, extra sleeping space, or a complete "in-law" apartment. When checking a basement, see if it's in use or why it isn't being used.
- Carpeting and Rugs: Carpeting typically stays with a property because it is attached and custom-fitted, while rugs are regarded as personal property and removed when the sellers leave. Large rugs are sometimes confused with carpeting, however, so make

sure you know what floor covering, if any, is to remain. If the carpeting is to remain, make sure it's in reasonably good condition. If not, get the seller to give either a cash credit or a replacement satisfactory to you.

Carpeting can hide a host of sins, so always lift a corner to see what kind of flooring is underneath. With modern properties it sometimes happens that the original purchasers had a choice of hardwood flooring or carpeting over plywood. After several years the carpeting will wear out and must be replaced, while hardwood floors typically last for the life of the property. If the carpeting is shot, buyers should adjust their offers downward.

- Clothes Washers and Dryers: Because they have few major parts (heating element, motor, timer), clothes dryers are easy to maintain and repair. Clothes washers, however, are far more complex. Look for clothes washers and dryers in good working condition and make certain they are included in the sale.
- Cracks: Most cracks are pencil-thin gaps caused by settlement over time and do not suggest that a house is coming apart. More serious, however, are wide cracks or cracks that go through a wall, problems that should be evaluated by a professional inspector or engineer.
- Electrical: With so many appliances in a modern home, it pays to look for houses with at least 100 to 150 amps, more in larger homes. Both circuit breakers and fuses work equally well, but circuit breakers are simply more convenient. In older homes, a property with circuit breakers means the electrical system has been upgraded and modernized. In all homes, look for 220-volt lines for large clothes dryers and air conditioners as well as special wiring for ovens. Make sure that proper grounding is in place.
- Fireplaces and Chimneys: Ask if fireplaces have been cleaned to remove flammable deposits. Beware of bowed or bent chimneys or bricks missing from chimney walls; call an engineer in such cases to see if the chimney is structurally sound.
- Freezers: Freezers allow families to stock up on food, a great convenience during sales or if the nearest supermarket is 80 miles away. Conversely, freezers—particularly older ones—can raise some problems. First, check to see if the door or doors can be

locked with a key, so children cannot get trapped inside. Second, make certain the freezer works. If it doesn't, removing such a large and heavy appliance can be a major headache, particularly if it's located in a basement. If the freezer is old, doesn't work, or doesn't work well, have the seller remove it from the property as a condition of the sale.

- Heating: Check for inspection tags to see if the heating system has been cleaned and adjusted recently, particularly if the property uses oil-fired heating. If there is a radiator system, ask if it is cleaned and flushed regularly each year.

  Heating systems are typically "sized" to give adequate warmth in a particular climate. However, if there has been an addition to the property, there is added cubic footage to heat, so either the system has to be upgraded or an extra heat source built in. If these changes have not been made, it's possible the system in place will not run effectively or efficiently.

  Wood- and coal-burning stoves have been added to many homes, and such devices should be carefully checked. Were they installed with a permit from the local government? Are they approved by an accepted testing agency? If not, they may be both a fire hazard and an addition to the property that can void insurance coverage.

- Kitchen Appliances: Try all appliances. Are they clean and in good working condition? What type of cabinets have been installed? Remember, wooden cabinets can readily be repainted or antiqued to upgrade a kitchen.

  Real estate agreement forms often state that appliances must be in "operating condition," a phrase that defies definition. Rather than debate what, if anything, this term means, it pays instead simply to test each appliance. If they need to be replaced, then buyers must consider how the expense of replacement should be reflected in an offer.

  As a matter of strategy, when appliances don't work, it usually makes sense for buyers to get a cash credit for new appliances or for the seller to replace defective appliances with new equipment. With replacements, however, make sure the seller is obligated to obtain appliances of a particular brand and model; otherwise you may wind up with the cheapest appliances on the market.

- Masonry: With brick homes, look for missing bricks, broken bricks, and missing or cracked mortar. Over time, say 40 or 50 years, pieces of mortar may come loose, allowing water to enter. To fix the leak it is necessary to dig out any loose mortar and replace it with fresh cement, a process called "repointing." This is labor-intensive, time-consuming, and expensive work—particularly with large jobs. In addition to checking the brick work itself, look at inside walls to see if there are broad areas where plaster has fallen away or discolored, possible signs of leakage caused by missing mortar.

- Outdoors: Check for dead or dying trees. A falling tree or heavy limb can easily cause extensive damage, and tree removal can be painfully expensive. If you see a dead or dying tree, make certain the seller is responsible for its removal.

- Plumbing: Run all spigots in the house at the same time. Does each deliver water with force? Also, check for construction (copper is generally regarded as best), rust spots in sinks (suggests that a cast-iron system may be eroding), drain flow, freezing (this can be a hazard in northern climates), and water pressure (if you can't get good pressure, then perhaps a pipe is blocked).

   Not only are plumbing repairs expensive, but they may also involve other expenses. To reach the cast-iron pipes in older homes, for instance, it may be necessary to break through plaster walls, a process unlikely to be cheap.

- Roofing: Roof repairs can be very expensive, so it pays to examine the roof with care. Are tiles missing? In an older house they may be difficult to match or replace. Is the roof lumpy? Even an apparently good roof may be hiding rotted areas. Does the roof sag? This may be a sign of rotted supports under the roof or it may be that there is too much roofing on the house.

   Shingle roofs typically have a life expectancy of 15 to 20 years, after which a new layer of roofing can be added to the old materials. But because roofing is so heavy, many jurisdictions allow no more than two roofing layers on a home at one time. Thus, if a house is 30 or 40 years old and needs a new roof, the old materials may have to be removed before new shingles can be added, a more expensive proposition than merely adding a new layer of materials.

- Utility Bills: Whenever you visit open houses, always ask to see utility bills, so that over time you can judge what constitutes a "high" bill and what is "low" for a given area. Ask for utility bills from the past year to see if utility costs for a particular house are higher or lower than for homes of similar size and construction. If higher, it may be because the current owners like lots of heat and air conditioning (not a serious issue), have a bigger family, have appliances that are inefficient (a cost factor to consider), are selling a property that lacks sufficient insulation for its location (a definite problem), or have a house with major problems, such as leaky pipes, poor wiring, or broken meters.

- Water: Homes have leaked ever since the first storm, and a major question for every home buyer concerns drainage: Where does the water go when it rains? Unless properly directed, water can harm foundations, make basements unusable, and crack walls. Most drainage difficulties can be resolved by installing gutters, redirecting and extending downspouts, building earthen slopes against foundations, or channeling water away from the house. Buyers should check basements for mildew, rotted fabric, and rust lines on major fixtures such as furnaces and hot water heaters. Always ask sellers or their agents, "Has the house leaked in the past two years?" If so, where?

Buyer's Strategy

The above list is but a layman's guide to home inspecting; it's not complete nor does it suggest that home buyers can be as qualified as professional home inspectors, experienced engineers, or professional builders. Moreover, it should be said that there is an emotional component to home buying, a factor that makes it difficult for many buyers to evaluate real estate objectively. Given these factors, it follows that buyers should take several steps.

1) Understand that no property is in perfect condition.

2) If a problem is found during the initial inspection of the property, the offer should be written to resolve the difficulty. For example, if the dishwasher doesn't work, the offer might state that the purchase is "contingent upon

replacement of the kitchen dishwasher with the installation of a new dishwasher satisfactory to Purchaser and the removal of the old dishwasher from the property prior to settlement." The make, model, and color of the new appliance should be specified. *Remember, if the offer does not specifically require replacing the old dishwasher, making repairs, or whatever, the problem is yours.*

3) Recognize that some purchasers do not want homes in pristine condition. Instead, they want properties in need of repair and improvement. By making improvements themselves, buyers can greatly increase the value of the property, a process known as "sweat equity."

4) It is the obligation of the seller to deliver the property at settlement in substantially the same condition that it was in when the offer was first accepted. *Take pictures of the property, inside and out, to make a clear record of property condition as of the date the contract was accepted by the seller.*

5) Since the average buyer is not qualified to make a detailed home inspection, it follows that purchasers should have a property examined by a professional home inspector.

REASONABLE REPAIRS

Model Language
Reasonable Repairs with Limitation

Lender Requirements: Seller agrees to comply with any and all reasonable repair requirements imposed by a lender financing subject transaction providing, however, that in no case shall the seller be required to expend more than $_____ for "reasonable" repairs as required by a lender.

In the event a lender requires the expenditure of more than $_____, then seller shall have the option to either pay the amount required by the lender or to terminate this Agreement/Contract/Offer. If the Agreement/Contract/Offer is terminated, then buyer's deposit shall be refunded in full.

Model Language
Provision for Reasonable Repairs

Lender Requirements: Seller agrees to comply with any and all reasonable repair requirements imposed by a lender financing subject transaction.

Buried within a growing number of realty contracts is a short and curious phrase that says that as part of the deal the seller will pay for "reasonable" repairs required by a lender.

If repairs were required by a purchaser such a clause would normally fall within the zone of negotiation—something to be debated by buyers and sellers. But here the deal is different. A lender is not a principal within the contract. In fact, at the time the contract is written, it's highly unlikely that a lender has even been selected to finance the sale.

We thus have a peculiar situation. Sellers are being asked to make a repair commitment without limitation. And the matter is not negotiable in the ordinary sense because there is no lender with whom to negotiate in most cases.

Why is a lender interested in repairs? Repairs are not a lifestyle issue to the lender, but they have importance.

To the lender, property is security for a loan. The more valuable the property, the less risk for the lender. The lender wants to assure that the property not only has an inherent worth but that it is well maintained so that it's easy to sell in the event of foreclosure. In normal circumstances a lender can't tell an owner to mow the lawn or fix a leak, but when a buyer is seeking a loan lenders have enormous leverage and power.

Under the VA program, for example, homes must meet what are generally termed "minimum property conditions"—meaning that they are safe, sound and sanitary. Before granting an FHA or VA loan, an appraiser evaluates the property and as part of the appraisal process must report any condition which causes the home to fall below minimum standards. If a home is less than satisfactory, then a loan will not be issued until repairs are made—thus the need for a contract clause allowing lenders to require "reasonable repairs."

However, there is *no* rule that says the repairs must be made by the seller. The only issue that concerns the VA is that repairs are actually made. Whether costs are paid by the seller, the buyer, the broker, or some combination is irrelevant to the VA.

The bottom line is that a contract clause requiring sellers to pay "reasonable repairs" without limitation is a potential blank check. There may well be a need for reasonable repairs to acquire a VA loan (and because of similar requirements, FHA financing), but there is no reason why a seller cannot limit such obligations.

If it happens that the Royce property needs $1,200 in repairs to meet VA standards, but the contract says owner Royce is not required to pay more than $500 for such improvements, several things can happen:

First, Royce can pay the additional money to make the deal work.

Second, Royce can refuse to pay more than $500, in which case the VA won't grant the loan, and the deal will be dead.

Third, Royce and the buyer can negotiate and share costs so the sale qualifies for VA financing.

There is a fourth choice as well, one that will make heads shake: The borrower and the lender can ask the VA to waive its minimum requirements.

The Buyer's Strategy

1) Any clause that requires sellers to pay money should be seen for what it is: wonderful.

2) Understand that lender requirements to make a property safe, sound, and sanitary should be viewed as the lowest-possible acceptable standards. A property that does not meet such base-line norms should be regarded as unfit for habitation.

3) Be aware that an appraisal is not a structural inspection. An appraiser is concerned with property values. A small crack in the foundation is not an appraisal issue—though it can be important to a structural inspector.

The Seller's Strategy

1) A "reasonable" repair clause should be seen for what it is: a bottomless obligation to make repairs according to someone else's definition of "reasonable."

2) You have every reason to limit repairs to an amount you regard as fair and appropriate.

3) If the value of required repairs exceeds the amount you regard as acceptable, then with a proper contingency you can pay the excess dollars needed to make the deal work, terminate the agreement, or get the buyer to chip in part of the cost.

4) Despite the fact that "reasonable" repair clauses are common, do not be bullied into accepting something that can hurt your interests.

HOW TO FIND A HOME INSPECTOR

Although many buyers rely on traditional methods of home inspection to find defects—namely a keen sense of observation—a growing number of

---

Model Language:
Purchaser's Clause for a Structural Inspection

This Agreement/Contract/Offer is contingent upon a property inspection which, in the sole judgment of Purchaser, is deemed "satisfactory." Such inspection shall be arranged and paid for by Purchaser and if Purchaser does not remove or act on this Contingency or notify Seller or Seller's agent in writing by _____M. (TIME) on _____ (DATE) of any dissatisfaction associated with subject property inspection, then this Agreement/Contract/Offer dated _____ shall be in full force and effect. If Purchaser or Purchaser's agent notifies Seller or Seller's agent by the time and date specified in this paragraph that subject property inspection is unsatisfactory, then this Agreement/Contract/Offer shall be null and void and any deposit made by Purchaser shall be returned in full.

The condition of the property is "unsatisfactory" to Buyer unless Seller will agree as of _____M. (TIME) on _____ (DATE) to repair or replace the central air-conditioning system in a manner acceptable to Buyer, such work to be completed prior to settlement, then the condition of the property shall be deemed "satisfactory." If Seller does not agree as of _____M. (TIME) on _____ (DATE) to repair or replace the central air-conditioning system in a manner acceptable to Buyer prior to settlement, then the condition of the property shall be deemed "unsatisfactory" and this agreement shall be null and void and Buyer's deposit shall be promptly returned in full.

---

purchasers are turning to professional home inspectors. The reason is not only that inspectors are expected to have extensive construction and building expertise, but also because inspectors—unlike buyers—can be objective and less emotional. When they look at a dining room, they see walls and floors, not family dinners. To an inspector, it's a job.

Inspectors may have experience as home builders, structural engineers, or architects, but whether it is better to have one or another is a debatable matter. The basic point is to find a knowledgable person to examine the property on the buyer's behalf. While inspectors are not licensed, some belong to the American Society of Home Inspectors, a group that requires 250 inspections before membership is granted.

A good inspection should include a thorough property examination, a written report describing its condition, and an estimate of both current repairs and those anticipated in the next three to five years. The report should cover the electrical, heating, air-conditioning, and plumbing systems, interior and exterior wear, and the condition of the basement, attic, roof, appliances, kitchen, bathrooms, and related buildings such as detached garages and sheds.

A buyer should accompany the inspector when he or she examines the property, not only to see what needs to be done but also because an inspector can offer maintenance hints and teach buyers how best to operate various household systems. This is the time to ask questions and to get some idea of how much energy, effort, and money will be required to get the place in top condition.

When considering an inspector, remember that your purpose is not to find every missing nail or loose screw. Rather, the inspector's job is to determine whether the property is in sound structural condition, to point out elements of the property that need to be repaired or replaced, and to estimate the cost of such work.

Do not be surprised if an inspector finds a lengthy list of minor problems with the property—that's to be expected. All homes have such problems. The real question is whether there are any problems that, alone or together, significantly affect the value of the property or its habitability. If so, then a buyer must either revise his or her offer or consider other properties.

Although most buyers can appreciate the value of a professional inspection when purchasing an existing home, the issue is somewhat clouded with new houses. After all, are not new homes delivered in the best possible condition?

Just before settlement on a new house, a buyer will have an opportunity to "walk through" the property with the builder's representative. Any work not then completed should be recorded on a "punch list," and the builder will then be responsible for completing such work, at his cost, after settlement.

Problems can develop, however, when items are left off the punch list ("Don't worry about that, we'll get it Tuesday") or when there are disagreements ("What's wrong with that wall? Sure it's a bit cockeyed, but when you get in the furniture and hang a picture on it no one will notice. Besides, that wall is built to the standards that are usual, customary, and traditional in our industry."). The builder in such situations has his representative at the property, and the buyer has, er, well, no one—unless a professional inspector is hired.

Buyer's Strategy

A structural inspection should be seen as a device to eliminate nasty surprises and as a bargaining chip in those cases where the condition of the property makes the seller's asking price unrealistic. Going further, a proper structural inspection should address these issues:

1) The inspector must be someone selected by the purchaser alone.

2) The inspection must be "satisfactory" to the buyer, or the deal is off.

3) If the deal is canceled, the purchaser's deposit must be promptly and completely refunded.

4) The buyer should have a reasonable time within which to schedule an inspection, say seven to ten calendar days after an offer is accepted.

5) In the case of a new home, a professional inspector should accompany the buyer during the pre-settlement walk-through.

6) Set aside enough time for a thorough inspection. Ask the inspector for a time estimate before making an appointment with sellers, agents, or builders to insure that there will be enough time to see the property completely.

7) When buying a new house, maintain your own "punch list," and make sure that at the end of the walk-through, your list and that of the builder's representative are identical.

8) When going through a new home, test all electrical, plumbing, heating, and air-conditioning systems.

9) If a home has one or two major faults but is otherwise attractive, an inspection clause can be used to get a better deal. Suppose the air-conditioning system is old and performs poorly. A buyer might deliver a letter to the seller or the seller's agent within the allowed time period stating that:

The condition of the property is "unsatisfactory" to Buyer unless Seller will agree as of _____M. (TIME) on _____(DATE) to repair or replace the central air-conditioning system in a manner acceptable to Buyer, such work to be completed prior to settlement, then the condition of the property shall be deemed "satisfactory." If Seller does not agree as of _____M. (TIME) on _____(DATE) to repair or replace the central air-conditioning system in a manner acceptable to Buyer prior to settlement, then the condition of the property shall be deemed "unsatisfactory" and this agreement shall be null and void and Buyer's deposit shall be promptly returned in full.

Note that in this situation the property has been declared "unsatisfactory," but if the seller wants to go ahead with the deal, the buyer has laid out an acceptable approach. If the seller doesn't want to replace the air-conditioning unit, then the deal is off.

Note also that as a matter of common sense one would not want to declare the inspection "unsatisfactory" if only minor items were outstanding (say two cracked windows in the basement) or if the property was a good buy otherwise. Even so, the buyer might point these items out to the seller, who then may agree to make repairs as a matter of goodwill or courtesy.

The Seller's Strategy

See previous section of this chapter: "Fixing-Up: The Seller's Perspective."

CREATING ESCROW ACCOUNTS FOR REPAIRS

Model Language:
Escrow Account to Assure Performance

Settlement provider shall establish an interest-bearing escrow fund from monies due Seller at settlement which Purchaser may use to _____. The settlement provider shall set aside $_____ from Seller's funds to create subject escrow account. It is agreed and understood that Seller's liability under this paragraph shall be limited to the dollar value of funds set aside in the escrow account herein created plus any accrued interest. On _____ (DATE), or at such time as all repairs specifically listed in this paragraph shall have been completed, whichever comes first, all funds, if any, remaining in the escrow account created herein shall be paid promptly to Seller without recourse or set-offs by Purchaser. Seller's approval shall be required for all expenditures of $_____ or more before work is started or purchases are made. All additional repair costs in excess of the funds set aside under the terms of this paragraph, plus all accrued interest thereon, shall be borne exclusively by Purchaser. The provisions of this paragraph shall not be extinguished by the merger of the deed and the sales contract but shall expressly survive the transfer of subject property.

Although settlement (closing) is usually seen as the end of a realty transaction, that is frequently not the case. There are sales where even though closing has occurred and title has been transferred to a new owner, the seller still has outstanding obligations.

When Mr. French, for example, bought the Appleton estate, his purchase was concluded in late November and settlement was held in mid-January.

Everything was fine between buyer and seller, but there was one problem: settlement occurred in mid-winter. In the cold of January the ground was frozen so Mr. Appleton, even with the best of intentions, could not complete promised repairs to the walks near the main house or the air-conditioning system.

So Appleton and French agreed to establish an escrow, or trust, account. Appleton was willing to do the repairs, but if for some reason the work was not completed French would have money to do the work promised by Appleton.

Having agreed in principle to an escrow account, there were five related issues to resolve.

First, Appleton—the seller—wanted to limit the amount of money to be set aside. French, on the other hand, wanted enough money in the account to insure that all repairs could and would be completed without any cost to him. They discussed the matter and agreed that $2,000 should be placed in the account.

Second, although Appleton agreed to the $2,000 figure, he felt the work could be completed for less than $1,500. He therefore required that any money left in the account after all repairs had been made would be returned to him.

Third, since French wanted the repairs made when the weather permitted and Appleton didn't want his money tied up for months or years, it was agreed that the buyer would be responsible for ordering repairs, but if such work was not completed by a particular date, all funds remaining in the account would be returned to Appleton.

Fourth, because several thousand dollars was to be set aside for a few months, Appleton wanted the money placed in an interest-bearing account so that his costs would be somewhat offset by the interest that the account generated. French approved the idea since the interest would also be available for repair work, if needed.

Fifth, although Appleton agreed to make the repairs and was not particularly bothered by setting aside funds to do the work, he was troubled by the possibility that repair costs could skyrocket or French might use gold-plated tools to finish the work. Therefore, Appleton limited his liability for repairs to the funds set aside in the escrow account.

Escrow accounts represent an excellent way to resolve potential disputes when promised work is incomplete or when other seller obligations are not fulfilled by settlement. Properly written, they limit a seller's liability while assuring that funds are available to buyers for promised purchases, improvements, replacements, and repairs.

The Buyer's Strategy

1) Always insist on the creation of an escrow account to assure the completion of promised work or repairs.

2) Be certain the escrow account contains enough money to accomplish your purpose.

3) Have enough time built in to the escrow agreement so that all necessary work can be completed.

4) Allow for an interest-bearing account so that the interest can be used by you, if necessary.

5) Be specific. For example, if the dishwasher is to be replaced, then describe precisely the make and model to be installed and the seller's obligation to pay for the removal of the old machine. Without specific requirements, you may wind up with a cheap dishwasher or perhaps a used model.

6) If you can't be specific, demand "satisfaction." For example, if the sidewalk needs to be repaired, require repair work in a manner "satisfactory to purchaser."

The Seller's Strategy

1) If you agree to an escrow account, make certain the agreement limits your liability to a sum no larger than that deposited in the account, plus any accrued interest.

2) Repairs required under an escrow account should be stated specifically. Don't allow yourself to be responsible for "roof repairs" when you really mean the "replacement of damaged shingles over the kitchen." Another example: Don't agree to buy "a new clothes washer" when you mean a specific make and model.

3) Make the buyer responsible for assuring the completion of all required work.

4) Put as little into the escrow account as possible.

5) Use an interest-bearing account to hold escrow monies.

6) Establish a specific date by which all work must be completed, after which any funds remaining in the account will be returned to you.

7) Recognize that an escrow fund and the agreement to pay for certain items represents a discount against the final sale price. Someone offering $128,000 for your property and requiring work worth $3,000 is making a less attractive offer than a second purchaser who offers $127,000 with no required repair costs.

8) The creation of an escrow fund represents, in a sense, a type of limited warranty. For instance, if you agree to pay not more than $500 to replace a bathtub, but such work ultimately costs $750, the purchaser will be forced to bear the additional expense.

9) Where appropriate, require the buyer to get your approval for any bid above an agreed-upon figure, perhaps $100, before the work is started. This assures that your money is being used for its intended purpose and that it is being well spent.

BUYING AND SELLING PROPERTY "AS IS"

> ### Model Language:
> ### Property to Be Sold "AS IS"
>
> Purchaser understands that subject property is being sold "AS IS" and that neither Seller nor Seller's agents, if any, make any representations whatsoever as to the condition of the structure being sold. No express or implied warranties have been made verbally or in writing, including whether the subject property is being used or can be used for any particular purpose or that it is habitable; whether the appliances, plumbing systems, electrical circuits, gas lines, and mechanical equipment are operational; whether any improvements thereon meet building, zoning, or health code standards; or whether any licenses, permits, or easements are or have been recorded or obtained. The provisions of this paragraph shall not be extinguished by the merger of the deed and contract for sale but shall expressly survive the transfer of subject property.

When we think about the proverbial "little house with a white picket fence," we expect that our model property will work as well as it looks. We assume that it's habitable, that it won't leak, and that appliances will run properly.

To some extent both buyers and sellers have a right to make assumptions about property. But unspoken and unwritten assumptions, as well as simple misunderstandings, often lead to trouble and conflict.

"Hey," says the buyer a week after closing, "you told me you kept meat in the basement freezer."

"Sure," replies the seller, "we keep steaks there before they're cooked. I never said anything was frozen. You want something frozen, go to Lake Huron in January."

To get around the issue of implied warranties, real estate is sometimes sold without any guarantees or assumptions; if something's wrong with the house, it's the buyer's responsibility.

Why would anyone buy property without some form of warranty? Several examples seem plausible:

- Mr. Watkins is selling a five-acre tract of land that includes an old, run-down house. Watkins does not want to be responsible for a house he expects will be torn down, so he offers his property for sale "AS IS."
- To get top value for his house, Mr. Burns will have to spend $12,000 for painting and repairs. Even with that investment, he's not sure the value of his home will rise the full $12,000. Rather than make any improvements, Burns sells his property "AS IS."
- The neighborhood where Mr. Wilson bought a house 25 years ago has changed radically. Where small ramblers once stood, high-rise office buildings are now being built. Wilson wants to sell his house and knows a commercial builder will pay the most for his property. But Wilson is not certain if his property can be rezoned for commercial construction and has no interest in going through a protracted zoning process. He sells his property "AS IS," without any assurance to the buyer that the property can be used for any particular purpose.
- When First National foreclosed on the Conklin residence, they found the house had been abandoned, pipes leaked, and a small fire had damaged the kitchen. Rather than make repairs, the property was marketed "AS IS."

Buying property "AS IS" is not necessarily a bad deal. The real question concerns *why* the property is being sold "AS IS" and how buyers may benefit. In the examples above, the condition of the Watkins house is irrelevant since it's going to be torn down; the Burns house may be an excellent buy for a handy purchaser who can do painting and repair work; the Wilson tract can be sold to developers; and the First National foreclosure will not only be priced far below market value, but the bank may even finance the deal at low rates just to get the property off its hands.

An "AS IS" sale should be seen for what it is: a deal where the seller offers no warranties of any type. At the very least, an "AS IS" clause is a warning, something that tells a buyer to slow down and pick through the deal with meticulous care.

The Buyer's Strategy

1) Do not exclude "AS IS" sales automatically. In some cases, such deals may be attractive.

2) Always find out why property is being sold "AS IS."

3) Always make an "AS IS" purchase dependent upon a structural inspection, title examination, and legal review satisfactory to you.

4) If you're handy, it may pay to look for "AS IS" properties. In some cases, a seller may not be able to complete repairs that you can do yourself.

5) Look for a steep discount when purchasing property "AS IS."

6) *Beware of hidden "AS IS" deals.* Sales that involve quitclaim deeds mean that the seller has not guaranteed title (and may not own the property or may be selling with debts remaining to be paid). *Never buy property with a quitclaim deed without a title search and legal advice from a knowledgable attorney.*

The Seller's Strategy

1) It may pay to sell property "AS IS" to avoid future warranty claims or to avoid excessive repair costs.

2) Be sure to check with a knowledgable attorney when preparing an "AS IS" sale. Some jurisdictions may require "AS IS" clauses to be expressed in a certain manner, such as with the term "AS IS" in quotation marks, underlined, or in capital letters. Also, be aware that in some jurisdictions it may not be possible to waive all warranties, something that again should be discussed with a knowledgable attorney.

3) It may be best to avoid an "AS IS" clause if a less visible sales approach can be employed. For instance, if plumbing repairs are a concern, perhaps a clause limiting repair costs would be less damaging to your marketing efforts.

4) Be certain your "AS IS" provision will remain in force after closing.

5) Check with your attorney to see how, if at all, "AS IS" sales limit or terminate implied warranties and future claims.

CONDITIONAL TRAPS

Model Language:
Notice of Owner Expertise

Notice is hereby given that any written statement concerning property condition and/or environmental information included in this Agreement/Contract/Offer or attached thereto has been made in good faith by the seller and/or the seller's agent.

However, unless written assurances to the contrary are contained within this Agreement/Contract/Offer and any attachments hereto, all parties to this Agreement/Contract/Offer and their agents are hereby on notice that neither the seller nor the seller's agent is an engineer, architect, structural inspector, licensed termite inspector, or surveyor; that while visible and readily accessible areas of the property may be examined from time to time, the property is not systematically inspected on a regular basis; that no information regarding areas of the property that are not visible or readily accessible can be made; and that terms such as "proximity," "traces," "elevated," "discoloring," "settling," "slippage," "sliding" and other like expressions are subjective matters not within the realm of absolute definition.

The buyer is advised to retain professional inspection services, as desired, to objectively determine the property's condition.

Consumerism has influenced the conduct of many professions and industries, so it should come as no surprise that real estate disclosure statements have become entirely common.

Property disclosure statements, at face value, appear to afford clear levels of consumer protection. In Virginia, for example, all existing homes must be sold either with a state-written disclosure form or "AS IS." Because properties marketed in "AS IS" condition are less desirable than competing homes, there is enormous pressure to complete the disclosure forms.

In addition to Virginia, a growing number of states require seller disclosure statements, a trend that is destined to spread. But while disclosure statements seem like a good idea, they contain serious pitfalls.

Condition is a major purchasing issue and brokers are generally required to disclose all material property defects that they know about or should know about. The catch is that brokers and their salespeople typically have no training whatsoever as engineers, architects, surveyors, or pest controllers.

Moreover, requiring people to disclose defects they "should know about" raises the matter of what we should expect brokers to know. In many cases, areas of a home are simply not accessible. Panelling installed 10 years ago may hide significant problems. Carpeting may cover damaged or discolored flooring.

Not only are brokers typically unqualified to spot subtle or hidden defects, but homeowners are likely to be equally untrained. The typical owner occupies a home but does not always understand how it works or what is wrong, especially when problems are minor, not visible, or in areas of the property that are not normally accessible.

Equally troublesome is the nature of various disclosure forms. Suppose someone asked you about the "proximity of the property to former or current waste-disposal sites." No one—obviously—wants to live next to a dump, but how much distance does "proximity" represent. And how far back in time are you expected to go with any declaration relating to "former" disposal sites? Ten years? A century?

What about a question that asks if your property has "depressions, mounds, or soft spots." To what does this question refer? The lawn? The roof? The floors?

Despite limitations, the drive for disclosure continues. Why?

One reason is that seller disclosure forms may reduce or eliminate broker liability in the event of a lawsuit. In California, for example, a broker was held partially liable for selling a home that slid down a hill.

A second reason for disclosure is that it seems like an inherently good idea.

But in no case should buyers regard seller disclosure forms as substitutes for professional structural inspections or other examinations. No one can seriously believe that an owner with a stake in the sale can evaluate a property with the independence and autonomy of a professional inspector.

As to sellers, the advice is threefold. First, if a disclosure form is required in your state, then it must be used. Second, you have every reason to state in the contract that your authority as a construction expert is limited and that your buyer should obtain a professional inspection. Third, there is now insurance available to home sellers that covers claims against hidden defects. Speak to your real estate broker for specific information concerning costs, coverage, deductibles, limitations, and related issues.

The Buyer's Strategy

1) Do not rely on seller disclosure statements to evaluate property condition.

2) Always have a professional inspector evaluate the property.

3) Be aware that oral statements regarding the property's condition are likely to be unenforceable expressions of opinion rather than fact.

The Seller's Strategy

1) Do not sign a property disclosure statement unless required by regulation.

2) If you must sign a disclosure statement, or if you elect to sign a disclosure statement, include a notice so that the buyer is aware that you are not an expert or authority in the field of residential construction.

3) If you have a seller disclosure statement, be certain to advise the purchaser to hire a professional inspector. At the very least, such a suggestion will show that the use of a professional inspector was proposed and that, in effect, you were not attempting to hide any defects.

20

Environmental Issues

There is little doubt that during the past decade environmental issues have become increasingly important. It's hard to imagine an industry or profession that is not making an effort to reduce, reuse, and recycle, and it's hard as well to imagine that real estate is without environmental concerns.

Because of the great complexity represented by a single home there is no end to the possible environmental issues that a given transaction can raise, but whether such concerns are significant is an open question. In many instances there is conflicting evidence, notable authorities disagree, and sometimes it's not certain if there is any risk even when environmental "hazards" are present.

If your home was built before 1973 it may well have lead paint. If you fertilize your lawn there can be a pesticide issue. If you have indoor plumbing, then lead pipes and lead solder may be a concern. If your house is not built on stilts then radon may be gathering below your basement and penetrating into the house.

The list of potential environmental risks is endless, but one needs to ask: Just how much risk is out there? Can the world ever be risk-free? Can we avoid all risk by living in a protective bubble? And even if the answer is "yes," who would want such a lifestyle?

In residential real estate at this time three environmental issues stand out: radon, EMFs, and FRT plywood, matters that buyers and sellers should at least examine.

RADON

Model Language:
Radon Addendum

Notice: Levels of naturally occurring radon gas can occur in residential housing that exceed guidelines developed by the Environmental Protection Agency (EPA). Studies have shown that extended exposure to high levels of radon gas can adversely affect your health. There are radon gas testing firms in this area that have equipment to detect levels of naturally occurring radon gas within residential structures. There are also firms in this area that can recommend actions to decrease interior radon gas concentrations to levels within EPA suggested guidelines.

Purchaser may elect to conduct his own investigation to determine radon gas levels, if any, within subject residence.

This Agreement/Contract/Offer shall be contingent until 5 PM on _____ (DATE) to allow Purchaser to obtain at his expense a radon inspection of all residential dwellings on the property by a radon testing firm that has met all standards and certifications required to perform radon tests in this jurisdiction. In exchange for access to the property, the Purchaser shall provide a copy of the test results to the Seller without charge.

Seller shall make the property accessible for and cooperate with conditions necessary for such a test. Within _____ hours of receipt of the test results, Purchaser shall deliver a copy of the test results to Seller.

If the radon reading is within the EPA's suggested guidelines as to limits of radon gas concentration for a habitable dwelling, this contingency shall be deemed satisfied. If the reading indicates a level of radon gas concentration that exceeds the EPA-suggested guidelines, then Seller shall take remedial action at his expense prior to settlement to correct unsatisfactory radon gas levels and shall deliver to purchaser prior to settlement a written certification from an approved testing firm or a licensed contractor showing that all required work has been completed. However, Seller shall not be responsible for such necessary remedial action to the extent that the cost thereof exceeds $_____. In the event repair costs exceed $_____ and the Seller does not elect to pay excess costs, then the Purchaser shall have the option, within _____ hours after notification by the Seller, to either pay the excess cost, thereby removing this contingency, or to declare the Agreement null and void. Purchaser's failure to respond within _____ hours of notice from the Seller shall be deemed an agreement to pay the excess cost and remove this contingency.

After remedial work done by the Seller has been completed, then the Purchaser, at his/her expense, may have the dwelling reinspected to verify that the radon level is within EPA-suggested guidelines.

Over the years there has been a growing concern about radon, a colorless, odorless, invisible gas that—according to the EPA—ranks second after cigarette smoking as a cause of lung cancer.

No one doubts that radon is potentially lethal, nor is there any question that radon can enter homes through basement cracks and fissures. Once within the confining walls of a residence radon can accumulate, and when levels exceed 4 picocuries per liter (pCi/l) you should at least consider more testing. (One pCi/l is considered normal for indoor air, says the EPA. By way of comparison, that's the equivalent of more than 20 chest x-rays in a single year.)

Given this background, it comes as little surprise that more and more buyers are interested in satisfactory radon tests before they purchase a property. Some in Congress want to make radon tests mandatory.

But while radon testing sounds reasonable, not everyone is so sure.

- Leonard A. Cole, with the Science, Technology and Society program at Rutgers University, maintains that a link between illness and home-based radon has never been established. (See "Radon Scare—Where's the Proof," *The New York Times*, Oct. 6, 1988.)
- A 1988 study by Bernard Cohen, a physicist with the University of Pittsburgh, showed that lung cancer deaths in 415 counties were low in areas with high average radon concentrations. (See "New Questions About Radon's True Dangers," *USA Today*, Sept. 29, 1988.)
- A 1991 study by Naomi Harley of the New York University Medical Center found that when testing kits are placed in basements—the location suggested by the EPA—the test results will be three to five times greater than in other parts of the home. (See "Kits May Overstate Radon Risk," *USA Today*, March 21, 1991.)
- A report in the *American Journal of Public Health* (Aug. 1990) showed that charcoal absorption tests were the most reliable, charcoal liquid scintillation units were acceptable, and alpha registration detectors were the least reliable. Thus, the type of test conducted can greatly influence results. (See "Accuracy of Radon Test Kits Varies Widely," *USA Today*, Aug. 22, 1990.)
- In 1989, Public Citizen exposed 34 radon test kits to radon-conta-

minated air obtained from the Energy Department and then shipped the kits to various testing laboratories. The result: numerous errors, some as great as 67 percent. (See "Accuracy of Radon Testing Challenged," *The Washington Post*, Jan. 7, 1989.)

- Douglas Mose, chairman of the Geology Department at George Mason University, found in 1989 that the most accurate radon test was with an alpha-track monitor. How accurate? It was off by 50 percent, plus or minus. Thus a reading of 4 picocuries could really mean 2 picocuries or 6 picocuries. Above 4 picocuries, of course, means there may be reason to be concerned. (See "Radon Tests Vary in Accuracy," *The Journal* [Montgomery County, Md.], Jan. 13, 1989.)

- *E Magazine* ("Radon Revisited: Invisible Gas Continues to Elude Scientists," Feb. 1994) says that the government continues to worry about radon while lacking solid evidence that radon is a significant health problem. The magazine, which specializes in environmental issues, claims the attention given radon distracts the public from known health concerns such as nuclear power emissions, industrial air pollution, and the use of tobacco. The magazine also points out that EPA's current guideline for indoor radon levels, 4pCi/l, is one-fifth the level set by the Canadian government.

The bottom line is that radon is a potential bonanza for fleet-footed entrepreneurs—a dangerous, odorless, invisible gas that test kits cannot accurately gauge. Since repairs to make homes radon-acceptable can cost thousands of dollars, you can bet that American homeowners are spending millions to fix something that's rarely broken.

Radon is an issue that should be approached with common sense. Despite claims that as many as 20,000 people a year die from radon-induced cancers (an assertion based on studies of long-term uranium miners), there are other claims that residential radon is simply not a health hazard.

Additional research may provide more evidence and then, perhaps, the issue of whether radon is, or is not, a significant health hazard can be resolved.

The Buyer's Strategy

1) Before actively searching for a home, decide how you wish to deal with the radon issue. Specifically, will you want a radon test? Will you accept a home that has high radon levels that can be reduced with remedial action? How much, if anything, are you willing to pay to underwrite radon-related improvements?

2) Check with community health or environmental officials to determine if radon is a common local hazard.

3) Ask local health or environmental officials if they have a list of certified or approved radon testers.

4) Feel free to obtain a radon test, but be aware that testing results may vary as a result of such factors as weather, indoor traffic patterns during the test period, the placement of testing devices, the type of device used, the quality of analysis, and other factors.

5) Be aware that while some structural inspectors are qualified to perform radon tests, many do not provide such testing and that a separate inspection is required.

6) Ask if the EPA has established official regulatory guidelines for airborne and waterborne radon in homes and, if so, if the property is within approved limits.

The Seller's Strategy

1) If the buyer wants a radon test, make the property available.

2) As a condition of conducting a radon test, require the buyer to give you a copy without cost.

3) If repairs are required, make certain that your financial obligation is limited to a specific dollar amount.

4) Sellers may want to have their house tested by a professional tester before putting it on the market simply to avoid this potential problem. If no radon problem exists you can then certify this fact to a potential purchaser with recent test results. If a problem does exist, you may want to have it alleviated, or may want to wait and negotiate with the purchaser as to who will pay for such work.

5) If you know there are high levels of radon in the home, you should reveal this fact to prospective purchasers, preferably in writing, to avoid future litigation related to excessive radon levels.

6) Ask if the EPA has established official regulatory guidelines for airborne and waterborne radon in homes and, if so, work with a qualified tester to determine if the property is within approved limits.

ELECTROMAGNETIC EMISSIONS

Model Language:
Electromagnetic Inspection

Notice: This property is located within _____ feet (+/-) of high-voltage power lines.

Some studies have shown that extended exposure to high levels of electromagnetic radiation, such as the radiation produced by high-voltage power lines, may adversely affect your health.

Purchaser may elect to measure electromagnetic radiation levels on the property. Purchaser is aware that specialized firms and/or equipment may be required to measure electromagnetic radiation on the property.

This Agreement shall be contingent until 5 PM on _____ (Date) to allow Purchaser to obtain at his expense an electromagnetic inspection of the property. Seller shall make the property accessible for and cooperate with conditions necessary for such a test. Within 48 hours of receipt of the test results, Purchaser shall deliver a copy of the test results to Seller.

In the event that the test determines that the electromagnetic radiation level on the property is in excess of _____ milligauss, Purchaser shall have the option to either declare this Agreement null and void, or Purchaser may elect to accept the property with said results and proceed with the Agreement. Purchaser's option to terminate the Agreement must be exercised within _____ hours after receipt of the inspection results.

In the event that Purchaser chooses not to terminate the Agreement, Purchaser hereby declares that Seller shall be held harmless and forever immune from liability to Purchaser, Purchaser's family, friends, and guests residing on or using the property, and Purchaser's assigns, heirs, and agents, for any injuries, losses, or damages (including but not limited to the advent or aggravation of physical conditions, injuries, illnesses or diseases, as well as any decrease in the property's recognized market value) incurred by the above-named parties resulting, in whole or in part, from the electromagnetic radiation levels on the property. This provision shall constitute a waiver by Purchaser, Purchaser's family, friends, and guests residing on or using the property, and Purchaser's assigns, heirs, and agents, of all claims against Seller that may arise with respect to electromagnetic radiation levels on the property.

In recent years concerns have arisen regarding the possible health hazards caused by high levels of electromagnetic radiation produced by high voltage lines and possibly other sources as well.

Although more than 100 studies concerning electromagnetic fields (EMFs) have been completed, the health effects of EMF radiation from power lines and other sources is not clear. Nevertheless, court suits concerning this issue have already arisen.

As an example, a San Diego couple sued the local power company claiming that power lines over their property caused their daughter's kidney tumors. The property owners sought medical payments for their daughter, compensation for lost property values, and other claims. Although the jury ruled for the power company in this case, other suits around the country are expected to emerge.

EMFs can be found wherever electricity is in use. Computer screens, refrigerators, and electric clocks all emit EMF radiation, but there is no reliable measure at this time as to whether or not such radiation creates a health risk.

Moreover, the fact that EMF radiation is produced may be less important than where it is generated. Physical space generally defeats EMF radiation. Seen another way, EMF radiation falls off as one gets farther and farther from the source. While this is generally good news, there are some instances where electrical products have value only when used in close proximity. Hair dryers, electric blankets, and electric shavers are examples.

Is EMF radiation a hazard? To answer such a question one would have to consider the radiation level, the distance between an individual and a radiation source, and the amount of time spent in close proximity to the radiation source. According to one Swedish study, exposure to 2 to 4 milligauss over a given period may be hazardous.

For buyers and sellers the issue should be seen in these terms: Many everyday EMF sources such as computers and electric shavers are not part of a property sale and thus are not an issue. A high-powered electric power line near the house or power-company equipment on the property are possibly more serious matters. Several states, for example, now limit EMF radiation from electric power lines.

Most EMF litigation to date involves local power companies and health-related issues. However, a second controversy lurks in the future: do power lines reduce property values?

Proving that the high voltage line running behind your house caused cancer is not a simple matter. Convincing a court that the fear of such health hazards resulted in decreased property value or salability may not be as difficult to demonstrate.

The Buyer's Strategy

1) Observe the property. Are there high-voltage wires nearby? Is power-company equipment located on the property?

2) Ask the seller if the property has ever been examined for EMF emissions. If so, when was the test and what were the results.

3) Be aware that the subject of EMF radiation is complex and that additional research may be able to prove, or disprove, a cause-and-effect relationship between EMF emissions and health risks.

4) Because local power companies are choice litigation targets when EMF suits arise, they may offer free or low-cost EMF testing, or they may be able to recommend knowledgable EMF testers. If you have any concerns about nearby power lines or electrical equipment, it may make sense to have the property tested as a condition of the sale.

The Seller's Strategy

1) An EMF clause may not be necessary if you are not near power lines or other power company facilities.

2) An EMF contingency may cause buyers to focus on an issue without substance.

3) EMF concerns, if realistic, can make properties more difficult to sell for a given price and in a timely manner.

4) Because local power companies are often litigation targets when EMF suits arise, they may offer free or low-cost EMF testing, or they may be able to recommend knowledgable EMF testers. If you have any concerns about nearby power lines or electrical equipment, it may make sense to have the property tested prior to marketing.

5) If the buyer wants an EMF test for the property, do not recommend a particular tester.

6) As a condition of allowing the buyer to conduct an EMF test, require that you receive a full copy of the test results without charge.

FIRE RETARDANT–TREATED (FRT) WOOD

It seemed like a good idea at the time: Why not make roofing materials that could prevent the spread of fire? Fire-retardant wood could stop

Model Language:
Fire Retardant–Treated Wood

Notice: Prospective purchasers of residential real estate should know that the home-building industry has acknowledged a problem in some dwellings constructed with certain fire retardant–treated (FRT) plywood and/or other wood roofing products. In certain instances FRT plywood and/or other wood roofing products have deteriorated as a result of a chemical process known as acid hydrolysis, which is thought to be caused by excessive heat and moisture present in attic areas. This process can result in a weakening of the wood and a breakdown in the structural integrity of the roof. The deterioration is sometimes characterized by a charred, brittle appearance combined with a whitish, powdery residue.

Purchaser and Seller acknowledge that they have been appraised by the Agents that there may be a structural problem if the roof in this property was constructed with certain FRT plywood and/or other wood roofing products. The parties further acknowledge that Agents have made no representations regarding the condition of the roof and that Agents have advised them to obtain an inspection of the roof by a qualified engineer or building specialist of their choice to determine the roof's condition and the extent of any deterioration.

Seller further makes the following disclosures to prospective purchasers of the property:
(Choose as applicable)

_____1) FRT plywood and/or other wood products are known by Seller to be present as a roofing material in this property.

_____2) Seller has no certain knowledge as to whether or not FRT plywood and/or other roofing products are on the property and has not made or caused to be made an inspection of the roof in this regard.

_____3) This roof has been repaired or replaced to correct problems caused by the presence of FRT plywood and/or other wood products.

the spread of flames, and beginning around 1979, tens of thousands of homes enjoyed the benefit of fire-retardant roofing. Unfortunately, while the treated wood really did suppress fire, it was also found that such wood could deteriorate with unusual speed when heated.

While there is little question that the chemicals, wood, and heat can form an unpleasant mixture, the issue of responsibility is less certain. Is the builder, the chemical company, the wood supplier, a home warranty organization, or a homeowner responsible for replacing bad roofing materials? And if a home is sold with FRT roofing, what is the responsibility of the seller?

As this is written the ultimate resolution of the FRT problem has not been established. One effort to create a nationwide compensation fund has failed, but such a fund could emerge in the future. Meanwhile, a compensation fund for homeowners in New Jersey has been established, a model—perhaps—for other states.

The Buyer's Strategy

1) If purchasing a property built after 1978, be certain to examine the roof with care, particularly when dealing with townhouses east of the Mississippi where much FRT roofing can be found.

2) In addition to an external examination, have a structural inspector enter the attic and carefully inspect the roof. Look for darkened wood; a white, dusty coating; a rough texture; visible deterioration; and leakage.

3) If FRT plywood or other treated wood is in place, determine what steps have been taken to resolve the matter.

4) If the roof needs to be replaced, get repair estimates from several sources and, as a condition of the sale, have the seller establish an appropriate escrow account to assure the completion of all work. See *structural inspection* material for detailed information.

5) If there is a third party that will cover some or all of the repair bill, then such funds should be used to reimburse any costs you pay out.

The Seller's Strategy

1) If you believe that your roof has been built with FRT plywood and/or other wood products, make repairs before placing your home on the market.

2) Keep all documentation that shows that FRT-related repairs will be underwritten by builders, insurers, chemical companies, wood firms, or any other party.

3) If you have made repairs, be prepared to show receipts and other documentation to buyers.

4) If you must make repairs as part of your sale, limit liability to the amount placed in escrow.

5) If repairs are required, obtain several written estimates.

6) If it's possible that repairs may be reimbursed in the future by insurers, builders, chemical companies, wood-products companies, or whomever, then provide in your Agreement for reimbursement up to the amount expended for FRT repairs.

21
Fixtures: What Stays and What Goes

Model Language:
Fixtures to Stay
The following items *shall be included* in the sale of subject property:

_____

Model Language:
Personal Property Not Part of the Sale
The following items are *not included* in the sale of subject property:

_____

In real estate, as in other types of activity, ordinary words may have special meanings. One such word, *fixture,* is particularly important to both buyers and sellers.

In technical terms, "real estate" is simply land. Anything in addition to raw land—buildings, fences, etc.—is usually regarded as an "improvement."

Within buildings, however, are items that, while not precisely part of the structure itself in the sense of walls or pipes, are *affixed* to the building and intended to remain in place, and their removal would cause "substantial damage" to the building. Such items include furnaces, central air-conditioning systems, and oil storage tanks—all of which are commonly regarded as "fixtures."

It may seem "right" and "natural" that equipment such as a furnace would automatically stay with a property when it is sold and convey without additional cost to a new owner. But not everyone defines "fixtures" in the same way, and for this reason it is important for contracts to show what remains with the property and is defined as a "fixture"— and what leaves with the sellers and is defined as personal property or "personalty."

For example, a dishwasher may or may not be a fixture. If the dishwasher is a portable model sitting on the kitchen floor and attached to the property only by a cord, then it would commonly be regarded as the seller's personal property. However, the same dishwasher, if built into a kitchen cabinet, would be considered a fixture, because it is firmly attached to the property and clearly intended as part of the kitchen. Pull out the built-in dishwasher, and you'll have a big hole in the kitchen, a void obviously not intended.

Having just shown how a dishwasher can be either a fixture or personal property, it must be said that such definitions may be nothing more than an academic exercise. Suppose, for example, that a buyer offers to purchase the above property and requires that the portable dishwasher—the one sitting on the kitchen floor—must be left to the buyer at settlement. Now, even though the portable dishwasher can be easily moved, it has been defined as an item that will be left for the buyers if the sellers accept the offer.

Definitions, then, depend not only on the facts and circumstances in each sale but also on how buyers and sellers define different items. Something can be a "fixture" if both buyer and seller say it is. Conversely, individual items can be a considerable source of dispute if buyers and sellers disagree.

What seems most important is to avoid nasty surprises at settlement. This can best be accomplished by carefully stating in the contract what goes and what stays with the property. Items of particular interest include clothes washers and dryers, drapes, curtain rods, rugs, storm windows and storm doors, trees, plants and shrubs, built-in stereo speakers and components, heating oil, freezers, portable dishwashers, outdoor swing sets, sheds, firewood, antennas, microwave ovens, special door knockers, wall telephones (if owned by the sellers), porch swings, outdoor barbecues, venetian blinds, cornices, septic tanks, built-in shelving and cabinets, wall-to-wall carpeting, all heating, plumbing, air-conditioning, and lighting equipment and fixtures, awnings, all stoves, refrigerators, ovens, built-in dishwashers and disposals and similar equipment, indoor shutters, shades, screens, and window air-conditioners.

The Buyer's Strategy

1) Recognize that fixtures are a key negotiating issue. The more that comes with the property, the less you will have to buy, install, or replace in the future.

2) Be careful to list every item that you want to convey with the property.

The Seller's Strategy

1) Use fixtures as a bargaining chip. For example, when you offer your house for sale, indicate that the basement clothes washer and dryer are "not included in the sale" even if you don't want them. Later, when bargaining with a buyer, you may want to include these items in the sale if only the purchaser will raise his bid ("Look, you can have the washer and dryer if you'll offer me $125,000 for the property.").

2) If there is something you want to keep when you move from the house, specifically exclude it from the sale. Don't take any chances; make sure the item is *listed in the contract* as something that will not be given to the buyer at settlement.

22
Making Adjustments

Model Language:
Adjustments to Be Made at Settlement
Settlement provider is authorized to adjust between Seller and Purchaser, as of the date of settlement, expenses, prepayments and credits associated with subject property including, but not limited to, property taxes, rents, service contracts, water bills, sewage costs, front foot benefit charges, fuel costs, insurance, operating charges, and condominium or cooperative fees. Property improvements, services, and repairs completed or rendered prior to settlement but not billed or paid as of the date of settlement shall be the responsibility of Seller. Flowers and crops not harvested as of the date of settlement shall be the property of Buyer.

A major function of the settlement process is to assure that the accounts of both buyer and seller are correct. While there is little difficulty calculating such matters as purchase prices and down payments, adjustments are more complex.

Adjustments at settlement are necessary because the transfer of property ownership invariably occurs in the midst of various billing cycles. Property taxes, for instance, might be payable from July 1st for the coming year. If a home is sold September 30th it means that the seller has prepaid property taxes for the next nine months. Rather than just give this money to the buyer, an adjustment is made at settlement by which the seller receives a credit for the tax prepayment. Sometimes unwary buyers or sellers fail to make proper adjustments.

Several weeks after settlement the weather turned cold and the

Andersons turned on their oil-based heating system. In the process of adjusting the furnace, they also discovered two 250-gallon oil tanks in the basement, both of which were filled. This was a pleasant surprise, particularly since the oil had been left behind by the sellers and no adjustment had been made at settlement. At $1.10 a gallon, the Andersons were ahead $550.00.

In certain situations, settlement providers may hold money due to sellers in an escrow account to assure the payment of specific expenses. Water bills, for example, are often issued by a governmental agency, and if they remain unpaid, a lien may be established against the property. Therefore a settlement provider will commonly set aside funds to assure payment of this debt, and any money remaining after payment will be refunded to the seller.

The Buyer's Strategy

1) Have the settlement provider explain each adjustment, so you know why a credit or debit was charged to your account.

2) Make certain that the seller is responsible for outstanding repair work, improvements, and services, whether billed yet or not.

3) Be sure that enough money is set aside at settlement to meet all unpaid bills, particularly water and sewage fees, which may be a lien on the property.

The Seller's Strategy

1) Make certain all credits to which you may be entitled are accounted for at settlement.

2) Check the property to see that full credit is given for items that may be overlooked such as fuel, firewood, service contracts, and club memberships that pass with the property.

23

Occupancy Agreements

Model Language
Pre-Settlement Occupancy Agreement

Address _____

    This Addendum made and entered into this _____ day of
_____, 19_____ is attached and/or made a part of the
Agreement/Contract/Offer dated _____, 19 _____, between
_____, Purchaser, and _____, Seller, and shall have the same
binding force and effect on all parties hereto as does the Agreement/Con-
tract/Offer, and shall take precedence over any and all conflicting or contrary language contained in the Agreement/Contract/Offer to which this
Addendum is attached and/or made a part, or any prior addendum or
addenda attached and/or made a part thereto, and states as follows:

    EXPLANATORY STATEMENT: The Seller and Purchaser have
entered into a contract for the sale and transfer of real property known as
_____ (ADDRESS) dated the _____ day of
_____, 19 _____. Prior to final settlement under subject contract the
Purchaser wishes to occupy subject property. The Seller is willing to permit
such occupancy even though Purchaser is not in a position to effect a complete settlement under the terms of subject sales contract with Seller. The
terms and conditions of the occupancy are specified in this Addendum and
are agreed to and will be binding on both parties.

    NOW IN CONSIDERATION of the promises contained in this Adden-
dum and other good and valuable consideration, receipt of which is
acknowledged by both parties to this Addendum, the Seller and Purchaser
agree as follows:

       1) The Purchaser shall have the right to the immediate possession of
the above-described property effective at _____M. (TIME) on
_____ (DATE).

2) The Purchaser shall have no legal claim upon said property until such time as a full and complete settlement has been made under the terms of subject contract between the Purchaser and Seller.

3) The Purchaser is entitled to an inspection and to prepare a checklist of defects within _____ days from occupancy date. Upon expiration of subject period of _____ days, Purchaser is liable for any and all defects not listed or provided to Seller or Seller's agent on said checklist. In the event a checklist noting defects is provided by Purchaser to Seller or Seller's agent, Seller shall be responsible for assuring that all subject systems, appliances, and facilities are in good working order at Seller's expense or by crediting said costs to Purchaser at settlement, at the option of Seller. All other listed defects shall, at the review and decision of Seller's agent, be the responsibility of the Purchaser.

4) Upon being notified by _____ (THE SETTLEMENT PROVIDER) that all of the papers in connection with settlement have been prepared and obtained and that a full and complete settlement can be made, Purchaser shall cooperate in effecting such settlement at the offices of said settlement provider.

5) Settlement on subject property shall be made not later than _____ (DATE). If Purchaser fails to make settlement within such time period, then the deposit or deposits made pursuant to the aforementioned sales contract may be forfeited as liquidated damages, at the option of Seller, unless Seller notifies Purchaser or Purchaser's agent that Seller has elected to avail himself/herself/themselves of any legal or equitable rights, other than the said liquidated damages, to which Seller may be entitled under subject sales contract.

6) Purchaser agrees to pay Seller an occupancy charge of $_____ per day beginning on _____ (DATE), through and including the day prior to the date of settlement called for under Paragraph 5 above. Said occupancy charge shall be payable monthly in advance at the rate of $_____ per month. An occupancy security deposit of $_____ shall be held by Seller's agent.

7) In addition to the aforementioned occupancy charge, Purchaser agrees to pay in full all utility charges, water bills and sewage fees as may be applicable and in such amounts as may be allocated to subject property beginning _____ (DATE) and continuing through the end of pre-settlement occupancy by Purchaser. Failure by Purchaser to pay said utility charges, water and sewage fees as may be applicable shall subject Purchaser to legal action and/or termination of this Addendum at the option of Seller. All costs incurred by Seller in this matter, including legal fees, shall be paid

by Purchaser either out of the occupancy security deposit or otherwise.

8) Seller shall continue to pay all real estate taxes through and including the day prior to the date of settlement called for under Paragraph 5 above.

9) Purchaser shall not make interior or exterior additions to or change or alter the subject property, structurally or otherwise, during the period of pre-settlement occupancy unless the prior written consent of the Seller is first had and obtained.

10) The Purchaser shall indemnify and hold Seller exempt and harmless for and on account of any damage or injury to any person or to any goods, wares, or merchandise of any person and all expenses, including legal fees, arising directly or indirectly from the use of the subject property by Purchaser. Any claim arising directly or indirectly from the failure of the Purchaser to keep the subject property in good condition or for injury or damage sustained in or upon said subject property, shall be the complete responsibility of Purchaser except where it affects the property itself or its value, and in that event the Purchaser shall be liable to the Seller for such damages occurring during this occupancy period and before said title transfer. Seller's agent is authorized to deduct a sufficient amount from subject occupancy security deposit created in this Addendum to repair, restore, and/or return subject property to its pre-occupancy condition and to return any remaining occupancy security funds to Purchaser. In the event that there are not enough funds to cover any said damage and/or repairs that may be necessary, Purchaser agrees to pay for said costs in accordance with this Addendum and as outlined in an inspection by Seller's agent.

11) Purchaser shall not assign, transfer, or convey, by sale or otherwise, all or any part of this Addendum nor attempt to lease or grant occupancy rights to the subject property without first obtaining the written consent of the Seller.

12) In the event that the Purchaser is unable to obtain a written commitment for financing as called for in the sales contract by _____M. (TIME) on _____ (DATE), then the Purchaser agrees to vacate the premises at that time and to pay the cost of restoring the property to its condition at the time of occupancy by Purchaser including, but not limited to, any outstanding utility charges and occupancy or legal fees; such costs are to be paid by Purchaser out of the occupancy security deposit or otherwise.

13) During the subject occupancy period, Purchaser shall maintain fire, theft, and liability insurance coverage on the property that is satisfactory to the Seller. Copies of documents showing said insurance coverage

shall be furnished to Seller. Failure of the Purchaser to maintain said insurance coverage or provide evidence of such coverage to the satisfaction of Seller may terminate this Addendum and said sales contract, at the option of the Seller.

14) If not prohibited by state or local regulation, this Addendum is not meant to and shall not be construed as creating a landlord/tenant relationship.

The principals to this Addendum mutually agree that this Addendum shall be binding upon them and each of their respective heirs, executors, administrators, successors, and assigns and that the provisions hereof shall survive the execution and delivery of the deed aforesaid and shall not be merged therein and that this Addendum contains the final and entire agreement between the parties hereto, and neither they nor their agents shall be bound by any terms, conditions, statements, warranties, or representations, oral or written, not herein contained.

We, the undersigned, hereby ratify, accept, and agree to the terms and conditions of this Pre-Settlement Occupancy Agreement, and acknowledge reading all pages of this Addendum and receipt of a copy of same.

(To be signed and dated by buyers and sellers.)

_____

_____

_____

_____

_____

Model Language
Post-Settlement Occupancy Agreement

Address_____

This Addendum made and entered into this _____ day of _____, 19_____ is attached and/or made a part of the Agreement/Contract/Offer dated _____, 19_____, between _____, Purchaser, and _____, Seller, and shall have the same binding force and effect on all parties hereto as does the Agreement/Contract/Offer, and shall take precedence over any and all conflicting or contrary language contained in the Agreement/Contract/Offer to which this Addendum is attached and/or made a part, or any prior addendum or addenda attached and/or made a part thereto, and states as follows:

EXPLANATORY STATEMENT: The Seller and Purchaser have entered into a contract for the sale and transfer of real property known as _____ (ADDRESS) dated the _____ day of _____, 19____. After final settlement under subject contract, the Seller desires to continue in possession of the property as described above. The Purchaser is willing to permit such occupancy. The terms and conditions of the occupancy are specified in this Addendum and are agreed to and will be binding on both parties.

NOW IN CONSIDERATION of the promises contained in this Addendum and other good and valuable consideration, receipt of which is acknowledged by both parties to this Addendum, the Seller and Purchaser agree as follows:

1) Possession: The Purchaser agrees to permit the Seller to remain in possession of subject property from the _____ day of _____, 19____, until the termination of the occupancy on the _____ day of _____, 19____, at _____M. (Time). The daily occupancy charge shall commence on the _____ day of _____, 19____. The Seller shall pay to the Purchaser or Purchaser's agent upon the signing of this Addendum, the sum of $_____ as an occupancy security deposit to be held in escrow by settlement agent. This occupancy security deposit shall be used by the Purchaser for satisfaction of any repairs that may become necessary under Paragraph 2 of this Addendum. The settlement agent shall promptly return any funds remaining from the occupancy security deposit being held to Seller upon termination of this Addendum minus costs of repair beyond normal wear and tear. The right to occupy created under this Addendum shall be considered a day-to-day occupancy. Should the Seller fail to vacate at the specified time, the daily occupancy fee shall be increased to $_____ per day.

2) Condition of Property: All appliances included in the sale and located in the property, including but not limited to air conditioning, heating, plumbing, and electrical systems are presumed to be operable and in working order at the time of possession, as specified in Paragraph 1 of this Addendum. Purchaser has the obligation to inspect these appliances and systems and advise Seller or Seller's agent of any defect within _____ hours of possession of premises after the termination of this occupancy. If the Seller or Seller's agent is not notified within the _____ hour period specified, the Purchaser waives any and all claims for the repair or placement of subject appliances and systems. Upon possession, the Purchaser accepts the dwelling in an "AS IS" condition and understands that there are no warranties with respect to the condition of the property other

than such items as to which Seller or Seller's agent are notified within the _____ hour time period. The Seller shall be responsible for any damage to the property during the occupancy, normal wear and tear excepted. The Seller agrees to be responsible for any defects that are noted within the time period above and agrees to have said damages subtracted from the occupancy security deposit held by settlement agent. If damages exceed said occupancy security deposit, Seller shall pay these amounts or have the premises returned to its original condition at Seller's cost and to the satisfaction of Purchaser.

3) Utilities: The Seller shall continue to have all utilities, including any water and sewer charges, remain in his/her/their account until the date of possession specified in Paragraph 1 of this Addendum and Seller shall be responsible for all such utilities until possession date specified in Paragraph 1 of this Addendum.

4) Sales Agreement: All terms and conditions of the original sales agreement between Purchaser and Seller shall remain in full force and effect, except as specifically modified by this Addendum. It is understood that with respect to the condition of the property and the condition of the appliances and systems, the provisions of Paragraph 2 of this Addendum shall supersede any contrary provisions in the sales agreement either expressed or implied.

5) Failure of Settlement: If for any reason settlement is not completed under the sales contract to which this Addendum is attached and made a part, this Addendum shall be considered null and void.

6) Insurance: During the term of this Post-Settlement Occupancy Agreement as indicated in Paragraph 1, Seller shall maintain fire, theft, and liability insurance coverage on the property that is satisfactory to Purchaser. Copies of said insurance shall be provided to Purchaser. Failure to maintain said insurance or provide said copies to Purchaser shall subject Seller to termination of this Addendum, at the option of Purchaser.

7) Problems: During the term of this Post-Settlement Occupancy Agreement as indicated in Paragraph 1, Seller agrees to promptly notify Purchaser of any major breakdowns, failures, or disasters that may occur on or about the property, which shall include but not be limited to flood, fire, theft, major leaks, and property damage and/or loss of value.

8) Changes: Seller agrees not to change, alter, and/or tamper with the appearance of the premises or the premises themselves in any way.

9) Assignment: Seller agrees not to assign, transfer, or convey all or any part of this Addendum nor shall Seller attempt to lease and/or grant occupancy rights to anyone other than parties named herein with respect

to the subject property without the prior written consent of Purchaser.

10) Relationship: If not prohibited by state or local regulation, this Addendum shall not be construed as creating a landlord/tenant relationship.

The principals to this Addendum mutually agree that this Addendum shall be binding upon them and each of their respective heirs, executors, administrators, successors, and assigns and that the provisions hereof shall survive the execution and delivery of the deed aforesaid and shall not be merged therein and that this Addendum contains the final and entire agreement between the parties hereto, and neither they nor their agents shall be bound by any terms, conditions, statements, warranties, or representations, oral or written, not herein contained.

We, the undersigned, hereby ratify, accept, and agree to the terms and conditions of this Post-Settlement Occupancy Agreement, and acknowledge reading both pages of this Addendum and receipt of a copy of same.

(To be signed and dated by both purchasers and sellers.)

_____

_____

_____

It would be wonderful to report that all real estate deals mesh with the precision of a fine watch movement, but rarely is this the case. Every deal involves a profusion of complexities and complications, including one of the most difficult issues of all: coordinated closings.

It's terrific to sell one house and to then turn around and buy another. And while coordinated settlements are common, not every deal works so smoothly.

Suppose Walton moved out of her home several weeks before closing. Suppose as well that her buyers, the Crawfords, want to move in before closing. This seems okay because the house is empty and maybe the Crawfords will pay some rent to offset Walton's costs.

Or, we could do it the other way. Closing on the Walton property is scheduled for March 1st, but Walton can't move into her new place until May 15th. The buyers have a lease and can't move into Walton's home until May 31st. In this situation everyone appears to benefit by having settlement on March 1st and allowing Walton to stay on for a few weeks as an occupant.

The above examples illustrate a pre-settlement arrangement (the buyers move in before closing) and a post-settlement occupancy (the seller stays in the property after closing). And while our examples are neat, tidy, and without problems, matters can fall apart very quickly without a written occupancy agreement between buyer and seller.

What can go wrong? Try these examples.

- The buyers move in before settlement but their financing falls through. Now there won't be a settlement and the buyers are simply tenants—probably unhappy tenants at that since the home that was to be theirs is now beyond reach.
- The buyer moves in before closing, paints the living room puce, and *then* financing falls through. The owner now has an unsold house with a puce living room.
- The buyer moves in before settlement, smokes in bed, and the property burns down. The seller's home insurance has no provision for renters, so the damage isn't covered. Even worse, the buyers refuse to go to closing because the property's condition has substantially changed since the Agreement was signed.
- The seller stays on after closing waiting for a builder to finish his new property. Floods worthy of Genesis rage for the next six months, construction of the new house is delayed, and the seller refuses to move out of the property.
- The seller stays in the property after settlement as a tenant for several weeks in a community with strict rent control regulations. Local rent control regulations require owners to pay a $750 moving allowance to assist any tenant who must move in less than a year. The seller demands $750 to vacate the property.

The solution to a host of occupancy issues is to go from an informal arrangement ("Yeah, sure, the place is empty so it's okay to stay for a few weeks"), to something more structured. While a lengthy addendum may seem awkward and stuffy, it does have the advantage of eliminating or moderating a host of problems before they can arise. Here are some of the major issues that an occupancy agreement should address.

- **Alterations.** While buyers may have a fervent desire to fix up the place from the moment they move in, the property is not actually theirs until closing. Alterations should be handled in two ways. First, there should be no alternations without the owner's permission. Second, in the event the deal falls through, any alterations become the owner's property.
- **Assignment.** To protect the owner's interests, it should not be possible to assign occupancy, nor should occupants have the right to sublet the property without the owner's approval.
- **Condition.** Before homes go to closing the buyer can usually walk though the property to assure that the house has not been damaged during the time between the contract signing and settlement. In a situation where the buyer will live on the property before closing, the approach must be somewhat different. A walk-through should be conducted prior to occupancy (not settlement) to find any substantial damage. Once the walk-through is finished the buyer is then responsible for maintaining the property.

  For a post-occupancy arrangement, the seller must be treated as a regular tenant. The property should be inspected prior to the owner's occupation and after—if there's any damage, then the owner must pay.
- **Deposit.** How much deposit money will be held by the owner? Under what conditions can some or all of the deposit be lost? It's generally a good idea to have the largest possible deposit; however, buyers and sellers should be aware that individual jurisdictions may limit the size of a deposit. Check with a local attorney for details.
- **Failure.** Buyers and sellers may assume that a deal will go through, but what if financing is not available or a major problem crops up? It's entirely possible to have a situation where buyer moves in before closing but the property never goes to settlement. In this situation a pre-occupancy agreement should provide that the buyer's residency will end as of a particular date, unless the seller agrees to an extension.
- **Heirs and Assigns.** An occupancy agreement must provide that it's binding on heirs, assigns, executors, administrators, and suc-

cessors. The logic here is that if a buyer or seller dies, assigns the sales agreement, or is hit by a bus, then the deal will still go ahead.

- **Hold Harmless.** This is an important clause, which says, in effect, that if there is an accident on the property during the occupancy period then the owner will not be liable for damages.
- **Insurance.** The occupancy agreement should require the resident to have fire, theft, and hazard insurance for the property. That said, a seller should always maintain insurance on the property until title is transferred in the public records, just in case the occupant's policy is faulty.
- **Legal Claim.** If purchasers move into a home before closing — or if sellers stay on after settlement — does occupancy create a legal claim against the property? Because a claim may be created by occupancy (think of squatter's rights), it's best to eliminate the problem before it can develop. A decision should be made as to whether in your jurisdiction it is better or worse to establish a landlord and tenant relationship.
- **Occupancy Charge**. Although it looks like rent, in many areas you want to collect an "occupancy charge" and not "rent." The reasoning is that some 200 communities have rent control regulations and by charging "rent" an occupant may gain special rights and privileges. To avoid rent control, if possible, it may make sense to charge an "occupancy fee" and to never ever use such terms as "rent," "lease," or "rental." See a local attorney for details if you live in a community with rent control.
- **Taxes.** The owner should be expected to pay property taxes during the occupancy period.
- **Term.** Usually we think of occupancy on a yearly basis or from month to month. However, in the case of an occupancy agreement the arrangement should run from day to day. Why? Because to end the occupancy it may be necessary to give notice in advance, sometimes the equivalent of a full month or however long the occupancy is defined. By making the occupancy day-to-day, it may be possible to remove the occupant with just one day's notice.

- **Utilities.** The occupant should pay all utilities, which means assorted meters may have to be read before and after the occupancy period to assure a proper accounting.

The Buyer's Strategy

1) If the seller wants to stay in the property after closing, be certain to create a post-settlement occupancy agreement.

2) Determine what rent control regulations, if any, may apply.

3) Collect an appropriate rent and require a solid deposit.

The Seller's Strategy

1) If the buyer wants to stay in the property before closing, be certain to create a pre-settlement occupancy agreement.

2) Determine what rent control regulations, if any, may apply.

3) Collect an appropriate rent and require a solid deposit.

24
Settlement: The Final Step

Model Language:
Establishing Settlement

Settlement is to be conducted by _____, an agent satisfactory to _____ (Purchaser or Seller), and settlement shall occur on _____ (DATE), or as soon thereafter as a title report, financing, and/or a survey, if required, can be obtained, time being of the essence. Settlement shall be held at _____ (LOCATION). Settlement agent shall be authorized to prepare all conveyancing papers and order a title examination and/or survey (if required). The settlement costs include survey expenses, tax certificate costs, notary costs, lender fees (except inspection costs), recordation costs, recordation and transfer taxes, and all other requisite expenses related to the transfer of title and completion of settlement. Of these costs, Purchaser shall pay the following: _____; and Seller shall pay the following: _____. Purchaser shall have the right to a walk-through inspection prior to settlement to examine the property and all improvements thereon. The party not selecting the settlement agent shall pay a reasonable cost for settlement services not to exceed $_____. *The party conducting settlement shall be responsible for assuring where possible that all settlement papers, documents and forms shall be completed and available to Purchaser and Seller or their representatives 24 hours prior to settlement.* If title is defective and cannot be remedied, Seller shall pay all settlement costs.

Few aspects of a real estate transaction are more perplexing than settlement (closing), a process that seems obscure, complex, and foreboding to many buyers and sellers.

Yet settlement is really a very simple process. It is nothing more than an accounting of who owes what to whom plus the completion of all the documents and paperwork necessary to finish the transaction. Clearly the buyer owes money to the seller, and the seller owes title to the purchaser. But, in addition, a number of accounts must be settled. Brokers, if involved, must be paid, title insurance purchased, termite inspectors compensated, and taxes collected or adjusted. The party conducting settlement must also be paid.

The key to these and other financial considerations can be found in the contract. It is the contract that governs settlement, and so it is the contract that must be properly written. If issues are left open, items are left out, or language is vague and unclear, then the settlement process may be delayed, belabored, or the scene of near-mortal combat. Time will have to be spent at the settlement table resolving issues and clarifying language that should have been been specified originally in the contract.

What can go wrong at settlement? Just about everything—at least in theory. In practice, most settlement disputes concern several major issues.

First, the specific date of settlement should be clear in the contract. The contract should allow some leeway for extra time to process a loan or resolve a small title problem, but there should also be a date set after which the parties can terminate the contract. The settlement date can be enforced with language stating that "time is of the essence."

Second, the contract should state who the settlement agent will be and the location where the settlement will take place. If you are responsible for selecting a settlement provider but do not have someone in mind at the time your offer is being made, you might write in "to be named" where a settlement provider is supposed to be designated on the offer form.

Third, the person paying for settlement should be clearly defined in the contract. This is a negotiable matter between buyers and sellers, and costs can be divided equally, borne entirely by one party, or shared unequally—all according to how the deal is negotiated. Beware, however, of contract language that allows one party, perhaps a buyer, to select a settlement provider but then obligates the other party, the seller, to pay "reasonable settlement costs." In such a situation, the seller will be obligated to pay just about any fee sought by the party conducting settlement. Sellers (or buyers) in this situation should instead place a specific dollar limit in the contract, such as "reasonable settlement costs not to exceed $150" or whatever figure seems appropriate. Note one major exception, however: If title is not good and cannot be remedied, the seller is typically responsible for all incurred settlement costs.

Fourth, the contract should allow for a pre-settlement walk-through and inspection to determine if the condition of the property and its components have changed since the offer was first accepted. Sellers are obligated to repair, replace, or correct any damage that occurred to the property between the time the contract was accepted and the day of settlement.

Fifth, the contract should specifically define what stays with the property and what goes. Debates at settlement concerning washers, dryers, plants, drapes, and other items are common in those cases where contracts are vague or unclear.

Sixth, the handling of miscellaneous items should be carefully spelled out, including adjustments such as rents, utilities, taxes, insurance, tenant deposits, and other prepaid items, the escrowing funds for water bills, lender accounts, repairs, and specific problem areas, the required payment of mortgages, judgments, or other liens against the property, and deposit interest credited to the appropriate party.

Seventh, help yourself. If you're a seller, bring required documents to closing. *Do not cancel your fire, theft, and liability insurance as of the date of settlement.* Instead, wait until title has been recorded in local government offices. If you're a buyer, follow the lender's instructions. Some will want you to bring your termite inspection and paid-up fire, theft, and liability insurance policy to closing. Other lenders will want the termite report and insurance policy delivered to them *before* settlement. Buyers should bring to closing a certified check or the equivalent in a form acceptable to the settlement provider.

Eighth, when hiring a settlement provider—whether an attorney, title company, escrow company, or other settlement provider—ask if they view themselves as your representative. Some settlement providers see themselves as "neutral" parties in the settlement process, while others believe they have a role as representatives of the party who engages them. Look for settlement providers who will act as your advocate in the settlement process.

Whenever you are buying or selling a home, it is very important to have a professional on your side during the closing process. If the person conducting settlement says that he or she is a neutral party, that's fine—get your own lawyer. If this means that at closing there is someone conducting the process, a lawyer for the buyer and a lawyer for the seller, that's okay.

There are important reasons why you want your own representative for closing. For example, as a buyer you may be purchasing title insurance. The party conducting settlement may well receive a commission for the sale of a title insurance policy. Can someone paid by the title insurance company advise you about your best choices, options, and coverage?

As a seller you want your representative to review all the closing papers because there may be an error. Errors worth thousands of dollars or unlimited future liability can emerge if the closing documents do not properly reflect the sale agreement.

The question is often raised: Should I, the person who did not hire the settlement provider, bring an attorney to settlement? The answer, in most cases, is that such legal presence is unnecessary. As an alternative, buyers and sellers may have their lawyers review settlement documents 24 hours before closing to assure that all matters dealt with in the contract have been properly addressed. If problems are found, then, of course, it makes sense to advise the settlement provider of any conflicts and to bring legal counsel to closing if the issue cannot be resolved. It also makes sense to bring an attorney to closing if the other party is ornery, offensive, combative, unlikely to fulfill their contractual obligations, picky, or needlessly aggressive.

Strategies for Both Buyers and Sellers

1) Try to shift as many settlement costs to the other party as possible, including sales, recordation, and transfer taxes.

2) Review settlement papers 24 hours before closing, if possible.

3) In the event of an anticipated dispute, bring photographs, notes, and

other supporting evidence to settlement. For example, if there wasn't a six-inch hole in the living room wall as of the contract date but there is as of settlement, it should be the responsibility of the seller to repair the damage.

4) If something promised has not been completed, require the establishment of an escrow account.

5) If you're hiring the settlement provider, get someone who views himself as your representative.

6) Be sure to bring to settlement all that is required of you, such as a proper insurance policy (buyers), money (buyers—in a form acceptable to the settlement provider), a termite inspection certificate (sellers), keys (sellers), and all other items required by the lender, settlement provider, and sales agents.

TITLE INSURANCE

A major issue at every closing concerns the subject of title insurance, which protects owners in case title to a property is faulty or invalid. Title insurance is purchased at settlement, and in the hustle and hubbub of closing, its purpose and function are often misunderstood. Here are the most common questions about title insurance as well as answers that explain how this unique form of insurance works.

Who buys title insurance?

Title insurance is purchased at settlement, either by purchasers directly or by sellers on their behalf.

How much is the annual premium?

There is no annual premium. Title insurance is bought at settlement, and the single premium paid at that time is the only cost.

What basic types of policies are available?

There are two fundamental types of coverage. "Lender's" title insurance protects the property up to the value of the mortgage. If a house costs $100,000, and there is an $80,000 loan, the policy will protect the buyer up to the $80,000 level—in effect, enough to pay off the mortgage if there are problems. With "lender's" coverage, as the size of the mortgage decreases over time, so too does the value of the policy. "Lender's" title insurance is universally required by—who else?—lenders as a condition of getting a loan.

A second general type of policy is called "owner's" coverage. Here the policy protects the buyer up to the purchase price of the property. If the title is invalid, a buyer with this policy would not only be able to pay off the mortgage, but his equity would also be protected. The buyer of a $100,000 home would have protection worth $100,000. "Owner's" coverage is optional and can be purchased at the buyer's discretion.

Why does a buyer need title insurance if there has been a title search just prior to settlement?

Many problems do not show up in a routine title examination. Such problems might include errors in the spelling of names, incorrect information regarding owners on deeds or mortgages, deeds containing forged signatures, and invalid deeds completed by people who didn't actually own the property. Also, it is possible that past owners were not competent to sell because of their age, physical condition, mental impairments, drug usage, or intoxication.

Are there any exceptions or risks that the insurance policy may not cover?

Yes! Most title insurance policies have standard exclusions for errors due to poor surveying, faulty boundary lines, limitations on land use and zoning requirements, failure of the attorney to do a competent title search, and liens for unpaid construction bills or repair work.

Can I get "endorsements" (additional coverage) for my title insurance policy?

Many title insurance companies sell additional coverage. Typical options include inflation clauses (coverage increases if the value of the property goes up) and coverage for specific easements, rights of way, and other encumbrances and restrictions. Speak to your settlement agent to see whether such policy options are available.

Who pays for title insurance coverage and how much is it?

Normally, the buyer pays for the title insurance coverage. In some states, however, both buyer and seller share the cost while in others the seller pays. Regardless of local custom, the cost of title insurance can be a negotiable matter.

Title insurance costs are a one-time charge paid at settlement. The expense of such policies varies from state to state and with the value of the property—as property values rise, so do title insurance costs and coverage.

How can I cut title insurance costs?

There are two ways to slash insurance expenses. First, you can sometimes obtain a discount rate if you buy your policy from the same company used by the previous owner, the so-called "re-issue" rate. Second, you may be able to get a discount if both the lender's and owner's policies are issued at the same time and by the same company.

What happens if a claim is made against my property?

If a claim is made, first notify the title insurance company immediately in writing and include copies of any letters or documents you may have received when the claim was first raised. It's wise to send such information to the insurance company by certified mail, with a return receipt requested, so there will be no question as to whether the company was notified.

Ask the title insurance company if the claim is covered under your policy and *get an answer in writing*. If the claim is covered, the company is required to settle the claim either through negotiation or the courts and to pay for all costs associated with the claim, including legal expenses.

If for any reason the claim is denied under your policy, have the title insurance company explain its position in writing. You may also wish to consult an attorney to assure that legitimate claims are covered by the insurance company and not erroneously denied. Another step is to check with an attorney to see if the parties who conducted settlement, surveyed the property, or searched the title may be liable for any claims not covered by your policy.

25

Damages and Rescission

Model Language:
Damage Clause: Buyer Liability Unlimited

It is mutually understood between the parties hereto that the agreement of the Buyer to buy the property is the sole inducement for the Seller to withhold same from the market. If the Buyer shall in any way breach said agreement or fail to comply with any condition of Buyer's loan commitment, the deposit being held by Seller or Seller's agent may be forfeited at the option of the Seller as liquidated damages and not as a penalty, in which event the Buyer shall be relieved from all further liability hereunder. In lieu of a forfeiture of the Buyer's deposit, the Seller may elect to avail himself/herself/themselves of any legal or equitable rights and remedies which he/she/they may have under this Agreement/Contract/Offer other than said forfeiture. In such event, the deposit shall be retained by the party holding same until complete resolution of any and all disputes or claims between the parties.

In the event of forfeiture of the deposit, or if the Seller shall fail to take any action or fail to pursue any legal or equitable remedies then, in such event, the Seller shall pay the Agent as compensation for his/her/their/its services one-half (½) of the deposit, said amount not to exceed the amount of the full brokerage fee. If, after a breach by the Buyer, the Seller shall release the Buyer from liability or authorize refund of the deposit money, the Seller shall pay the Agent as compensation for his/her/their/its services one-half (½) of the amount of the Buyer's deposit, not to exceed the amount of the full brokerage fee. If, after a breach by the Buyer, the Seller obtains an award of damages from a court or enters into a compromise agreement with the Buyer, the Seller shall pay the Agent one-half (½) thereof, said amount not to exceed the full brokerage fee.

Unlike a good children's story, not every real estate deal has a happy ending. Some transactions are marred by deliberate efforts to renege on a sale or the failure to meet specific terms, while other sales fall through because conditions change or misrepresentation is alleged.

Individuals rarely file lawsuits when a dispute first develops. Usually there are phone calls or letters to the other party, requesting or even demanding performance or change. If, after all the conversation back and forth, nothing satisfactory emerges, a visit to an attorney may then become likely.

At this point, an attorney may still suggest that a lawsuit is *not* the best way to resolve the dispute. Additional contacts may be made through the attorney in the hope that such communication will resolve the matter.

If the dispute still cannot be resolved, however, three major types of damage claims may emerge: forfeiture, specific performance, or action on the contract (or action for breach of the contract).

In a "forfeiture," one party cannot complete the contract and is willing to pay certain damages to end the matter. A forfeiture means therefore that there will be no attempt to enforce the contract, to obtain further damages, or to revise the contract on more positive terms. Additionally, if the purchaser has been occupying the property and the contract is declared a forfeiture, the occupancy must end.

"Specific performance," another kind of remedy, presents a paradoxical situation in the complex world of contracts and lawsuits. Essentially, specific performance means forcing someone to comply with a contract. If Mr. Stapleton agreed to sell his house to Mr. Ridgewell for $145,000 and Stapleton later refused to sell, a successful suit for specific performance would compel Stapleton to go through with the deal.

Yet, specific performance, as a remedy, is rarely granted by the courts. The basis for this reluctance is a practical one—if a person cannot perform under a contract, it may well be due to a business failure or some other problem that would make a court order meaningless or overly burdensome.

Thus, even if someone, say a buyer, wins a suit for specific performance, it is quite possible that the seller will not be able to meet the terms of the court order. As a result, a situation may emerge where there is an ongoing breach of a court order, but no real satisfaction for the purchaser.

Another reason suits for specific performance often fail concerns the notion of fairness. When someone is unwilling to perform but offers instead monetary compensation, there may be a perception of unfairness if a court requires the individual to continue with the contract. After all, how much more should a court demand; aren't monetary damages sufficient?

The more common type of lawsuit seeks money damages. There are three basic kinds of money damages:

- Direct damages due to the breach of a contract.
- Damages caused indirectly by the breach.
- Damages for legal costs and other expenses.

What are typical *direct damages?* They include money expended to sell a property or to fix it up for a specific buyer, the buyer or seller's "loss of bargain," and brokerage fees or money expended as a result of the transaction itself, such as the expense of a termite inspection. With direct damages, there is an attempt to return the party who is suing, the plaintiff, to the position he was in before the contract was created. Direct damages are easier to calculate than other forms of money damages, and they are at the center of most damage claims.

Indirect damages are more difficult to calculate. What, after all, should be regarded as an indirect but related cost? Suppose Mr. Hoffman offers to buy the Carsworth house if Carsworth will repaint the property a deep yellow. Carsworth repaints, but when it comes time to settle, Hoffman can't come up with a down payment. Hoffman is clearly in default, and the cost of repainting the house is certainly a direct damage he caused. But what about the marketing time Carsworth lost by taking his home off the market? Is not Carsworth entitled to some compensation for this loss as well? If so, how much should he get?

A third type of damage claim is for *related costs* arising out of the lawsuit itself, items such as attorneys' fees and case preparation costs. While courts will usually grant court costs to the winner, there is often a reluctance to award attorneys' fees and costs. One exception: When contracts specifically allow lawsuit winners to collect attorneys' fees from the losers, courts will commonly abide by such provisions.

Another option in the event of a dispute is called "rescission," a remedy that, if selected, must be acted upon promptly once a problem arises. Rescission means that both parties go back to where they started. Suppose Mr. Flowers put a $5,000 deposit on a property after being told by the seller that it could be used as a small trailer park. Suppose also that Flowers later found out that use of the property was restricted and that it could not be used by trailer owners. Flowers could demand rescission, giving up all contract rights to the property but getting back his $5,000, if successful.

Related to the subject of damages is the matter of compensation for realty brokers when deals fail. Standardized form agreements commonly provide that brokers are to receive one-half of any damage award, up to the value of their commission. Buyers should be aware of this fact in a situation where a larger deposit is suggested in order to make a "stronger" offer.

How can damages and litigation be avoided? Deal fairly and in good faith, commit every aspect of an agreement to clear and understandable written language, avoid surprises, and try communication and compromise before litigation.

The Buyer's Strategy

1) Limit potential damages. For example, if a standardized agreement allows a seller to collect both a deposit and other damages, limit your liability to the deposit alone.

2) Keep notes concerning matters that may evolve into conflicts and litigation, including names, dates, places, comments, and related information.

3) Put down the smallest possible deposit to limit liability.

4) Place a provision in the contract that if you must sue the seller, the seller will be responsible for attorneys' fees if you win.

The Seller's Strategy

1) Maximize potential damages. Look for standardized agreements that allow you to collect both the deposit and other damages in the event the buyer defaults.

2) Keep notes concerning matters that may evolve into conflicts and litigation, including names, dates, places, comments, and related information.

3) Get the largest possible deposit from the purchaser to maximize your leverage.

4) In case of forfeiture, make certain your liability to your broker is limited to one-half the amount of the deposit or any award you receive up to the value of a full commission. Also, make sure you will have no liability in the event that the deposit or an award of damages is not granted.

5) Place a provision in the contract so that if you have to sue the purchaser, he or she will be responsible for your legal fees if you win.

6) Consider placing a mandatory arbitration clause in the contract. With such a provision, the matter would be arbitrated rather than litigated, a possibly cheaper and faster process.

III
Special Situations

It is clear that no single contract form can possibly cover all the issues that might arise in a realty sale. Not only are there too many issues, but a form that works well for a seller might be intolerable to a buyer and vice versa.

Form agreements generally outline selected contract issues, which means, by definition, that many potential topics are left uncovered. Many forms favor one party or the other and needlessly concede important negotiating points. While this guide (or any other for that matter) cannot possibly describe or discuss all the myriad issues and concerns that might affect real estate buyers and sellers, it can at least touch on the subjects that are most likely to arise but are rarely addressed in form agreements.

The fact that so many special situations exist should suggest to readers that a wide variety of issues are open to negotiation. While it is unlikely that most buyers and sellers would want to address any more than one or two of the following subjects in a given contract, there are situations where many addenda are both appropriate and necessary.

26
Adjustable Rate Mortgages (ARMs)

> **Model Language:**
> **Sale Subject to Acceptable Adjustable Rate Mortgage**
>
> It is agreed and understood that Purchaser shall not be required to accept an adjustable rate mortgage (ARM) that fails to provide any of the following terms: 1. Subject financing may be prepaid, in whole or in part, at any time and without penalty; 2. Purchaser shall not be required to pay points (loan discount fees) equal to more than _____ percent of the first mortgage or first deed of trust; 3. Purchaser shall not be required to pay loan placement fees equal to more than _____ percent of the first mortgage or first trust; 4. there shall be no prepayment penalties; 5. the initial interest level shall not exceed _____ percent annually; 6. the interest rate shall not exceed _____ percent annually at any time during the life of the loan; 7. the maximum year-to-year interest increase shall not exceed _____ percent annually; 8. the margin above the index shall be limited to _____ basis points; 9. negative amortization (deferred interest) shall be prohibited; and 10. all the terms and conditions in this paragraph, or terms and conditions otherwise acceptable to Purchaser, shall be included in writing in any loan agreement. If all of the terms and conditions of this paragraph cannot be met, or terms and conditions otherwise acceptable to Purchaser cannot be obtained, then subject Agreement/Contract/Offer shall be terminated and Purchaser's deposit, if any, shall be returned in full.

Model Language:
Recognition of ARM Risk

Purchaser has been told and understands that interest rates, monthly payments, and other matters associated with adjustable rate mortgages (ARMs) may increase or decrease over time. This paragraph shall not be extinguished by merger of the deed and the contract of sale but shall expressly survive the transfer of subject property.

Until the late 1970s, virtually all home mortgages in this country fell into several easy-to-identify categories. There were 15-, 20-, 25-, and 30-year loans with fixed rates (so-called "conventional financing"), second trusts, and mortgages backed by VA, FHA, and private mortgage insurance.

But the simple world of real estate finance collapsed in the face of sharply higher interest rates. Rates rose in the mid-1970s until 1978 when home interest costs hit an "astounding" 9.46 percent for fixed-rate financing by mid-year. That record was soon broken, however, as rates skyrocketed. By late 1981, home mortgage costs rose above 17 percent.

For a country that had traditionally enjoyed low mortgage costs, typically between 4 and 6 percent during much of the past 50 years, the new mortgage rates were both stunning and largely unaffordable.

Lenders faced a major problem in this situation. They held billions of dollars in low-rate, long-term mortgages financed by billions of dollars in high-rate, short-term loans. Thus, when then-current interest rates rose, lenders lost billions of dollars. Borrowers with fixed-rate financing at, say, 6 percent interest were in heaven, while lenders, who were paying 14 percent, 16 percent, or higher to bring money into their coffers, were somewhere else.

To resolve this multi-billion-dollar fiasco, lenders devised what was then called the "variable rate mortgage," or VRM. Basically, VRMs had an interest rate that floated up or down with an index, possibly the cost of one-year Treasury securities. Add a set amount to the index, the margin, and you could calculate the total interest rate. If the margin was 2 percent (what lenders call "200 basis points") and the index was at 4 percent, then the interest rate on the loan was 6 percent. Since the mortgage rate changed from time to time, lenders could finance VRMs with short-term borrowings and not worry too much about interest rate changes.

The early VRMs stirred considerable opposition because payments could rise or fall monthly and there was no interest limit, whether in the form of a year-to-year cap or an interest ceiling over the life of the loan—a system that virtually guaranteed havoc with family finances. In response to public criticism and the threat of legislation at the state and national levels, VRMs began to evolve. Interest caps became common, and payment changes were generally limited to once a year. The old VRMs, now refined and more acceptable to the general public, became known as adjustable rate mortgages, or "ARMs."

Today ARMs are often available with initial interest rates substantially lower than fixed-rate financing, sometimes two points or more. Why? Because lenders want to encourage the use of ARMs. They believe ARMs represent less long-term risk for them than fixed-rate financing. Besides, if ARMs and fixed-rate financing had equal interest rates, most people would take fixed-rate loans and avoid possible interest increases in the future.

As simple as the ARM concept may seem, it is fraught with complexities, and buyer/borrowers should understand that such financing inherently represents more risk than fixed-rate loans, if only because monthly costs can rise unpredictably, and because the risks of inflation largely pass from lender to borrower. Questions arise with ARMs that are simply irrelevant with fixed-rate mortgages. How often does the interest rate change? Will monthly payments soar if interest rates rise? Is there any limit to how much interest a lender can charge over the life of the loan? Unfortunately, however, standard agreement forms remain largely unchanged; they still ask about interest rates and points while saying nothing about the new issues raised by ARMs.

The Buyer's Strategy

1) Review the offer form with care. Where, in writing, is the interest rate limited? Where, in writing, is the obligation to pay points limited? Is there a clause that allows lenders to raise interest rates or the number of points above levels written into the purchase offer?

2) Have the offer form show that you are seeking an ARM mortgage so the seller will clearly understand how the sale is being financed.

3) Make the offer form show ARM limits. For example, state the maximum initial interest rate you are willing to pay, the maximum interest rate you are willing to pay over the life of the loan, the margin, the maximum annual interest increase allowed each year, and the maximum monthly payment increase.

4) Make certain to address the issue of "negative amortization" (also called "deferred interest"), a situation where monthly payments are held down by a payment cap and do not cover interest costs. For example, suppose interest rates rise, and a borrower should pay $750 per month to cover interest and amortization. Suppose also that a payment cap limits the borrower's required monthly cost to a maximum of $650. What happens to the missing $100? If negative amortization is permitted, the $100 will be added to the borrower's debt.

Many ARMs not only allow negative amortization, but also provide that if the size of the loan grows to 125 percent of the original amount borrowed, the lender can call the loan on 30 days' notice! Since few people can refinance or sell a home in 30 days, what is likely to happen is that a lender will "accept" a cash infusion—perhaps several thousand dollars—rather than foreclose. The bottom line: When considering ARM financing, always ask if negative amortization is permitted.

5) ARM rates can be based on any index over which the lender has no control. Look for indexes that cover the longest possible span of events (five-year Treasury securities rather than a daily stock market index), since long-term measures tend to change more gradually than short-term indexes.

6) Compare rates for both ARMs and fixed-rate financing. Are ARM rates at least 2 percent lower? If not, would you be better off with a simple fixed-rate loan?

The Seller's Strategy

1) Limit the number of points you are required to pay at settlement. See Chapter 12.

2) When a buyer wants to use ARM financing, insist that a statement of risk, showing that ARM interest rates and monthly payments can rise or fall, is included in the offer and signed by the purchaser. This statement, which should be designed to survive after the sale is completed, may prevent or limit future claims by purchasers who might otherwise say they were not aware that ARM rates and monthly costs could increase.

27
Balloon Payments

Model Language:
Buyer Acknowledges Balloon Payment Obligation

Purchaser has been told and understands that, under the terms of subject Agreement/Contract/Offer, Purchaser shall borrow $_____ for a term of _____ years and at the end of this term a single, lump-sum payment, commonly called a "balloon payment," of approximately $_____ (+/-) representing the entire remaining loan balance, shall be due and payable. The provisions of this paragraph shall not be extinguished by the merger of the deed with the contract for sale but shall expressly survive the transfer of subject property.

When Mr. Howe made an offer to buy the house on Tremont Lane, his offer included the creation of a $25,000 second trust. With interest at 12 percent and a five-year term, Howe should have paid $556.11 per month. However, Howe could not afford such a high additional monthly cost and agreed instead to pay just $300 monthly. The result: At the end of five years Howe will owe nearly $21,000—money that must be paid back in a single lump sum, a so-called "balloon payment."

Buyers throughout the country use loans with balloon payments to acquire property, and there is nothing inherently wrong with such financing. Buyers assume that by the end of the loan term they will be able to either refinance the property, pay off the balloon payment from savings, or sell the house in time to settle their debt.

But it's not always possible to refinance, raise needed money from savings or investments, or sell. Sometimes interest rates rise, expected money doesn't materialize, or housing values decline—all problems that can sink buyers who used balloon financing.

To avoid foreclosure, buyers may claim they didn't know they had a balloon note to pay. This may seem difficult to believe, and it usually is, but what the purchasers are really doing is laying the groundwork for suits against the seller, broker, lender, and everyone else associated with the sale.

Potential claims of this type can be limited or eliminated by having a purchaser state in writing at the time of the sale that he or she knows balloon financing is being used to finance the deal and that a balloon payment is due at the end of the loan term. Such language, of course, should be designed to survive settlement.

The Buyer's Strategy

1) Always ask if any loan, particularly a second trust, requires a balloon payment.

2) Determine the size of the balloon payment.

3) Ask yourself: "How will I pay off a balloon note?" Through refinancing? Savings? A killing in the stock market? Sale of the property prior to the end of the loan term?

4) Before you place a balloon note, find out if you have the right to extend the term of such financing, thereby delaying the balloon payment. Borrowers have this privilege in at least one state, and it may come in handy if you cannot make a timely final payment. Ask what notices are required and if any other steps must be taken to delay the final repayment.

The Seller's Strategy

1) Always have the purchaser acknowledge his or her understanding, in writing, if a balloon note is being used to finance the property and have the acknowledgment survive settlement.

2) Check balloon financing rules in your community with a knowledgable attorney. In one state, for example, certain borrowers can extend the term of second-trust balloon loans without the seller's permission, thus postponing the final payment. If you, as a seller, had such financing and were dependent on receiving a balloon payment at a particular time, you could be in trouble if the borrower decided to extend the loan term. If you are making a real estate loan, always have your attorney review applicable laws and regulations to make certain you are not unknowingly entering into a bad deal.

28

Creating a Back-up Contract

Model Language:
Back-up Agreement—No Order of Preference

This Agreement/Contract/Offer shall not become binding on the parties until Seller or Seller's agent notifies Purchaser or Purchaser's agent in writing that this Agreement/Contract/Offer has been accepted. *It is clearly understood that this is a back-up Agreement, contingent upon the voiding of one or more earlier Agreements/Contracts/Offers by one or more other parties to purchase subject property and the removal of this contingency.* If Purchaser or Purchaser's agent has not received written notice at or before _____M. (TIME) on _____ (DATE) that Seller has removed this contingency, then subject Agreement/Contract/Offer shall automatically terminate and Purchaser's deposit shall be refunded in full, with accrued interest, unless there is a written agreement by Purchaser and Seller to continue subject Agreement/Contract/Offer.

Selling real estate can be a tough proposition, and most homeowners are both relieved and delighted to receive a single offer for their property. But there are cases where a home is so attractive that more than one offer is presented. Sellers in these situations must wrestle with a delightful question: Can I accept a second offer when I have already agreed to a first offer?

The answer is "yes," but with an important condition. If one offer has been accepted, another offer cannot have equal standing; it must be a back-up agreement contingent on the termination of the earlier contract.

Even more delightful (at least for sellers) is a related question: What if I get three good offers for my home? How can I accept each one?

Three offers can be conditionally accepted but one must have priority. If one offer is accepted, the other two are back-ups. But what is the order of preference for the two back-up offers? That is, if a seller accepts the Able offer first, the Baker offer second, and the Cramer offer third, must he accept the Baker offer if the Able deal falls through?

It is possible to write a back-up contingency where an order of preference is created, but sellers have little incentive to agree to such language. For instance, in the case above, Cramer may have made a higher bid than Baker even though his offer was received later.

The solution for sellers is to conditionally accept a back-up agreement. It can then later be fully accepted if the seller desires *and* the first deal falls through. If there are several back-up contracts, sellers can select the best offer they have or hunt for still additional offers, provided that they have not established an order of acceptance.

For buyers, the idea of a back-up agreement presents several problems. Several offers mean a property is in demand, at least at a given price, and the seller has leverage in the marketplace. Equally distressing, a given buyer cannot be certain about the content of other offers. Sellers and their brokers have no more incentive to reveal the terms of other offers than poker players have to show their cards.

Back-up agreements, however, should not be seen as wholly negative for buyers. Deals *do* fall through, and back-up offers are frequently accepted, particularly when sellers no longer have the incentive, energy, or interest to again market their properties.

To protect themselves, however, buyers should insist on a specific termination date when their offer will automatically lapse. Otherwise, buyers will be in the position of having made an open offer, which will effectively prevent them from bargaining for other properties. If a buyer has an open offer outstanding *and* makes a second offer to purchase another property, it is possible that *both* might be accepted, a "success" few buyers can afford.

The Buyer's Strategy

1) Find out if any other offers, other than the deal accepted by the seller, are being held on a back-up basis.

2) Ask why the first offer may fail and how long it will take before termination.

3) Create a termination date in your back-up agreement, based on common sense and the seller's representations.

4) Remain in contact with the seller to follow the progress of your offer.

The Seller's Strategy

1) *Always tell buyers in writing and as part of your acceptance of their offer if there is a prior contract on a property.*

2) Do not set an order of priority for accepting back-up agreements—a better offer may come in later.

3) Do not show earlier contracts to competing buyers—even strong agreements may give away your bargaining position.

4) Stay in communication with the buyers so that you can get in touch with them immediately if an earlier contract fails.

5) Once a contract is accepted, promptly notify all other potential buyers. Do not, however, reveal the terms that you have accepted because if the offer you accepted falls through, you may again want to contact your potential purchasers.

6) If you have more than one back-up offer (or if you simply have more than one offer), always pick your first choice on the basis of objective criteria, such as the best price after concessions (if any), the largest deposit, or the best income qualifications. To avoid discrimination claims, *never* judge an offer on such terms as race, religion, color, marital status, national origin, disability, ancestry, sex, source of income, sexual orientation, presence of children, or age. In fact, make a point to never mention such matters; they are irrelevant to the purchase and sale of real estate. If you find two offers exactly alike (an implausible event), then—with both parties present so there can be no claim of favoritism or bias—flip a coin.

29

Looking at Condos and PUDs, Co-ops, and Timesharing

A significant portion of all residential transactions involve the purchase and sale of condominiums, properties in planned unit developments (PUDs), cooperatives, and both resort and urban timesharing. These forms of real estate ownership raise issues and questions not normally found in transactions that involve "fee simple" ownership, where a seller sells, and a buyer buys, all rights to the property.

CONDOMINIUMS AND PUDS

Model Language:
Sale Contingent on a Review of Condo and/or PUD Documents
  This Agreement/Contract/Offer is contingent on a review satisfactory to Purchaser of all condominium and/or PUD documents, including but not limited to the public offering statement, management agreement, declaration, current budget, budgets for the past two years, projected budgets (if developed), all bylaws, rules and regulations, engineering reports, and all other requisite documents associated with subject property. Said review shall be arranged and paid for by Purchaser. If this contingency is not removed and/or acted upon by Purchaser for any reason whatsoever, or if Seller or Seller's agent is not notified of Purchaser's dissatisfaction in writing by _____M. (TIME) on _____ (DATE), then this contin-

gency shall be removed automatically and this Agreement/Contract/Offer shall otherwise be in full force and effect. Purchaser shall receive aforesaid documents upon execution of this contract, or as soon thereafter as possible. Purchaser shall provide a signed and dated receipt evidencing each document received from Seller or Seller's agent. If Purchaser or Purchaser's agent notifies Seller or Seller's agent by the time and date specified in this paragraph that subject review is unsatisfactory, then this Agreement/Contract/Offer shall be null and void and Purchaser's deposit, if any, shall be returned in full.

With a condo, an individual owns a unit of real estate, such as an apartment or townhouse, plus an interest in the "common areas" on which the property is located. Common areas might be anything from hallways to tennis courts, depending on how the condo is organized and structured.

Owning a condo means that one not only owns a unit, but that an owner is also automatically a member of the condo association, the group of unit owners who govern the project. The decisions of this group are important and include everything from the size of monthly condo fees and what such fees cover to the hours that the pool will be open.

Condo units are bought, sold, and financed separately, according to the wishes and needs of individual owners. They, like typical single-family homes, are also taxed individually by local governments. However, because condos are part of a governing body or "regime," they are quite unlike private homes in many respects. The value of a property and the lifestyle of the owner may be greatly influenced by the decisions of the condo association. It therefore becomes critically important to look at the condo and its documents with great care.

Major condo documents include the "declaration," which establishes the condo, "by-laws," which govern the operation of the project, "rules and regulations," which concern specific administrative matters, and the budget, which describes how the condo will allocate its funds. Taken together, these documents may total several hundred pages of carefully worded legal language.

Important information is often buried in these papers. Can you have a pet? How big? How old is the roof and when will it need to be replaced? What voting scheme is used? One unit-one vote or a proportional vote based on the size of a unit?

Because condo documents are so complex, buyers usually have several days by law to review the papers or to have them reviewed by an attorney; if they are unsatisfied with the documents, they may then terminate the deal without penalty. Review times vary according to the jurisdiction where the property is located and sometimes depend on whether the unit is new or used.

Like condos, planned unit developments (PUDs) are distinguished by the fact that they have central associations and boards that govern the activities of the unit owners. A major function of the PUD concept is to allow developers to mass-market single-family homes or condominiums by creating an atmosphere that encourages ownership with such facilities as golf courses, swimming pools, tennis courts, and other recreational features. The PUD concept also permits a developer to manage the growth and direction of a development, to plan for utilities and other requirements such as schools and shopping areas, and to spread the cost of development over a period of many years. Nationally known and highly regarded examples of the PUD concept include Columbia, Maryland, and Reston, Virginia, both near Washington, D.C.

Planned unit developments have been quite successful in this country because they offer open spaces, quiet streets, and many other convenient amenities that have proved to be strong selling points. Raising the concept to the level of an entire community or city has also demonstrated that a variety of housing options can be fitted into a comprehensive plan and that the atmosphere and lifestyle created in such communities is itself of great value.

PUDs often include a home or city association and a board of directors. Also, there may be a town manager and professional staff who run the community on a day-to-day basis. The decisions of these organizations and individuals can greatly influence PUD ownership, as can the covenants and restrictions that are often found with PUDs. These understandings are generally non-negotiable and may carry fines or other penalties if violated. Covenant provisions may prohibit the use of certain colors on outside front doors, clotheslines or television antennas, certain fences on the property, or certain changes in or to the property.

Future development, which should also be considered in any PUD purchase, might involve the construction of bike paths, schools, recreation areas, shopping centers, and parks. Future development is an important matter because what looks like unspoiled woods today may emerge tomorrow as a light industrial park. The good news with PUDs is that such future development won't be a surprise; it's all set in advance and available for review to anyone who is interested.

In terms of "future prospects," PUDs raise many of the same questions one would want to ask about any community. Is there a mixture of housing styles and options—condominiums and cooperatives as well as single-family homes? Are there duplexes or townhouses? Are the homes well built? How does PUD development mesh with surrounding areas? How are complaints and disputes resolved? How is representation on the board allocated within the PUD? These issues are important because with a PUD, you are essentially purchasing both a home and a community.

The Buyer's Strategy

1) Speak to current condo and PUD residents about the project or community. With a condo or PUD, you're buying an environment, not just real estate.

2) Have all papers reviewed by a knowledgable attorney. Make sure to raise questions about your particular needs. For example, what do the papers say about pets, renting property, and exterior decor?

3) Be aware that condominium purchasers typically have a "rescission" period of several days in which to review condo documents. How long do you have to review the papers and what steps must you take to end the sale if you are unhappy with the documents?

4) Always check condo and PUD budgets. Is the project in debt? Have reserves been set aside for emergencies such as substantial repairs or replacements?

The Seller's Strategy

1) Have all documents and budget papers available for a buyer as soon as an offer is accepted. Rescission periods usually begin only after a buyer has received all papers and documents, so not having such materials available only gives a buyer more time to get nervous.

2) Offer to introduce the buyer to neighbors and association officials. This will give the purchaser a better sense of the project and the community.

CHECKING CO-OP DOCUMENTS

Model Language:
Sale Contingent on Review of Co-op Documents

This Agreement/Contract/Offer is contingent on a review satisfactory to Purchaser of all co-op documents, including but not limited to the articles of incorporation, management agreement, current budget, budgets for the past two years, projected budgets (if developed), all bylaws, rules and regulations, engineering reports, and all other requisite documents associated with subject property. Said review shall be arranged and paid for by Purchaser. If this contingency is not removed and/or acted upon by Purchaser for any reason whatsoever, or if Seller or Seller's agent is not notified of Purchaser's dissatisfaction in writing by _____M. (TIME) on _____ (DATE), then this contingency shall be removed automatically and this Agreement/Contract/Offer shall otherwise be in full force and effect. Purchaser shall receive the aforesaid documents upon execution of this contract, or as soon thereafter as possible. Purchaser shall provide a signed and dated receipt evidencing each document received from Seller or Seller's agent. If Purchaser or Purchaser's agent notifies Seller or Seller's agent by the time and date specified in this paragraph that subject review is unsatisfactory then this Agreement/Contract/Offer shall be null and void and any deposits made by Purchaser shall be returned in full. It is agreed and understood that sale and settlement are subject to approval by the cooperative board and if such approval is not given then any deposits made by Purchaser shall be returned in full.

Although cooperative units are generally perceived as "real estate," owning a co-op is not the same as owning fee-simple property or even a condo.

Co-ops are found throughout the country but arguably have found the greatest measure of success and acceptance in New York City. With a co-op, what you purchase is stock in a corporation that owns real estate, the exclusive right to use a particular unit, and a non-exclusive right to share in the use of common facilities. Since individual units are actually owned by the co-op and not individual shareholders, all sales are subject to the approval of the co-op organization. Taxes on the property and mortgage interest on the underlying mortgage are paid by the cooperative association rather than individual unit-owners, but owners will get income tax deductions if the co-op is properly organized.

Co-ops are usually financed—at least at first—with an "underlying" mortgage. Suppose a rental building with 100 units, all of equal size, is bought by the tenants and converted to co-op status. If the building costs $6.6 million and $6 million of that amount was financed with a mortgage, it would mean that each unit has a proportionate debt of $60,000 ($6 million divided by 100 units). Unlike a condo fee, a monthly co-op charge is likely to include mortgage payments, property tax costs, and other operational expenses. Thus the two fees—while sounding similar—are actually quite different since a condo fee will not include mortgage payments or individual property taxes.

Let's say that after five years one of the original unit-owners, Mr. Royal, wishes to sell his interest. He prices his co-op at $85,000, and a buyer, Mr. Luter, offers $80,000. Can Luter go out and get a mortgage for a co-op in the same sense as someone trying to finance a condo?

The answer is generally no. Why? Because within the $80,000 sales price there is the remaining underlying balance of the mortgage, perhaps in this case $58,000 per unit. However, neither Luter nor Royal can simply pay off a proportionate share of the underlying mortgage. What will probably happen is that Luter will buy the co-op stock owned by Royal by putting some money down, then finance the difference between the purchase price and the underlying mortgage balance.

There are now some programs being developed where lenders make co-op loans with what are called "recognition" agreements. Under these arrangements, a lender will finance an individual co-op unit if the co-op organization grants certain concessions to the lender. One concession, for example, might be a willingness to give property rights automatically to a lender without further co-op approval in case of default.

Because co-op sales normally require approval of the co-op board, sellers should be aware that they must not only find a buyer who is "ready, willing, and able" to purchase their stock ownership in the property, but also one who will be approved by the co-op board. Buyers have been disapproved because they were in the "wrong" profession (acting or politics) and for other reasons not particularly related to the purchase or sale of real estate.

On the positive side, because cooperative ownership involves stock rather than real estate, transferring title is far quicker and cheaper than with fee-simple real estate such as a single-family house or a condo. As a result, both buyers and sellers can expect fewer settlement costs than with other forms of real estate ownership.

The Buyer's Strategy

1) What are the restrictions and covenants associated with the project? Can you rent a unit? Have pets? Entertain guests past a certain hour?

2) What is the composition of the co-op fee? How much of the fee is tax deductible?

3) Speak with members of the co-op board and project residents. Is there any reason why you would not be accepted as a shareholder?

4) Make absolutely certain that your deposit will be returned if you cannot get financing or if you are rejected by the co-op board.

The Seller's Strategy

1) Gather all papers and documents so they will be available to a purchaser as soon as an offer is made.

2) Introduce your prospective purchaser to board members and others to help gain board approval.

TIMESHARING

Model Language:
Sale Contingent on a Review of Timesharing Documents

This Agreement/Contract/Offer is contingent on a review satisfactory to Purchaser of all timesharing documents, including but not limited to the public offering statement, management agreement, declaration, current budget, budgets for the past two years, projected budgets (if developed), all bylaws, rules and regulations, and all other requisite documents associated with subject property. Said review shall be arranged and paid for by Purchaser. If this contingency is not removed and/or acted upon by Purchaser for any reason whatsoever, or if Seller or Seller's agent is not notified of Purchaser's dissatisfaction in writing by _____M. (TIME) on _____ (DATE), then this contingency shall be removed automatically and this Agreement/Contract/Offer shall otherwise be in full force and effect. Purchaser shall receive aforesaid documents upon execution of this contract, or as soon thereafter as possible. Purchaser shall provide a signed

---

and dated receipt evidencing each document received from Seller or Seller's agent. If Purchaser or Purchaser's agent notifies Seller or Seller's agent by the time and date specified in this paragraph that subject review is unsatisfactory then this Agreement/Contract/Offer shall be null and void and any deposits made by Purchaser shall be returned in full.

A recent arrival to the real estate landscape is timesharing, a variation on the condominium theme.

Timesharing takes the condominium concept and divides it not only among owners of individual units in a single building or project, but also among owners of a single unit. The proposition is that the owner, instead of owning the condo year-round, owns it just a few weeks a year. Thus an owner would have, say, Week 42 of condominium unit 12, while the other weeks of the year for that unit would be sold to other owners.

Although one may own Week 42, that does not mean an individual will be forced to vacation forever at that time. Timeshare units of "like value" are readily exchangeable, both within projects (say Week 42 for Week 31) and among projects (perhaps a week in Florida for a week in Colorado). In addition, an owner may elect to rent his unit rather than occupy it. Such rentals are commonly arranged by managers at the project.

Not all timeshare units represent interests in real estate, however. Some, called "vacation leases," "vacation licenses," or "club memberships," are merely right-to-use leases where ownership rights are limited. Such leases typically have a life of 12 to 40 years, after which they expire.

When timeshare units are sold on a fee-simple basis, however, owners are generally entitled to all the rights and privileges that one would normally find in condominium ownership—with one important exception: financing. Lenders generally treat timeshare units as personal property rather than real estate, even though fee-simple ownership can be deeded and recorded. Financing is commonly available from lenders on an installment-loan basis, a form of financing that means title is only transferred to purchasers when much or all of the loan is repaid.

Unit prices will vary according to the location of the project, amenities, and the time of year. Buying at the height of the season will be most expensive; many purchasers choose instead to buy during "shoulder" periods, either just before or after the season. The attraction of shoulder periods, it is sometimes claimed, is that they are easy to exchange.

Timesharing is generally associated with resort areas, but in the future we may see more of this practice in major cities. Many people would like a place to stay in, say, New York, San Francisco, or Washington for a week or so, and urban timesharing may well emerge as an alternative to downtown hotels. Corporations also may take to the urban timesharing idea since it would then be possible for them to house traveling executives at a known cost.

The Buyer's Strategy

1) Check with a CPA or tax attorney to determine if interest payments on timeshare units are tax deductible. The central issue here is whether the financing used to buy the unit is considered a secured real estate debt with interest that is tax deductible or simply a personal debt. Note that timeshare units are commonly financed with personal loans rather than mortgages.

2) Look for timeshare units as an alternative to future vacation costs and not as a realty investment.

3) Be certain that you are buying a fee-simple interest in real estate and not a mere lease.

4) Ask if all facilities, such as pools, tennis courts, and spas, have been deeded over to the timeshare project or if they are being held by the developer for rental to unit owners.

5) Ask who owns the ground under the project. Beware of land-lease deals.

6) Ask about the experience of the management company, what its relationship is to the resort developer, what the management policies are with respect to guests, and what restrictions there are regarding the use of the property.

The Seller's Strategy

1) Make certain you have a fee-simple interest to sell; otherwise the unit may be unsalable or restrictions may apply.

2) Recognize that you may be competing for buyers with the developer, particularly if many units remain unsold.

3) Try to sell during a good season. Marketing timeshare units in Miami is much easier in December than July.

SPECIAL ASSESSMENTS

> **Model Language:**
> **Special Assessment Warranty**
>
> Seller warrants that no special assessments are pending or scheduled for a period of _____ months following the date of settlement and Seller shall indemnify Purchaser for the full amount of any special assessment(s) charged during subject period. The provisions of this warranty shall not be extinguished by the merger of the deed and sales contract but shall expressly survive the transfer of subject property.

Condo, co-op, and PUD unit owners typically pay a fee each month for services provided their project. Included within that fee may be money for maintenance, insurance, and management, as well as a reserve fund for unexpected emergencies. But it sometimes happens that the money collected for reserve funds is not sufficient to meet certain costs, and when such conditions arise, unit owners may be charged a "special assessment," a one-time fee in addition to regular monthly payments.

What kind of emergency might cause or require a special assessment? The need for special assessments usually arises in three situations. First, there is an emergency that the reserve fund cannot finance, such as a sudden crack in the pool, a leaky roof, or asbestos insulation that needs to be removed. Second, there are costs that arise just after a project has been built or converted when there simply has not been enough time to build up the reserve fund. Third, the owners may decide to make a major change in the project, such as the conversion to individual electric meters from a single central meter—a change which in the long run means electric bills will be paid by each owner rather than through a common monthly fee but, in the short run, requires a substantial one-time payment.

Special assessments, like monthly fees, are a lien against each unit. Unlike monthly charges, however, special assessments by their nature are unpredictable—you don't know when, if ever, a special assessment may be required and you don't know the size of such assessments. While special assessments are typically less than $1,000, special assessments in excess of $10,000 are not unknown.

Special assessments should be of particular interest to purchasers for two reasons. First, if left unpaid, special assessments can lead to fore-closure. Second, if units in two different projects are priced equally, but a $500 special assessment is suddenly announced for one project, the two units no longer have the same value.

The Buyer's Strategy

1) Check with the board of directors or the management to see if any special assessments are scheduled or anticipated.

2) Check the budget to see if a reserve fund has been established. Projects with small reserve funds—or no reserves—should be viewed with caution.

3) Have the seller agree to indemnify you if a special assessment is charged during a certain period after settlement, say 12 to 24 months.

4) Read engineering reports with care, since they may offer important information concerning the condition of the property. For example, if the report says that the roof has a life expectancy of 20 years and the 25-year-old building has its original roofing, you can anticipate roof repairs in the near future.

The Seller's Strategy

1) Check with the board of directors or management company to see if any special assessments are planned or anticipated. Always tell a purchaser if a special assessment is pending, as this information is a material consideration in the purchase of a unit.

2) If you accept an offer that includes an indemnification clause for special assessments, negotiate for the shortest possible indemnification period—for example, 3 months rather than 12 months.

30
Making an Irrevocable Gift

Model Language:
Gift Clause

_____ (Donor) agrees to provide the sum of $_____ as an irrevocable gift to Purchaser on which repayment, in full or in part, interest, or valued consideration of any kind shall not be required or expected. Donor shall place subject funds, on or before _____M. (TIME) on _____ (DATE), in an escrow fund established by a party acceptable to Purchaser. At settlement, subject funds shall be deposited with settlement provider as a credit to Purchaser. If for any reason Purchaser does not complete subject transaction, subject gift funds shall immediately be returned in full to Donor. If Donor does not deposit subject funds with a party acceptable to Purchaser by the time and date established in this paragraph, then this Agreement/Contract/Offer may, at the option of Purchaser, be deemed null and void, in which case Purchaser's deposit, if any, shall be returned in full. Donor has read this gift clause and agrees that it shall be binding on him/her/them and each of his/her/their respective heirs, executors, administrators, successors, and assigns. *(To be signed by buyer, seller, and donor.)*

Many home sales, particularly first-time realty purchases, are dependent on gift contributions. But standardized agreement forms rarely define gifts or describe how gifts should be handled in the context of a transaction.

A "gift" is an outright grant made without condition or reservation and for which nothing is expected in return. "Nothing" means no principal, interest, or any other form of consideration.

The willingness of someone to make a gift is of little, if any, value if the funds are not accessible. If a buyer makes an offer to purchase property based on the presumption of a gift but the donor fails to provide the money, the buyer could lose his or her deposit—depending on how the agreement is written—because he can't complete the purchase. Thus, buyers need to use caution when buying with the expectation of a gift. They must make their offer subject to the gift: that is, no gift, no deal, in which instance all deposit money is returned.

Gifts raise four issues from the donor's perspective.

First, if the gift is intended only for the purchase of a particular property, the money should be returned to the donor if the deal falls through.

Second, any gift money should be held in an escrow fund until settlement, separate and apart from the buyer's or seller's funds.

Third, donors should ask: What are the tax implications of a gift? This issue should be reviewed by a CPA, tax attorney, or other knowledgable source *prior* to making a gift commitment.

Fourth, when making a gift, the donor's commitment should be binding on heirs, successors, executors, and administrators. If the gift commitment is not binding and something happens to the donor prior to settlement, the sale can be lost because of family bickering—before he was hit by a bus, did Uncle Ned really mean to give Freddie $15,000 in cash or should that money be divided among the heirs?

For sellers, an offer that depends on a gift commitment should be viewed with both interest and caution. How realistic is the buyer? Can the donor deposit the gift prior to settlement so everyone is sure the money is available? Will the donor make a commitment in writing? If the money is readily available and the donor will make a written commitment, there should be few, if any, problems with the deal.

The Buyer's Strategy

1) Line up any gift commitment before entering the marketplace.

2) Have a donor who is willing to sign a gift commitment.

3) Know how much money is involved and when it can be delivered.

4) Be sure the deal can be terminated and your deposit returned in full if gift funds are not delivered by a given time.

5) Have the donor examine the tax aspects of a possible gift commitment with an attorney or CPA.

6) Require the donor, if possible, to bind heirs, successors, and others to the gift commitment.

The Seller's Strategy

1) Beware of gift commitments made by individuals other than a donor with a formal, signed gift commitment in hand.

2) Insist on delivery of the money within a reasonable period, say 10 to 15 days after the contract is ratified.

3) Require the donor to bind heirs, successors, and others to the gift commitment.

31

Legal Reviews, Lawyers, and Representation

Model Language:
Sale Subject to Approval by Buyer's Attorney

This Agreement/Contract/Offer is contingent on a review satisfactory to Purchaser's attorney, and such review shall be arranged and paid for by Purchaser. If this contingency is not removed and/or acted upon by Purchaser for any reason whatsoever, or if Seller or Seller's agent is not notified of Purchaser's dissatisfaction in writing by _____M. (TIME) on _____ (DATE), then this contingency shall be removed automatically and this Agreement/Contract/Offer shall otherwise be in full force and effect. If Purchaser or Purchaser's agent notifies Seller or Seller's agent by the time and date specified in this paragraph that subject review is unsatisfactory then this Agreement/Contract/Offer shall be null and void and Purchaser's deposit, if any, shall be returned in full.

Few commonplace transactions are more complex than the purchase and sale of real estate, a process that can include zoning, easements, contracts, title questions, financing, warranties, and taxes. With so many complications and with so much at stake, it is little wonder that lawyers are commonly involved in realty matters.

Unlike brokers, lawyers are not typically concerned with the pricing and selling of property. Instead, attorneys are active in preparing contracts, performing title and settlement work, and providing legal advice to buyers, sellers, and brokers. Lawyers can assure that contract lan-

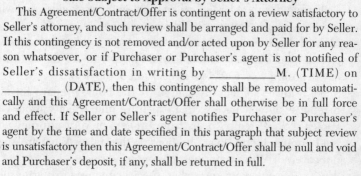

Model Language:
Sale Subject to Approval by Seller's Attorney

This Agreement/Contract/Offer is contingent on a review satisfactory to Seller's attorney, and such review shall be arranged and paid for by Seller. If this contingency is not removed and/or acted upon by Seller for any reason whatsoever, or if Purchaser or Purchaser's agent is not notified of Seller's dissatisfaction in writing by _____M. (TIME) on _____ (DATE), then this contingency shall be removed automatically and this Agreement/Contract/Offer shall otherwise be in full force and effect. If Seller or Seller's agent notifies Purchaser or Purchaser's agent by the time and date specified in this paragraph that subject review is unsatisfactory then this Agreement/Contract/Offer shall be null and void and Purchaser's deposit, if any, shall be returned in full.

guage says what the parties intend, refine agreements with contingencies, addenda, and contract changes, explain the legal issues that may result from various purchase or sale strategies, assist in the event of disputes, and, if qualified, outline the tax consequences of the transaction. In addition, lawyers conduct a large portion of all settlements.

The need for legal services arises not only from the complexity of real estate transactions, but from the need for separate representation for buyers, sellers, and sometimes brokers as well.

As a matter of tradition, brokers are commonly hired by sellers, and so it is sellers who benefit from the broker's sales, marketing, and negotiating skills. While brokers are obligated to get the best possible price and terms for their clients, brokers cannot offer legal services unless also qualified as attorneys.

Buyers, also as a matter of tradition, are regarded as "customers" by brokers in the real estate marketplace rather than as "clients" to whom an agency obligation is owed. Buyers do not have representation in the marketplace unless they hire either an attorney, a broker, or both.

The use of attorneys raises several issues that should be considered by both buyers and sellers:

- Plan ahead. *Find an attorney who can do your legal work before you sign a contract.* Look for lawyers who are knowledgable about real estate in the jurisdiction where the property is located, who charge an hourly fee (not a percentage of the property's value), who are available with reasonable notice after office hours (many real estate deals are hashed out at night or on weekends), and who express a genuine interest in working with you.

- Make the offer or its acceptance *subject to a legal review satisfactory to your attorney,* and be certain to provide for the return of any deposit if you're advised to back out of the deal.

- Since attorneys generally charge by the hour, prepare for any meetings you may have so that expensive time is not wasted. Get copies of local realty forms from brokers or your attorney and read through them. What questions do they raise? What areas are not covered? Write your questions out in advance.

- Always consult an attorney when special circumstances arise such as transactions involving minors, estates, divorces, separations, or possible incapacity. For example, if someone is in a hospital under medication, his or her ability to make a contract may be questioned later and the agreement voided. In such situations, you may need a note from a physician stating that the individual was alert, coherent, and able to enter into a contract at the time documents were being signed.

- Look for attorneys—and brokers—who are mutually respectful and who have a desire to work together.

- Recognize that the right of a broker to amend or adjust a realty contract is limited in many states, and in such jurisdictions the use of an attorney is essential.

- Do not select an attorney on the basis of a recommendation from the other party or their broker. Get your own lawyer.

- If your lawyer is conducting the settlement, ask if he or she will act as your representative. Some settlement providers see themselves as "neutral" parties in the settlement process, while others believe their role is to represent the party who engages them. Look for settlement providers who will act as your advocate in the settlement process.

Note that there are some within the real estate community who believe that lawyers are often "deal killers," attorneys who needlessly find fault with every transaction and frighten buyers and sellers. While there are undoubtedly cases where inept and unprofessional lawyers complicate transactions, it must also be said that the attorney's role is to protect a client's interest, and sometimes that interest is best served by advising against a deal. While this may not be a happy thought, it is, nevertheless, a reality.

32
Opening and Closing Offers

Model Language:
Offer Is to Remain Open

Purchaser agrees that this offer shall not be withdrawn before _____M. (TIME) on _____ (DATE).

Model Language:
Offer Is to Terminate Automatically

This offer shall terminate automatically at _____M. (TIME) on _____ (DATE), unless accepted on or before that time and date.

When an attractive offer to purchase is made, it is in the seller's interest to accept it as quickly as possible and to communicate acceptance to the purchaser. The logic behind this point is both a matter of common sense and legal procedure. Sellers will certainly want to accept quickly to prevent purchasers from getting cold feet and backing out of a deal. In addition, *unless otherwise agreed, buyers have the right to withdraw an offer at any time prior to acceptance, without penalty*.

However, while speed is often important, there are also situations where a quick acceptance is not possible or desirable. Consider these examples:

- Broker Pitman receives an attractive offer for the Ruiz house. The Ruiz family, however, is vacationing in Canada and cannot be reached quickly.

- Seller Holmes gets an offer from a buyer that seems attractive but contains several clauses and conditions that Holmes wants her attorney to review. She delays responding to the offer until she has checked with her lawyer.
- The Cramer house is the best home on the block and when it goes up for sale three offers are received the first time the property is held open. Mr. Cramer wants time to examine each offer to see which produces the highest net benefit and so delays accepting any proposals.

In each of these examples, sellers might ask purchasers to write offers that remain open for a set period of time so that they can be reviewed carefully without the possibility of a sudden withdrawal.

Another value to an offer that remains open until a certain time, at least from the seller's viewpoint, is that with a signed offer in hand a seller can "shop" the market with the hope of finding a better deal. If a higher price or better terms are not available, the seller can always accept the open offer. While buyers may be appalled at this idea, shopping offers—without revealing the terms of the offer in hand—is not uncommon.

Suppose a purchaser agrees not to withdraw an offer until a certain time. Does that mean the offer closes once the deadline passes? Not necessarily. When a buyer agrees not to withdraw before a specific time he has not said the offer will be withdrawn at that moment. It is entirely possible that the offer will continue to remain open and that it could be accepted even after the buyer's deadline has passed, depending on how the contingency is written.

Sometimes, however, buyers want to limit the period of acceptance so that they will not be forced to wait eternally for a seller to respond. If the offer isn't accepted by a particular time and date, the deal is off, and the buyer's deposit will be returned. Note, incidentally, that setting a time limit may place some pressure on the seller to make a decision, be it acceptance or rejection. This is generally an advisable way for the purchaser to proceed.

The Buyer's Strategy

1) Feel free to write an offer that terminates at a specific date and time.

2) Explain why you want a specific termination time inserted in the offer so that the seller understands your bargaining position.

3) Beware of demands to leave an offer open until a certain time without clear and convincing evidence that the seller has a pressing need for additional time.

4) If you have left an offer open with one seller but want to make an offer on another property, be sure to withdraw the earlier offer, otherwise you may wind up purchasing two houses at once.

The Seller's Strategy

1) As circumstances require, feel free to insist that a buyer's offer remain open until a specific time and date.

2) Tell the purchaser why you want the offer left open.

3) Recognize that an offer that remains open until a specific time is not necessarily terminated once a deadline has passed.

33

Permits and Zoning

Model Language:
Sale Subject to Permits and Zoning

This Agreement/Contract/Offer is contingent on the Purchaser securing building, health and occupancy permits, sewer hookups and zoning requirements which are satisfactory to Purchaser. If this contingency is not removed and/or acted upon by Purchaser for any reason whatsoever, or if Seller or Seller's agent is not notified of Purchaser's dissatisfaction in writing by _____M. (TIME) on _____ (DATE), then this contingency shall be removed automatically and this Agreement/Contract/Offer shall otherwise be in full force and effect. If Purchaser or Purchaser's agent notifies Seller or Seller's agent by the time and date specified in this paragraph that Purchaser is unsatisfied for any reason then this Agreement/Contract/Offer shall be null and void and Purchaser's deposit, if any, shall be returned in full.

The value of real estate depends not only on how the property is currently being used but also on potential: how the property *can* be used. The use of property, in turn, is typically controlled not only by economic demand but also through zoning, the issuance of building permits, health and fire code regulations, and the availability of sewer hook-ups.

It is easy to demonstrate how use affects value. When the Quade family sold The Tidewater, a 100-unit downtown apartment complex, they were getting average monthly rentals of $750 per unit, or a gross revenue of $900,000 annually. A buyer, Mr. Hempstead, offered $2.5 million for the property when it became available.

Hempstead chose his offering price with great care. Assuming rentals could not be raised, he would clear $100,000 a year. Wanting to make at least 20 percent on his investment, Hempstead offered the sellers $500,000 down if they would take back a $2 million mortgage at 10 percent interest. Since the interest on $2 million was greater than their annual profit from owning the building, and since they would get another $500,000 up front, the Quade family agreed.

In his offer, however, Hempstead made the deal dependent on his ability to obtain satisfactory zoning within a 120-day period following acceptance of his offer. He wanted to convert the apartment building into a hotel, a project that would cost at least $20,000 per unit in repairs, furnishing, and other costs, or a total outlay of $2 million above the purchase price.

Hempstead got his zoning, made his conversion, and became affiliated with a national hotel chain. With units now used as suites and priced at $75 per night, and with an 80 percent occupancy rate, each unit produced $1,800 per month ($75 × 30 = $2,250 less 20 percent) and the entire project generated $2.16 million ($1,800 × 100 units × 12 months) in its first year.

When the next buyer came along and saw that Hempstead's building could now generate profits of $400,000 a year, he offered to buy the building with $2 million down if Hempstead would take back a $6 million loan. Hempstead said the price was agreeable, but the buyer would have to get financing from a regular lender. In the end, Hempstead got $8 million for the project, paid off his $2 million mortgage to the Quades, repaid the $2 million loan he made to fix up the property, replaced the $500,000 he originally invested, and shared the remaining $3.5 million in profits with Uncle Sam.

Deals that depend on zoning or the issuance of various governmental permits are common in commercial transactions and in evolving neighborhoods, but such transactions raise major questions for sellers: Why sell? If a zoning change can greatly increase the property's value, why not get the new zoning yourself and sell from a stronger negotiating position? Or, alternatively, why not get the new zoning, upgrade the property, and hold it for possible further appreciation?

The Buyer's Strategy

1) Look for properties that can be converted to higher and better uses.

2) Tie up the property, through a purchase offer or option, while seeking zoning and permits.

3) If you do not want the property unless and until you have appropriate governmental approval, make sure your offer gives you an out and that it insures the return of your deposit.

The Seller's Strategy

1) If someone offers a deal dependent on zoning changes or specialized governmental permits that may substantially increase the value of the property, consider making the conversion yourself.

2) If the zoning and permit process is lengthy, have the buyer pay you a non-refundable fee for an option to buy the property. That way, if needed zoning and permits do not come through, you will have compensation for not having had your property on the market and available to other purchasers.

3) Set a time limit on the option period. Zoning can be a long and cumbersome process that may take longer than anyone expects. With a time limit on the option, you may be able to collect a second option fee or be the beneficiary of the buyer's zoning efforts if he does not want to continue with the option.

34
When There Are Tenants

Model Language:
Sale Subject to Existing Leases

It is agreed and understood that this Agreement/Contract/Offer is made subject to an existing management agreement, existing leases and tenant rights under applicable laws. This paragraph shall not be extinguished by the merger of the deed and the contract of sale but shall expressly survive the transfer of subject property.

Model Language:
Sale Contingent on Property Being Lease-Free

Seller warrants that as of 24 hours prior to settlement the property shall not be under lease; there shall be no tenants on the property; Seller shall be responsible for the payment of all tenant moving allowances, if any; Purchaser shall have no obligation to lease subject property at settlement or after settlement; and all tenant deposits shall have been returned in full. Seller shall hold Purchaser harmless and shall indemnify Purchaser from any and all costs, including legal fees, which may result from landlord/tenant conflicts associated with leases written, signed or authorized by Seller, including all agreements which Seller has accepted as assignee. This paragraph shall not be extinguished by the merger of the deed and the contract of sale but shall expressly survive the transfer of subject property.

Model Language:
Notice Regarding Landlord/Tenant Matters

Seller and Seller's agents make no representations or warranties as to how many units, if any, are under lease; as to whether any of the existing leases are valid; as to whether any of the tenants have a right to buy and stay in his/her/their units at this point in time or after the sale of the property; as to whether tenants have a first right of refusal to purchase subject property; as to whether any tenant improvements form a part of the premises offered for sale; and/or as to whether there are any landlord/tenant matters which have yet to be resolved. Purchaser has carefully read this paragraph, understands its content and shall not hold Seller or Seller's agents liable for any matters arising from circumstances described in this paragraph. This paragraph shall not be extinguished by the merger of the deed and the contract of sale but shall expressly survive the transfer of sub-

---

Model Language:
Seller to Provide All Requisite Tenant Notices

Seller shall be responsible for providing all tenant notices as required by local law and/or as directed by Purchaser. Seller shall deliver tenant notices in a timely manner and maintain records showing when tenant notices were sent and delivered and the mode of delivery. Seller shall promptly inform Purchaser of all tenant responses and communications.

About 25 percent of all single-family homes are occupied by renters, and these properties raise special issues not normally found with owner-occupied real estate.

Of central importance is the fact that, unless otherwise stated, leases remain in effect regardless of ownership changes. This means that the purchase of rented real estate involves not only the acquisition of property, but a willingness to accept existing leases as well. In turn, existing leases may enhance the value of a given property—or detract from it. If a property is leased for $3 per month for the next ten years, whoever buys it must honor the lease and all its terms.

Leases, like purchase agreements, are all different—there is no standard lease, and therefore the purchase of rented property should be contingent on a legal review satisfactory to the buyer's attorney. That review should include a careful examination of all lease documents to assure that tenant agreements do not adversely affect buyer interests.

In particular, leases should be checked for monthly rental terms, tenant repair obligations (if any), termination dates, and renewal options. The seller should be asked for records showing tenant payments for the past year.

Rent control regulations govern landlord/tenant matters in several major cities, and such rules may profoundly affect realty values and owner rights. These rules may limit rental increases, create special benefits for elderly, handicapped, or poor tenants, mandate moving allowances for tenants in certain circumstances, and create special purchase rights for renters. Rent control regulations may also require special sale notices for tenants, notices that should be the responsibility of the seller.

One special consideration, for instance, may be a tenant's "first right of refusal," the right of a renter to match any purchase offer accepted by a seller. If owner Duggin accepts a $125,000 purchase offer from buyer Hurst and tenant Long has a right of first refusal, Long can buy the property at the same price and terms as Hurst. In accepting Hurst's offer, the seller in this example, Duggin, should be careful to note that acceptance is conditional, based on the prior rights of his tenant, Long.

From the seller's viewpoint, the issue of who buys a property, whether tenant or purchaser, is irrelevant. In some cases, it may actually be easier to sell to a tenant because in many communities special financing programs have been established to help renters acquire the property they inhabit, usually with low-interest loans and sometimes with outright grants. Such programs are generally directed toward low and moderate income earners who are purchasing a first home or who have not owned real estate for at least three years.

Sellers with renters may wish to sell their property without guaranteeing a variety of issues: how many units are rented, lease terms, prior tenant rights, etc. For buyers, the seller's refusal to warrant lease arrangements should be taken as a clear signal to examine a prospective purchase with great care and proper legal assistance.

The opposite situation concerns sales where purchasers want the property lease-free and without tenants. Here, both parties should be certain that all tenant deposits have been returned and that all tenant rights and obligations have been satisfied by the seller prior to settlement.

The Buyer's Strategy

1) Do not buy rental property unless all leases are "satisfactory" to you or your attorney.

2) Be certain that all tenant deposits are turned over to you, or in some other way accounted for, at settlement.

3) Be aware that in certain jurisdictions tenant rights take precedence over purchaser rights.

4) Obtain a statement from each tenant, or have the seller provide such a statement, showing that the tenant has no claims against the landlord.

5) Have the settlement provider prorate rents and any pre-paid tenant items. Tenant deposits should be passed on to the new owner.

The Seller's Strategy

1) Have all leases and payment records available for review by potential purchasers.

2) Do not show the property without giving tenants at least 24 hours notice, if possible.

3) In rent control areas, make sure you are familiar with all tenant purchase rights and provide all notices required under local laws.

4) Do not hesitate to sell to a tenant, particularly if the tenant qualifies for local purchase assistance programs.

5) Get a release from each tenant showing that the tenant has no claims against you.

35

What to Do When the Purchaser Has a House to Sell

Model Language:
Sale Contingent on Sale of Purchaser's House

This Agreement/Contract/Offer is contingent on the sale and settlement of Purchaser's property located at _____, which Purchaser shall make every effort to sell expeditiously and in good faith, time being of the essence. Settlement on subject Agreement/Contract/Offer shall take place on or about the same time settlement is conducted on the sale of Purchaser's property. It is agreed that if Seller obtains a back-up Agreement/Contract/Offer, Purchaser shall have _____ hours following receipt of written notification from Seller or Seller's agent within which to remove this contingency, as well as any other addenda and contingencies still unfulfilled (except financing addenda and financing contingencies) that are contained in the Agreement/Contract/Offer made by Purchaser or any contingencies or addenda attached thereto and/or made a part thereof. In the event Purchaser fails to remove this contingency or any other contingencies or addenda (except financing addenda and financing contingencies), then this Agreement/Contract/Offer shall be null and void and Purchaser's deposit shall be returned in full; provided, however, that should the sale and settlement of Purchaser's present property, the location of which is shown herein, not be accomplished by _____M. (TIME) on _____ (DATE), then Seller herein may declare this Agreement/Contract/Offer null and void by written notification to Purchaser, in which event Purchaser's deposit shall be returned in full.

Most people have enough trouble affording one house, and the idea of owning two at the same time is financially frightening. And yet, buyers may find that they indeed own two houses at once—at least for a little while—in those situations where they buy one home but have yet to sell their old property.

Mr. Murphy, for example, figured he could sell his house for $125,000 and use the accumulated equity—the sales value of the house less marketing costs and unpaid mortgages—for a down payment on a new home in Sunset Acres. With this strategy in mind, Murphy bought a new home and set a settlement date 120 days into the future.

Unfortunately, when the old house didn't sell, Murphy was in a bind. To get out, he got a "bridge loan" from a local lender so he could have enough money to settle on his new home. The bridge financing will be paid off as soon as the old property is sold. Until then, Murphy not only has a new and larger mortgage to pay, but the cost of his old mortgage and a bridge loan as well.

Most buyers do not want to be in Murphy's position, so rather than face the possibility of dual ownership, buyers often make offers contingent on the sale of their current residence.

The idea of a contingency that makes the purchase of one home dependent on the sale of another is certainly reasonable from the buyer's perspective, but for sellers such clauses must be viewed with care. Suppose the purchaser's property is poorly located, ridiculously priced, horribly decorated, unpainted in 30 years, or under water each spring? Surely no seller should simply agree to an offer saying, "Settlement on this property shall not occur until Purchaser's current residence has been sold and settlement completed."

A more reasonable approach, if no better deal is available, is to accept an offer that makes a purchase dependent on the sale and settlement of the buyer's home *and* also provides that if the seller gets another offer, the buyer will have some time—say 24 to 72 hours—either to eliminate the contingency or to back out of the agreement. This is commonly referred to as a "kick-out" provision. In addition, the offer can provide the seller with an option to terminate the contract after a certain time period even if there is no alternative offer, in which case the buyer's deposit will be returned.

The Buyer's Strategy

1) As a matter of necessity, you may be forced to make the purchase of one home dependent on the sale of another. This is not unusual, but your offer will not be as strong as that of a buyer who can make a non-contingent bid.

2) Your goal is to have both the "sale *and* settlement" of your first house before buying the second. Merely having an offer to buy your property does not mean that it will go to settlement. Your buyer's financing could fall through or a hundred other problems could arise.

3) If your deal with a seller is terminated, be sure your deposit will be refunded.

4) *Although the model contingency in this chapter gives the seller a uni-lateral right to terminate the agreement, the purchaser does not have a similar option to withdraw.*

5) Be certain that in the transition between homes you have a place to stay at all times. Consider contract provisions allowing a post-settlement occupancy agreement to reside in your old home after closing or a pre-settlement occupancy agreement to live in your new house before closing.

The Seller's Strategy

1) Beware of simple offers that do nothing more than tie the sale of your property to the sale of the buyer's home.

2) Require a kick-out clause so that if you get another offer the purchaser will have a short period of time within which to either back out of the deal or commit to the transaction.

3) Require an absolute cut-off date after which if you elect not to sell the property, you have an option to terminate the deal.

4) Do not require the purchaser to use your broker or any particular broker to market his property. Such an arrangement may lead to considerable conflict and confusion.

36

What to Do When the Seller Needs a New House

Model Language:
Sale Not Final Until Seller Finds Replacement Home

This Agreement/Contract/Offer is subject to Seller purchasing and settling upon a replacement house, and said Agreement/Contract/Offer shall not become effective until and unless Seller or Seller's agent gives written notification to Purchaser or Purchaser's agent that Seller has purchased and settled on a replacement house. Purchaser and Seller shall make a good faith effort to arrange settlement on subject property and settlement of Seller's replacement house at or about the same time. Purchaser may elect to provisionally withdraw subject Agreement/Contract/Offer at any time, in which case Seller shall have _____ hours from receipt of written notification from Purchaser or Purchaser's agent to commit to this Agreement/Contract/Offer and remove in writing all addenda and/or contingencies attached thereto. If Seller does not commit to this Agreement/Contract/Offer within the time period set forth herein, then this Agreement/Contract/Offer shall automatically become null and void and Purchaser's deposit shall be refunded in full. If Seller does not remove this contingency by _____ M. (TIME) on _____ (DATE), then Purchaser may declare this Agreement/Contract/Offer null and void, in which case Purchaser's deposit shall be refunded in full.

It wasn't long after Mr. Clockton placed his home on the market that he received a solid offer. The money was good and the terms were right, but Clockton had a problem: he didn't have any place to move. Rather than say "no" to his buyer, Clockton accepted the offer on the condition that he be allowed to first buy another home.

Another seller, Mr. Longworth, had a similar problem. He got a good offer for his house and had already made a deal to buy a replacement home. But Longworth was troubled by the fact that he had yet to go to settlement on the replacement property. What would happen if he sold his house and the deal for the new home fell through? Instead of giving a blanket "yes" to his buyer, Longworth said he would accept the purchaser's offer provided he went to settlement on his new home.

Both Clockton and Longworth—and their buyers—needed to work out one of the most vexing problems in real estate. It is entirely possible that the sale of one house will occur before the settlement of another, a situation where sellers are likely to find themselves on vacation, staying with relatives, or otherwise living in a motel.

Moreover, the problem may not be limited to a few days of disruption. What happens if an owner sells his house but cannot quickly find another suitable home and interest rates rise in the interim or incomes suddenly decline? A seller could be living out of a trunk for months.

Rather than face such risks, sellers may instead opt to make a deal contingent on the purchase of a replacement home. But if a seller merely said, "I accept this offer subject to the purchase and settlement of a replacement home," the deal would not go through. No reasonable buyer would want to depend on the seller to find a replacement property. For all the buyer knows, the seller may not have enough income to qualify for a new mortgage, or the seller may not find a satisfactory property for months.

Instead, there must be accommodation on both sides. The deal can be contingent on the seller finding a new place but the buyer must have the right to withdraw the offer at any time. If, in turn, the buyer wants to withdraw for any reason, the seller should have time—say 24 to 72 hours—either to finalize the sale or terminate the deal.

With a more balanced approach, we now have a situation where both buyer and seller have risk and opportunity. No one else can buy the property unless the purchaser backs out of the deal, and the seller can search for another home with a solid offer for his old property in hand. If the seller is unable to find a second home, the purchaser can force the issue by provisionally terminating his offer. At that point, either the seller goes ahead with the sale or the deal is off and the buyer's deposit will be refunded.

The Buyer's Strategy

1) Do not enter a deal where the seller has an unlimited amount of time to purchase a second home. The seller may be inept, indecisive, or poorly financed.

2) Understand that a seller's desire to find a second home is not unreasonable.

3) Look for an arrangement where you can cause the deal either to terminate or to be accepted within a reasonable time period.

4) In the event of termination, provide that your deposit will be returned in full.

The Seller's Strategy

1) Try to arrange settlement on your old and new homes at the same time and place. Not only is this convenient, but parallel settlements will also eliminate the need to store goods for several days, to stay in a motel, or to obtain a bridge loan.

2) Be sure you have tied the sale of your first house to both the purchase *and* settlement of a second home. It is not enough merely to have a contract on a second property; deals can fall through.

3) If the buyer wishes to withdraw, get as much time as possible to accept the offer—72 hours rather than 24.

4) *Using the contingency language above, the purchaser has a right to terminate his offer without penalty after a certain date, but the seller does not.* It is possible that a purchaser would want to continue with this agreement in force until the seller finally finds a second home, a process which may take weeks or months.

5) Consider including a pre-settlement occupancy agreement in the contract so that you can reside in the new house before closing or a post-settlement occupancy agreement so that you can live in the old house after closing.

37

Breaking Off: When Deals Don't Work

Model Language:
Termination and Mutual Release

1) Subject Agreement/Contract/Offer between the parties dated _____ and all related addenda and transactions are hereby terminated.

2) In consideration of a mutual exchange of valued consideration, as of the date this "Termination and Mutual Release" is ratified, the undersigned parties to subject Agreement/Contract/Offer forever release each other, and all brokers, heirs, assigns, agents, executors and administrators associated with either party, from any and all claims, demands and actions of any nature, kind and/or character whatsoever to which either party may have been entitled as a result of subject Agreement/Contract/Offer and/or any related addenda or transactions thereto.

3) The undersigned Purchaser hereby acknowledges return of a deposit in the amount of $_____, with interest if required by subject Agreement/Contract/Offer, from _____ (Deposit Holder), in settlement of all claims.

Almost every day there are real estate deals that fall through. Interest rates rise and marginally qualified buyers can no longer get financing, gifts are not made, potential co-signers don't sign, sellers refuse to make repairs, structural inspections are unsatisfactory, and a hundred other things go wrong to destroy deals where both buyer and seller have acted in good faith.

It was a home Mr. Reynolds absolutely loved, a downtown brownstone with a basement apartment and two parking spaces. Reynolds felt the $185,000 asking price was a bargain and rather than haggle and possibly lose out to another purchaser, he agreed to pay the seller's price in full.

In developing his offer, however, Reynolds had made his deal contingent on a structural inspection. When the inspector looked at the property he found the old radiator system was rusting through and would have to be replaced, a huge cost that Reynolds could not possibly afford.

While deeply depressed over his situation, Reynolds at least had the forethought to use a proper inspection clause. Not being "satisfied" with the property, Reynolds was entitled to get his deposit back.

When sales fall through, both buyer and seller must take care to terminate their relationship properly. The seller wants to continue marketing the property, the buyer wants his or her deposit returned, and neither wants to face protracted legal battles. For these reasons, a formal termination agreement is important.

A proper termination agreement resolves several problems. First, it ends the contract between buyer and seller. Second, the purchaser's deposit is returned. Third, there is a *mutual, general release of all liability*. Fourth, the release applies not only to the buyer and seller but also to their agents, heirs, assigns, and others, and as a result the potential for future legal claims is minimized if not ended.

Note that both parties want a "mutual, general" release of liability, not merely a release. With a simple release, for example, it is possible that buyer Reynolds might agree to release the seller from all liability. However, while the seller has been released from liability the buyer has not, and Reynolds could be sued by the seller.

In a transaction where a realty broker is holding the deposit, the agreement of both buyer and seller will be needed to release funds held in the broker's escrow account. If buyer and seller do not agree to release the deposit, an experienced broker will turn the money over to a court and let the buyer and seller settle the matter.

But what happens if the broker says, "Look, there's only $2,500 in this account and I should get that money for putting the deal together. Since I have possession of the money, you try to get it back." While such instances are extremely rare, it can happen if the broker is unscrupulous and believes that the cost of litigation will deter a purchaser (or seller) from suing or feels that he is entitled to a commission because he found a buyer.

Money held by a broker in an escrow account is not the broker's property and a broker has no right to such funds. Moreover, it should be said that since the broker is typically the agent of the seller, both broker and seller may be liable to the purchaser if a deposit is not returned. In addition, the broker is likely to have violated local real estate commission regulations and may face the suspension or revocation of his or her license as well as the possibility of a fine or jail sentence. Given the possible consequences of wrongfully withholding a deposit, a broker would be foolish to interfere with the joint instructions of buyers and sellers. But should this happen, don't hesitate to contact a knowledgable attorney immediately.

The Buyer's Strategy

1) Always get a release in the event a transaction fails.

2) Always get your deposit returned.

3) Do not accept a termination agreement that relieves only the seller of liability.

The Seller's Strategy

1) Always get a release in the event a transaction fails.

2) Make certain the buyer's deposit is returned in full if held by a broker.

3) Do not accept a termination agreement that relieves only the buyer of liability.

IV
The Broker's Perspective

Although contingencies, addenda, and contract changes are designed largely to enhance the negotiating posture of buyers and sellers, such clauses have potential value to brokers and salespersons as well. Today, because members of the brokerage community are faced with an ever-increasing volume of litigation, realty practitioners must understand and use the contracting process for their own protection.

In many instances, language that is valuable to brokers can be incorporated into material required by a buyer or seller. For example, a seller may have a right to obtain a purchaser's credit report. Model language might say that, "Neither Seller nor Seller's agent shall be liable for any statements, reports, or documents included in or resulting from the report," thereby protecting both seller and broker.

Sometimes, however, the interests of the broker will be decidedly different from those of the principal. In such cases, a broker has an understandable right to protect his interests in the transaction because he may later be held responsible for acts, errors, or omissions.

While it is not possible for brokers to anticipate every complaint, dispute, or action, it is feasible to take steps that radically diminish one's potential liability. Here are several basic strategies designed to protect brokers and agents in realty transactions.

38

How Brokers Can Protect Their Interests

Because real estate transactions have grown more complex over the past several years, contract modifications have become an integral part of almost every sale.

The new contracting procedures and trends that have emerged raise significant issues for realty brokers and agents: If a real estate contract must conform to all relevant legal requirements, then who is allowed to prepare this document and its modifications? Should brokers or salespeople prepare or modify sales agreements, or is this an exclusive domain for attorneys?

The answers to these questions vary from state to state. According to a study funded by the Department of Housing and Urban Development (HUD), real estate brokers and salespeople in many states are expressly prohibited from preparing real estate contracts and addenda. In other states, brokers are authorized to prepare only "simple instruments"—that is, basic outlines that include only fundamental information such as the names of the parties, the date of the sale, pricing terms, and a settlement date. In these jurisdictions, only an attorney can draw up a contract and its addenda.

Some states, however, view the preparation of a sales contract as "incidental" to the real estate brokerage business and allow more freedom. These jurisdictions give express authority to brokers and their salespeople to assist in the contracting process as part of the services they offer.

In all cases, brokers and salespeople must follow the dictates of the laws and regulations in the states where they practice and, if there are any questions about their role and authority in the contracting process, they should consult a knowledgable attorney.

Brokers and attorneys have distinct educational backgrounds, training, and experience. Brokers, typically, are not lawyers and, therefore, do not possess a legal education. At the same time, it is equally true that attorneys do not automatically or necessarily possess the same degree of expertise in the valuation, marketing, or management of real property offered by members of the brokerage community. Indeed, there are large numbers of attorneys who are adept with patents, corporate mergers, or whatever, but have *no* real estate experience or expertise.

Nevertheless, it should be recognized that legal writing has evolved over time and that certain words and phrases may have an entirely different meaning when used in a legal context than when used in daily conversation. Thus, material that has been originated or reviewed by an attorney must contain acceptable legal wording. Likewise, material prepared by a broker in the contracting process will be held to the same standard in the event of a dispute. Brokers and salespeople should recognize the responsibility—and potential liability—they may face by amending and, in some instances, even selecting "standardized" contract forms.

Regardless of the functions and duties ultimately delegated to brokers and agents in the contracting process, it is obvious that brokers and agents possess a fundamental understanding of the real estate marketplace and therefore should have a significant role in the negotiations. Whether a broker's ideas are ultimately transcribed into contract form by a broker or attorney, the point remains that the ideas of the brokerage community should be valued and considered.

In those cases where brokers and agents are permitted to assist in the development of realty agreements, there are three crucial issues that real estate professionals must consider when changing, deleting, or adding contract language.

First, does the suggested addendum or contingency meet the precise needs of the client? Careful thought should be given to the client's goals, limitations, concerns, intentions, and motivations.

Second, is the suggested language and format consistent with the requirements of the transaction? Proper care must be taken to avoid language that violates public policy or contradicts the understandings of the buyer and seller. In addition, the language of the addendum or contingency should mesh properly with the basic contract document.

Third, do the changes or new language conform to all relevant legal requirements applicable to the sale? In addition to those legal matters that directly affect real estate transfers, such as statutes and regulations dealing with subjects like usury or zoning, there may be other legal concerns related to the basic transaction. For example, what if the sale is associated with a divorce or the disposition of an estate? What if court approval is needed? What if the interests of minors are involved? These and other issues must be carefully addressed and reviewed.

MAKE REPRESENTATION CLEAR

Model Language:
Broker Represents Seller Only

It is agreed and understood by Purchaser and Seller that _____, a licensed real estate Broker in the jurisdiction where subject property is located, and all agents associated with said Broker, represent Seller alone. Purchaser has no obligation, and does not owe a fee, commission or other consideration of any nature to said Broker or agents associated with said Broker, unless otherwise stated in writing and attached to this Agreement/Contract/Offer. Settlement provider is directed to collect and pay said Broker from the funds of Seller and to disburse said funds, as per the contractual relationship between Broker and Seller, to Broker at settlement. Settlement provider is directed to collect and pay the Broker, if any, who represents the Purchaser as per the agreement between Purchaser and the Broker representing Purchaser. If Purchaser requires representation or assistance, the services of a competent professional person should be sought. (*To be signed by buyer and seller.*)

Across the country real estate regulators are requiring brokers to state in writing that they work for sellers or, if that is not the case, that they are employed by purchasers. While this may not seem like an important development, the implications of this trend are significant.

Model Language:
Broker Represents Purchaser Only

It is agreed and understood by Purchaser and Seller that _____, a licensed real estate Broker in the jurisdiction where subject property is located, and all agents associated with said Broker, represent Purchaser alone. Seller has no obligation, and does not owe a fee, commission or other consideration of any nature to said Broker or agents associated with said Broker, unless otherwise stated in writing and attached to this Agreement/Contract/Offer. Settlement provider is directed to collect and pay said Broker from the funds of Purchaser and to disburse said funds, as per the contractual relationship between Broker and Purchaser, to Broker at settlement. Settlement provider is directed to collect and pay the Broker, if any, who represents the Seller as per the agreement between Seller and the Broker representing Seller. If Seller requires representation or assistance, the services of a competent professional person should be sought. (*To be signed by buyer and seller.*)

Realty brokers have traditionally represented sellers in property transactions. It is the seller who hires the broker, and, thus, it is the broker who is the seller's agent. In those cases where there is a multiple listing service (MLS), the broker retained by the seller is the listing broker, and other brokers within an MLS system are typically considered "subagents" who have the right to market the property through the agency relationship established by the listing broker. The bottom line: In virtually all brokered sales today, it is the broker's job to get the best possible price and terms for the seller.

In practical terms, however, the relationship between broker and seller is often not clear to purchasers. A broker may show many houses to a prospective buyer over a period of weeks or months. In this period buyer and broker get to know one another, the buyer confides in the broker and shares financial information and bargaining strategies—all of which the broker is required to disclose to a client/seller.

But in real life a broker who acts as a subagent may not even know the seller. He or she may, on the other hand, know the buyer very well. The buyer may be the broker's friend, neighbor, or fellow club member. The broker may have been sought out because the buyer regards the broker highly, trusts the broker, and views the broker as a professional. The broker may have spent many hours over a period of weeks or months talking with the buyer and even providing insights into the negotiating process by talking about past deals or current transactions.

Yet with all the faith placed in the broker by a purchaser, the basic point remains: Unless the broker is hired and paid by the purchaser—a relationship called "buyer's brokerage"—the broker is the agent of the seller and must get the best possible deal for his principal.

Several problems can emerge when relationships are not clearly defined, known, or understood. For instance, a broker may disclose information that materially harms a seller ("Well, the property is listed at $145,000, but I think they'd take $130,000"). Alternatively, a buyer may give away valuable negotiating information ("I'm willing to pay $128,000 for the property, but let's offer $120,000 first and see if they accept it").

Most significantly, from the broker's viewpoint, the possibility of a "dual agency" relationship can arise. A broker may only represent one party in a transaction unless he has prior approval, in writing, to the contrary from both buyer and seller. For example, in a property exchange a broker might be paid by both parties. With advance knowledge and approval this is an acceptable dual agency relationship.

Dual agency relationships without prior approval, however, are commonly banned in real estate law. The catch is this: While brokers list property through the use of written listing agreements, agency relationships can be created by *acts* and therefore it is entirely possible to inadvertently create a dual agency situation.

It is a fact that we live in an increasingly litigious society and that brokers must view their activities with an eye toward possible claims and actions. Because the issue of representation has become so important, brokers must clearly and promptly disclose their relationships and avoid acts that may lead to dual agency conflicts.

In their own defense, one of the best actions brokers can take to defuse the agency issue is to identify and define their representation when first meeting prospective buyers and sellers face to face and getting a signed disclosure statement at that time, a statement that the individual has been advised and understands the broker's role in the realty marketplace.

There are several advantages to disclosure forms. First, if all brokers use them, no broker can gain a competitive advantage by not employing disclosure statements. Second, disclosure forms issued at the first substantial meeting between broker and buyer or broker and seller will limit potential claims concerning misrepresentation. Third, it's tough to claim misrepresentation when the broker has a signed disclosure statement in hand.

When this guide was first published in 1987, the idea of universal disclosure was regarded as unnecessary by many within the brokerage field. The old system worked for years, some said, so why change?

The case for change seemed compelling to us, and with this new edition we see that more than 40 states have now adopted mandatory disclosure regulations for real estate brokers and their agents. The National Association of Realtors and Consumer Federation of America have actually joined together to assure that state-mandated disclosure becomes a standard practice nationwide.

Why then do we still include disclosure forms in this edition? Several reasons stand out.

First, a number of states at this time do not have disclosure requirements. Brokers and agents in these jurisdictions—in consultation with local attorneys—may find that the disclosure forms provided here are useful and appropriate for their needs.

Second, state disclosure requirements vary. Not all states have mandated language that all brokers must use. In situations where brokers are allowed to prepare their own disclosure language, the wording provided in this guide can represent a starting point.

Third, it is possible that mandated state language will not go far enough or be sufficiently clear. In this situation, *in addition to the state form*, brokers may want to have a second disclosure document that meets their particular needs.

In those cases where states specify that brokers and agents must use specific wording, then—obviously—follow state requirements. Do not substitute the model language found in this guide for mandated wording required in your state.

The Broker's Strategy

1) Always identify the seller as your client when you first meet a prospective buyer, if that is the case.

2) Be aware that as of this writing, many states require written contract disclosures showing the broker's relationship in a sale. For specific language in

the area where you practice, consult with a knowledgable attorney or with your local professional association.

3) If you are representing a purchaser, be certain to tell sellers and other brokers of your relationship when you first speak with them.

4) Keep records showing when and where you disclosed your agency relationship.

5) In situations where an agency relationship is complex, brokers should insist on a disclosure statement. For instance, with a referral service a purchaser may be met in a new city by a broker who works for sellers—something the purchaser may not understand. This lack of understanding may lead to future claims if left unclarified.

TAKE NOTES

As simple as it may seem, many brokers and agents cannot adequately respond to complaints and suits because they lack adequate documentation to support their positions. As a matter of practice, brokers and agents should take notes whenever they speak to either clients or prospects, whether in person or by phone. Such notes, which need not be formal, typed memos, should show the time and date of the conversation, the topics covered, and the points raised by the buyer or seller. In particular, be certain to record matters that may be significant in the future, such as disclaimers or when notices were given.

DEFEND YOUR CLIENT'S INTERESTS—AND YOURS

When a real estate deal goes wrong, it is frequently the broker who is blamed by both seller and buyer (about 75 percent of all lawsuits against brokers are initiated by purchasers). Brokers can defuse or defeat many potential suits by forcefully defending client interests in two specific areas: property condition and representation.

Brokers should always seek to have a structural inspection included as a condition of purchase. Why is this a good idea, particularly when brokers commonly work for sellers?

The reason concerns potential liability. If there is no independent source of information, a buyer who discovers damage or defects after the sale may claim to have relied upon the seller or the seller's agent— the broker—for structural information. Clearly such a claim would be ridiculous if a buyer had a structural inspection performed by an inspector of his or her choice.

Another major issue concerns the matter of representation. If you represent the seller, who represents the purchaser? Or, if you represent the purchaser, who represents the seller? The potential problem here is a future claim that the broker in some way acted in a manner where the "customer," not the "client," believed he or she was represented by the broker. This claim is best defeated by making the sale contingent on a review satisfactory to the customer's attorney.

But wait, how does this help the client? If, for example, the broker works for the seller, how does the seller benefit from a purchaser's legal review? The answer is that with a contract review by an attorney of his choosing, a buyer cannot later say in a credible fashion that he thought the broker was "negotiating" on his behalf when the broker merely transmitted a basic offer form to the seller.

Just as importantly, with a legal review everyone will know in a few days if the buyer is going ahead with the deal. Chances are, if the buyer wants to back out, the sale would have had problems at some point before reaching settlement anyway, if settlement occurred at all.

Two caveats: First, don't suggest a structural inspector or attorney by name—that's a matter for the customer to decide. If the buyer, for instance, uses your favorite structural inspector, your claim that the buyer did not rely on you concerning the condition of the property will have far less credibility. Second, if a customer refuses to utilize a structural inspection or legal review, make notes showing the time, date, and place where the opportunity was offered and the prospect's precise response.

DISCLOSE RISKS

By their nature, all real estate transactions involve some element of risk. The list of potential problems is endless: financing can fall through, buildings can leak, mortgage payments can be late or unpaid, tornados can flatten garages, and on and on. In the midst of these and other prospective calamities, we have the broker, who more and more is being held accountable when something goes wrong.

For brokers, risks can be divided into two categories: those not possibly the fault of the broker (falling meteors, nuclear war) and those risks for which a broker may conceivably have some responsibility and, therefore, potential liability.

Model Language:
Sale Contains Certain Risks to Buyer and Seller

Seller and Purchaser are aware that this transaction contains certain inherent risks and agree not to hold _____ (Broker), and any individuals associated with said Broker, responsible for any loss or losses which may occur as a result of this transaction and to indemnify and hold harmless, including attorneys' fees, said Broker and associated individuals from all claims, actions and lawsuits which may be brought in connection with subject sale or any claims, actions and lawsuits which may arise from subject Agreement/Contract/Offer. The provisions of this paragraph shall not be extinguished by the merger of the deed and the contract of sale but shall expressly survive the transfer of subject property. *(To be signed by buyer and seller.)*

In the latter category we have several areas where brokers should act with care:

- Sales where the purchaser puts no money down.
- Sales where an owner takes back financing.
- Transactions where settlement is scheduled for an unusually long time in advance, say six months to a year.
- Timeshare sales.
- Sales involving the transfer of cooperative interests.
- Sales featuring adjustable rate financing, graduated payment loans, zero-interest payment mortgages, growing equity financing, and balloon payments.

In these cases, and in others, brokers should recognize that there is a greater element of risk than in the proverbial sale of the single house with a white picket fence and a 30-year, fixed-rate mortgage. Don't be shy about defending your interests and don't be reluctant to get a lawyer involved. If you use an attorney, try to do so without telling either the buyer or seller at first (or at all). Disclosure could raise the level of confrontation. Get disclaimers in writing if possible, and in any event, at least make extensive notes, which may be valuable in the event of a claim against you.

WHAT IF YOU'RE TOO SUCCESSFUL?

Model Language:
Offer Above List Price

Purchaser is aware that the listed price of this property is $_____ and that neither Broker(s) associated with this transaction nor their agents(s) recommended, suggested or encouraged Purchaser or Purchaser's agent(s), orally or in writing, to make an offer greater than subject property's listed price. (*To be signed by buyers and sellers.*)

It sometimes happens that a property is more desirable than anyone might have imagined, and in such cases it is possible to get an offer above list price.

Offers above list price happen most commonly when seller and broker have underestimated the property's value or when two or more buyers compete for a single desirable home. In either case, sellers should be enormously happy.

For brokers, however, there is a concern. If a listing agreement provides that a broker has the right to market a home for $130,000, that means only $130,000—not more and not less without written authorization. A purchase offer above $130,000 may raise an ironic issue: Has the broker violated the seller's instructions by asking for more than the listing price? Did the broker tell the buyer of the correct price? Rather than get into a debate about the broker's actions, it is much simpler to have the purchaser acknowledge that he or she knew the correct list price and freely made a higher offer.

PROTECT YOUR COMMISSION

Within the cooperative system it often happens that purchasers contact many brokers in their search for the perfect home. Since commission claims may, in part, be based on the issue of who first "introduced" a prospective buyer to a property, both brokers and sellers may wish to shift the burden of possible commission claims from themselves to purchasers, particularly if the buyer has worked with several agents or has a "friend" in the business.

Model Language:
Only One Broker Entitled to Commission

All parties agree that only _____, a real estate broker licensed in the jurisdiction where subject property is located, is entitled to claim a commission as a result of subject Agreement/Contract/Offer. Purchaser shall save and hold both Seller and Broker herein harmless and indemnify either and/or both from any and all actions or claims, including attorney's fees, in the event of a demand for a commission instituted by another broker as a result of any act or acts by Purchaser. The provisions of this paragraph shall not be extinguished by the merger of the deed and the contract for sale but shall expressly survive the transfer of subject property. *(To be signed by buyer and seller.)*

SELLING OTHER SERVICES

Model Language:
Notice Regarding Compensation to Broker for Other Services

All parties to this Agreement/Contract/Offer are aware and approve of the fact that the purchase or placement of _____ (product or service) through _____ (individual(s) or organization(s)) may result in a fee, commission or other consideration to the individual(s) and/or organization(s) named herein. The provisions of this paragraph shall not be extinguished by the merger of the deed and the contract of sale but shall expressly survive the transfer of subject property. *(To be signed by buyer and seller.)*

Real estate has traditionally been a business dominated by cycles and events—such as rising and falling interest rates—that are beyond the control of individual brokers. To protect themselves against these and other marketplace vagaries, brokers frequently offer additional products, including insurance and mortgage loans.

There is nothing inherently wrong with brokers who offer multiple services, except perhaps that such marketing may expose the broker to claims of dual agency.

For example, broker West sells the Hartman home and also arranges financing for buyer London. West gets a commission for the sale of the house *and* the placement of a loan. Has the purity of West's agency relationship been diluted in this transaction? What happens if seller Hartman claims that he could have gotten a better deal if the buyer had found more advantageous financing? And what if such financing was, in fact, available, financing on which West would not have gotten a commission?

Suppose further that Hartman claims he didn't know West was getting a fee for the placement of the mortgage, but that such a fee was evidence of conflicting interests? For West, and for most brokers, a better approach is simply to disclose all fee arrangements in advance.

NOTICE OF MORTGAGE OPTIONS

Model Language
Notice of Mortgage Options

Notice is hereby given to all parties that financing related to this transaction may be obtained from _____ (Broker), a licensed real estate broker representing _____ (Seller or Buyer). Should financing be obtained from Broker, then all parties should understand that a commission, fee, or thing of value may result from the placement of financing through the broker named herein.

It should be clearly understood, however, that no party to this agreement shall be required to use the services of any particular financing source, title insurance company, settlement provider, or other service or product vendor.

If more than one offer is made to purchase subject property, the decision to select one offer and not another will be made without regard to the use of a particular financing source, title insurance company, settlement provider, or other service or product vendor.

In 1993, the Department of Housing and Urban Development (HUD) and a major realty company reached an out-of-court settlement in a complex case that involved allegations of steering, kickbacks, and unearned fees.

While the real estate company denied all allegations, it did agree to settle the matter by paying $500 each to consumers involved in 783 transactions as well as $100,000 each to HUD and the Minnesota attorney general; $95,284 to the state of Minnesota for consumer education; and $15,000 to the New Jersey Division of Consumer Affairs. In total, more than $700,000.

The issue in this particular case involved allegations that brokers and agents with a real estate company steered business to affiliated firms in exchange for money that HUD alleged were kickbacks and unearned fees.

Under the Real Estate Settlement Procedures Act (RESPA), fees and commissions can be okay if fully disclosed and earned in exchange for actual work. Not allowed, however, are so-called "naked" referrals, the practice of receiving payment for providing client names or steering business to one company.

As real estate companies diversify and offer more services, either directly or through affiliates, the obligation to disclose increases. No less important, there is a need to say that the acceptance or rejection of an offer will not depend on the decision of a buyer to use a particular lender, title company, or any other product or service vendor.

To the extent required by law and regulations, buyers and sellers should be advised up front and in writing of any potential fee, commission, or thing of value that a broker may earn in addition to a realty commission. Buyers and sellers should also be advised to shop around, to compare prices and services, and to make certain they are getting the best possible deal. If it turns out the best deal is from a broker, that's okay—as long as all disclosure requirements have been met.

Disclosure requirements are in flux as this is written, so brokers and their agents are best advised to speak with a knowledgable real estate attorney in their community for the latest information and requirements.

THE ISSUE OF SELF-DEALING

Because brokers are in the real estate business, it is not surprising that they frequently purchase and sell property. Most jurisdictions require brokers to disclose in writing that they are licensed when participating in a real estate transaction. Less clear, however, is the matter of self-dealing, a situation where a broker lists a property and, during or after the listing period, makes a purchase offer.

The problem here is obvious: the seller depended on the broker to place a market value on the property and to assist in the sale. In this process the seller may have revealed confidential information that would not normally be made known to purchasers. The broker, who was supposed to be the agent of the seller, is now an adversary.

It may be to the seller's advantage to market the property to a broker, but such deals can collapse if brokers are not careful. Suppose, for example, that a broker lists a property for $125,000 and later offers to buy it from the seller at that price. Has not the seller gotten full value? Maybe. But what happens if the seller finds out that like properties in the same neighborhood have been selling for $145,000? Has the broker in such circumstances dealt fairly with the seller? It's not a question with which most brokers would want to deal.

If you have listed a property that you want to purchase, it makes sense to terminate the listing agreement, make certain the deal is dependent on an appraisal satisfactory to the *seller,* and have both the seller and yourself consult with lawyers (separately) to assure the matter is handled fairly and to prevent future claims.

HOW TO GET TWO COMMISSIONS

Brokers are sometimes in a situation where, having sold a home, the sellers ask if the broker will now assist in the purchase of a new property. Brokers in this situation face an interesting issue: If the sellers were "clients" when their home was sold, what is their relationship to the broker when they are purchasers? If, in this situation, the broker will collect a commission from the sellers of the second home—either as a listing broker or as a subagent—then the sellers-turned-buyers are now surely "customers" and not "clients" represented by the broker.

But at what magical point did the broker's allegiance change? How, in human terms, can a broker deal with someone as a client one moment—and be obligated to get the best price and terms possible for the sale of a property—and as an adversary the next—obligated to get the best price and terms for a different client?

Since brokers cannot turn their allegiances on and off like light bulbs, there must be a better alternative. That alternative: represent the seller as a listing broker, and when he or she enters the marketplace as a purchaser represent him or her again, only this time through a buyer's brokerage arrangement. In this way there will be one broker/client relationship, even though the goals of the relationship have evolved.

FACILITATION

During the past decade much of the debate concerning representation, notification, and liability has revolved around traditional forms of brokerage. While real estate prior to the 1990s was absolutely dominated by seller representation, subagency, and Multiple Listing Systems (MLS), such traditional forms of practice now vie with buyer brokerage and disclosed dual agency for consumer interest. Behind the new practice options are two factors: consumer demand and the potential for litigation.

Within the marketplace are buyers who want professional representation and who are able and willing to pay for it. But the practical reality is that most purchasers do not have the funds to engage buyer brokers and the result is that the buyer broker's compensation must come from somewhere else.

One approach is for the buyer broker to receive 50 percent of the commission paid by the seller—the money that usually goes to a cooperating broker who brings in a buyer. In other words, if a home is listed for $150,000 with a 6 percent commission, the listing broker will receive $9,000 for selling the property directly. If the property is sold with a cooperating broker, then the listing broker and the cooperating broker each receive $4,500.

But in a deal with a buyer broker, there is no cooperating broker to pay. Instead, $4,500 from the $9,000 commission is assigned to the buyer broker, an arrangement that is possible only if the listing broker agrees or if the listing agreement provides for such a payment.

Another approach, and a far better one, is to write a deal that looks like the following:

Suppose the Green property is available for $150,000. Suppose, as well, that Green has a listing agreement with broker Wilkens to pay a 6 percent fee if the property sells.

Buyer broker Reese, representing buyer Goodwin, makes a

$150,000 offer for the property. Seller Green, through his broker, accepts.

We know that seller Green has a listing agreement with a broker and therefore the listing broker will be paid. The buyer broker, Reese, gets his money this way.

In the offer for $150,000 is a requirement for the seller (Green) to pay the buyer (Goodwin) $4,500 at closing. Most likely, Green will say to his broker: "Look, if you'll take 3 percent rather than 6 percent—the same fee you would get in a co-op deal, I'll pay the $4,500 demanded by the purchaser at closing. To me, the result is the same as paying a full commission, and to you the result is the same as a co-op sale. If you don't agree to the better commission split, we may not get another offer, and both of us will suffer."

The attraction of the deal with a $4,500 seller credit is this: at no point did the buyer broker receive money from the seller or the seller's broker. Reese, the buyer broker, was paid at closing directly by the purchaser. Everyone is in sync. The buyer and seller have a deal, and the brokers are being paid by their respective principals.

In addition, the deal between Green and Goodwin involves no sub-agency, and thus no additional liability for seller Green or the listing broker for errors, misrepresentations, or biases that a subagent might make known. It is the lure of reduced liability which has caused so many brokers to realize that cooperation with a buyer broker may well be a good idea, especially when cooperating brokers and their agents are likely to be unknown.

If we're going to have agents for buyers and agents for sellers, then we need to know who represents whom, thus the rationale for full, early, and complete disclosure. And if a broker is uncertain as to whom or what he ultimately represents, then a little representation is better than no representation; so we have disclosed dual agents.

So far we have agents, subagents, buyer brokers, seller brokers, and cooperation. What we don't have is non-agency, and that's where facilitators come in.

According to a 1992 study by the National Association of Realtors' Presidential Advisory Group on Agency, a facilitator is defined as a "person who assists the parties to a potential real estate transaction in communication, interposition and negotiation, to reach agreement between or among them, without being an advocate for the interests of any party except the mutual interest of all parties, to reach agreement. Also known as an intermediary."

Facilitation, says the NAR study, has both pros and cons. The good news is that facilitators can reduce consumer confusion concerning representation because there is none. And, since there is no agency relationship, broker facilitators have fewer liabilities because they have no fiduciary obligations.

The down side is that neither buyers nor sellers have their own representation and as yet there is no widely accepted method that allows facilitators to handle multiple purchase offers. In addition, once someone works as an agent, that individual cannot suddenly transmute into a facilitator and work with a former client.

Other problems include uncertain liability because there is no established case law and debatable economic benefit.

In addition to pros and cons, the agency group points out that practical questions still exist: Will the public want to buy facilitator services? Will it be possible to purchase errors and omissions insurance? How will individual state licensure regulations cover facilitators? How can facilitators work within traditional MLS rules and ethical codes?

Many communities, perhaps most, now offer traditional brokerage, discount brokerage, and flat-fee brokerage—an array of services that can easily be expanded to include facilitation.

Roughly 18 to 20 percent of all residential real estate transactions involve direct sales by owners—a percentage that translates into 500,000 to 600,000 sales per year. Marketplace experience tells us that some proportion of all self-sellers use For Sale By Owner (FSBO) status to find a broker, so there is a natural opening for the provision of professional services.

To date, FSBOs have commonly turned to flat-fee firms with a menu of services, and to discounters who offer lower total costs for a given package of services. Traditional firms have also found business among self-sellers by converting FSBOs to full-service clients.

Brokers who act as facilitators may thus find a ready market for their services among FSBOs, many of whom want the benefits of professional brokers, but not the usual mix of traditional offerings.

But if there is a ready market for facilitators, how should such services be valued?

One approach is to have an hourly fee, an incentive for both buyer and seller to get on with their deal and not rack up onerous mediation expenses.

A second choice is to charge by the deal, say "x" percent of the transaction value. In this situation, no sale means no income, so it is likely that brokers will want an up-front, non-refundable fee to assure that all participants are serious.

A third concept is a flat-fee arrangement for all deals, or for deals within a certain price range. As auto dealers have begun to discover, one-price, no-hassle shopping draws consumers and cuts operating expenses, a good approach for everyone.

In the usual brokerage arrangement, compensation is based on performance rather than time. The result is that much professional energy is expended with prospects who don't buy and owners who don't list. Even when a deal is made, compensation is commonly chopped into little pieces as brokers split with brokers and then brokers split with agents.

Facilitation, like consulting, allows relationships that can be straightforward—"this is what I charge, this is what you get." If the client goes elsewhere, at least the broker has not lost valuable time or provided professional services without compensation. While an individual facilitator deal is unlikely to produce as much income as a traditional transaction of equal size, it is entirely possible that a facilitator will be able to conduct more transactions with the same effort—and with no commissions to split.

Easy money and short hours are not guaranteed, however. Facilitators will have to deal with a very powerful competitive reality, the fact that most buyers and sellers do not want a neutral party to assist in the deal. If history is any guide, what principals want is not just representation, but representation that is better than their adversary's.

To this point we have considered brokers as facilitators, but what happens if non-brokers enter the field?

While the real estate industry and state regulators surely support licensure, licensing facilitators to "protect the public interest" may not be feasible. Facilitators need do no more than act as information providers, and regulating the flow of real estate information is virtually impossible. Any facilitation regulations would have to contain exceptions for books, newspapers, magazines, newsletters, electronic bulletin boards, schools, educators, divorce counselors, financial planners, psychologists, and lenders.

And if facilitation becomes attractive, then the biggest competitive threat to brokers is likely to come from attorneys. A surplus of law school graduates coupled with possible tort reform has caused lawyers to seek new markets. Facilitation is as natural to law as it is to brokerage, a matter that should concern those in the real estate industry.

In addition to lawyers, another competitive threat could come from non-broker facilitators such as unions or neighborhood housing coalitions that offer individual counseling with regard to such matters as home buying, selling, negotiating, pricing, and financing.

There is little doubt that utility and economics will make facilitation appropriate in some transactions, but not all. Most people, most of the time, will continue to rely on traditional marketing approaches even though a variety of alternatives are available, as is the case today.

And facilitation, as a business option, does not seem destined to stand alone. Instead, it is likely to emerge as one of many services offered by brokers who represent sellers one day, buyers the next, and then perhaps no one.

As to ethical codes and MLS systems, it is worth noting that real estate counselors have long been active within the industry, though usually as agents and not as neutral parties. MLS systems need not be modified to accommodate facilitators because—as appraisers have shown—an agency, subagency, or cooperative posture is simply not required to use an MLS.

What can brokers do to protect their professional turf? Several strategies stand out:

- Licensure programs and continuing education efforts should be expanded to include facilitation.
- To maintain market share and professional status, the industry should promote such institutional values as representation, training, skills, marketplace experience, and licensure status.
- Brokers who wish to act as facilitators should have full use of local MLS systems.
- Thought should be given to the idea that while facilitation does not involve representation by the facilitator, parties to the process

can bring their own advisers to the table, including, of course, real estate brokers.

Because facilitation is a new concept, brokers will need to originate specialized arrangements, agreements that should include these elements:

Term. How long will the agreement be in effect? A specific cut-off date should be shown.

Compensation. How will the facilitator be paid? By the hour? For the project? If no deal is made will the facilitator receive less money? Will the facilitator be paid at cost for such expenses as phone calls, copying, and messenger services, or will there be add-on fees? Will there be up-front fees? If so, are up-front fees refundable in whole or in part?

Relationship. A facilitation agreement needs to clearly state that the facilitator works for neither the buyer nor the seller.

Notice of expertise. A facilitation agreement should state where the facilitator has experience, training, certification, licensure status, and education, and where he or she does not. If appropriate, a broker who acts as a facilitator should say that he or she is not an attorney, architect, structural inspector, loan officer, or appraiser.

Scope. The facilitator's job should be clearly stated. What is it that the facilitator is expected to do? At what point has a facilitator done his or her job? As what point is a facilitator entitled to a fee?

Arbitration. What if everyone hates the facilitator, or feels that the facilitator has made significant errors? In the event of a dispute, an arbitration clause can save time and legal fees, and it can also limit damages if properly written. (See arbitration material elsewhere in this guide.)

To fully develop a facilitator agreement appropriate for your jurisdiction, speak with a knowledgable attorney in your community.

THE PREVENTIVE APPROACH: LIST IT RIGHT

Model Language:
Notice of Broker's Expertise

Unless otherwise stated in writing, it is agreed and understood that Broker herein is not an attorney, tax authority, lender, architect, loan officer, structural engineer or surveyor. Client shall contact an attorney for legal advice and seek other professional assistance as required. *(To be signed by broker and client as part of a listing agreement.)*

> **Model Language:**
> **Arbitration Agreement**
>
> Any controversy or claim arising out of or relating to this Agreement/Contract/Offer, or any breach thereof, shall be settled through binding arbitration by a mutually acceptable third party. In the even t the parties cannot agree within _____ working days as to who the mutually acceptable third party shall be, then arbitration shall be conducted by the American Arbitration Association in accordance with that organization's Commercial Arbitration Rules. The judgment of the arbitrator shall be binding on all parties and may be entered in any Court having jurisdiction thereof. The costs of any arbitration matter shall be paid in accordance with the ruling of the arbitrator or, if there be no ruling as to costs, then by the party who is adjudged to be in the wrong at the hearing. No damages, other than actual damages, shall be awarded; no money whatsoever shall be awarded for legal fees or costs. Both parties agree that there shall be no appeal of the arbitration decision. *(To be signed by broker and client as part of a listing agreement.)*

Relationships between brokers and their clients are commonly created through written listing agreements, employment contracts that typically cover such items as listing prices, down payments, household items that convey, and the willingness to pay points. In addition to these matters, brokers should see listing agreements as an opportunity to limit future claims.

One element not normally found in such agreements is a statement of expertise—that is, a statement that the broker is a broker and not a lawyer, tax authority, surveyor, or whatever. A notice clearly listing those areas in which the broker is not professionally qualified can do much to prevent or limit potential suits where clients claim they relied on the broker's advice and counsel not knowing the broker's limitations.

A second concept involves arbitration. Rather than letting matters fall into the province of the court system, some brokers instead opt for binding arbitration. While arbitration does not relieve a broker from liabilities and may, in the same manner as a lawsuit, result in a broker paying an award to an aggrieved client, arbitration may reduce or eliminate legal fees and speed the settlement of disputes.

A key point concerning arbitration is that such agreements are most likely to be of value if established when relationships are positive, which means—basically—at the time a home is listed or a buyer's brokerage agreement is signed. Trying to get parties to agree to arbitration once problems have arisen may be difficult if not impossible, particularly if the agreement will limit damages. Think ahead and you may be spared considerable grief, turmoil, and, not incidentally, money.

ADA AND BROKERAGE

In 1990 new civil rights legislation was passed to assure that disabled individuals have equal access to public accommodations, jobs, and opportunities. Known as the Americans With Disabilities Act (ADA), this federal law has important implications for the real estate industry.

At first the term "disability" may suggest application only to individuals with clear and visible limitations such as those who require wheelchairs, but in the context of ADA the definition of "disability" is broadly drawn. For example, someone with HIV can be regarded as disabled, even if there are no overt symptoms and the disease has not progressed to an advanced and disabling stage.

Census Bureau figures from 1990 show that of the 115 million people who belong to the labor force, 4 million have disabilities which limit workplace activities and another 1 million have severe disabilities.

The President's Committee on Employment of People with Disabilities defines ADA as a law which "covers people whose disabilities typically cause great difficulties in such daily activities as walking, talking, seeing, hearing, communication, learning, or working." The total number of such individuals is substantial. For example, the Committee notes that 23 million people have hearing impairments, 7.5 million have visual impairments, and 6.2 million have diabetes—impairments which may be regarded as disabilities in some circumstances.

Given that millions of people are included within the scope of ADA, as a broker you will inevitably meet such individuals and it is your responsibility to assure that disabled people not only have full access to your services and facilities, but also opportunities to work within your organization.

ADA requires "reasonable accommodation" when dealing with disabled individuals, an expression not clearly defined. That said, how difficult is it to construct a wheelchair ramp? Why not install a TDD (telephone device for the hearing impaired) in your office? How hard is it to install grab bars in bathrooms?

The list could go on, but the basic point is this: brokers—and all people in business—have a clear obligation to reduce and eliminate barriers and to end workplace discrimination based on physical and mental disabilities. Those who fail to comply with ADA requirements may find themselves in court, an expensive adventure when one considers that maximum fines for small businesses—those with as few as 14 employees—can total $50,000 plus such costs as back pay, damages, and legal fees. And bigger organizations, it should be said, are subject to even larger penalties.

ADA addresses certain issues related to companies with as few as 14 "employees," but since real estate agents are typically "independent contractors," some might argue that ADA may not apply to many brokerage firms. The view here is that ADA casts a wide net, accommodation is typically inexpensive, the penalties for being "wrong" are substantial, and it's simply good business to accommodate those with disabilities—individuals in your community who rent and own property and who can provide referrals to friends, family, neighbors, and co-workers.

ADA is a new and unfolding concept, something that should concern all brokers and agents. While it is not possible to review all ADA issues in this guide, here—as a start—are several baseline ADA matters to consider.

Facilities. Is your office physically accessible? If not, what steps should you take to increase access? For example, to accommodate an agent who uses a wheelchair you might raise a desk or rearrange furniture to create wider aisles.

Taxes. When you spend money to comply with ADA it may be possible to earn both tax credits and deductible write-offs. For specific information speak with a tax attorney, CPA, or enrolled agent.

Agency. As you work for another and for a fee, be aware that you can be hurt by clients who ignore ADA obligations. For instance, a shopping center or multi-tenant office building must be accessible to all, otherwise how can disabled people find employment, shop, or go to work? If you are the manager and the owner does not make "reasonable accommodations," you could be involved if the matter goes to court.

Outreach. When dealing with disabled individuals be certain to accommodate special needs. As an example, hire an interpreter when dealing with deaf clients or provide readers for the blind.

If the individual is a customer and not a client, then matters become more complex. After all, if you are an agent of the seller and the buyer is blind, then the reader you supply is obligated to work for the best interests of the seller. In such situations, make certain that customers have access to required support services from independent sources of their choice.

Hiring and Retention. ADA does not require that you retain unqualified people. It does require equal access to jobs and opportunities. Thus, asking about someone's prior sales experience is fine. Rejecting someone merely because they use a wheelchair is clearly prohibited.

Marketing. Tell people about your outreach efforts. Include TDD numbers in advertisements and on business cards. Note the availability of ramps and other special facilities in brochures and booklets about your organization. Speak with local special-interest organizations that represent the disabled and ask how you can better serve their needs.

Additional Information

Successful Real Estate Negotiation is part of a series of real estate books designed to raise ideas, provide information, and suggest strategies that can have value for consumers nationwide.

In addition, you may want to consider other ways to gain real estate information.

First, speak to as many lenders, brokers, and agents as possible. Many will have bargaining ideas and suggestions that have value.

Second, consider taking a basic, low-cost licensure class. Such classes—which can be available from colleges, universities, real estate organizations, and private schools—will show you how the real estate marketing system works in your jurisdiction and qualify you to take an agent's licensure test.

Third, read local newspapers. Many real estate sections offer solid advice and information, so clip and save the items most interesting to you.

Fourth, visit real estate expositions, particularly those sponsored by local newspapers, real estate organizations, and builder groups. Such expos often have a variety of booths, little or no selling pressure, plus a goodly amount of information.

Fifth, check out personal finance publications such as *Money*, *Consumer's Digest*, and *Kiplinger's Personal Finance* that often carry extensive, timely articles of value to real estate consumers.

Sixth, if this guide has been helpful, then consider the other books in this series: *The Common-Sense Mortgage* (published annually), *Successful Real Estate Investing*, *Buy Your First Home Now*, and *How to Sell Your Home in Any Market—With or Without a Broker*. These books, published by HarperCollins, are available from booksellers nationwide.

Seventh, go electronic. Millions of people have a computer, modem, and mouse—all you need to be a part of the network nation. Local electronic bulletin boards may have real estate information, while a national service such as the real estate forum hosted by Mr. Miller on America Online has an MLS open to brokers and non-brokers, current mortgage rates, real estate software, online questions and answers, and much more. For additional information, call 800-827-6364. Be certain to mention extension 5764 for such free software, online time, and introductory pricing as may be available when you call.

Lastly, if you do well negotiating and bargaining, pass on what you've learned and make the marketplace easier for the next person.

Index